# STUDY GUIDE WITH READINGS

TO ACCOMPANY PAPALIA/OLDS

# HUMAN DEVELOPMENT

FIFTH EDITION

## THOMAS L. CRANDELL

Broome Community College

## GEORGE R. BIEGER

Indiana University of Pennsylvania

McGRAW-HILL, INC.

New York   St. Louis   San Francisco   Auckland   Bogotá
Caracas      Lisbon      London      Madrid      Mexico      Milan
Montreal    New Delhi    Paris      San Juan
Singapore    Sydney    Tokyo    Toronto

This book was designed and set in Century Old Style with Optima by SG/TN Associates.
The editors were Renee Shively Leonard and Susan Gamer.
The production supervisor was Annette Mayeski.
Cover illustration by Steve Karchin.
Malloy Lithographing, Inc., was printer and binder.

## PERMISSIONS AND CREDITS

Sharon Begley, "Brother Sun, Sister Moon," *Newsweek,* October 29, 1990. Copyright © 1990. Reprinted by permission.

Gerald W. Bracey, "Culture, Science, and the Concept of Child," *Phi Delta Kappan,* May 1990. Copyright © 1990. Reprinted by permission.

Carla Cantor, "The Father Factor," *Working Mother,* June 1991. Copyright © 1991. Reprinted by permission.

Stephanie Ericsson, "The Agony of Grief," *Utne Reader,* September-October 1991. Copyright © 1991. Reprinted by permission.

Barbara Kantrowitz, "The Dangers of Doing It," *Newsweek,* Special Issue, Summer/Fall 1990. Copyright © 1990. Reprinted by permission.

Barbara Kantrowitz, "The Good, the Bad, and the Difference," *Newsweek,* Special Issue, Summer 1991. Copyright © 1991. Reprinted by permission.

Nancy Kelton, "Dating at Forty," *Parents,* September 1989. Copyright © 1989. Reprinted by permission.

Richard Lacayo, "Do the Unborn Have Rights?" *Time,* Special Issue, Fall 1990. Copyright © 1990. Reprinted by permission.

Charles Leershen, "Helping Themselves," *Newsweek,* Special Issue, Summer 1991. Copyright © 1991. Reprinted by permission.

Leah Levinger and Jo Adler, "How Children Learn," *Good Housekeeping,* September 1990. Copyright © 1990. Reprinted by permission.

Leslie Lindeman, "Beating Time," *Modern Maturity,* June-July 1991. Copyright © 1991. Reprinted by permission.

Michele Block Morse, "Fitting into the Family," *Parents Magazine,* July 1990. Copyright © 1990. Reprinted by permission.

Jill Neimark, "They've Got to Have It," *Mademoiselle,* December 1990. Copyright © 1990. Reprinted by permission.

Carla Rohlfing, "Are You a Victim of Silent Stress?" *Family Circle,* September 3, 1991. Copyright © 1991. Reprinted by permission.

Michael Ryan, "Here, They See Age as an Asset," *Parade,* July 14, 1991. Copyright © 1991. Reprinted by permission of the author and the author's agents, Scott Meredith Literary Agency, Inc., 845 Third Avenue, New York, New York 10022.

Rollene W. Saal, "On My Own," *New Choices,* June 1990. Copyright © 1990. Reprinted by permission.

Grace Slick, "Highs and Lows," *Newsweek,* Special Issue, Summer/Fall 1990. Copyright © 1990. Reprinted by permission.

Rob Waters, "Young and Old Alike," *Parenting,* Time Publishing Ventures, Inc., October 1991. Copyright © 1991. Reprinted by permission.

 This book is printed on recycled paper containing a minimum of 50% total recycled fiber with 10% postconsumer de-inked fiber.

# CONTENTS

# PREFACE

## TO THE STUDENT

This *Study Guide with Readings,* which accompanies *Human Development,* Fifth Edition, by Papalia and Olds, is designed to help you master the material presented in the textbook.

As educational psychologists, we recognize that people differ with respect to their learning styles and preferences. Consequently, we encourage you to continue using the study methods and techniques which you have found successful. At the same time, however, you should recognize that each new learning experience brings with it a unique set of objectives, vocabulary, and applications. We have written and organized the Study Guide with the express purpose of making the important facts, terms, and concepts discussed in the textbook easier for you to identify, learn, and recall.

Also, we believe that if you follow our suggestions for using the Study Guide and for studying and taking tests, you will improve your performance on classroom quizzes and avoid—or at least reduce—the anxiety which often debilitates students at exam time.

While the Study Guide is designed to help you process and learn information more effectively, remember that there is no "fast track" to learning. Learning is the result of motivation, organization, and hard work. The student who wants high grades and has the diligence to study for them should find this Study Guide especially helpful. In addition, the student who has been away from formal schooling for some time will find that the Study Guide provides an easy-to-use framework for identifying and learning important material in the text, organizing study time, and preparing for tests and examinations with more confidence.

Enjoy your course in human development!

## ORGANIZATION OF THE STUDY GUIDE

Each chapter in the Study Guide corresponds to the same chapter in the textbook. The chapters are all organized according to the following scheme.

### Introduction

The first section—the introduction—provides you with a brief overview of the main topics discussed in the textbook chapter.

Use the introduction to familiarize yourself with some of the important issues in the chapter and to organize your thinking in preparation for learning the major facts and concepts that will be presented.

### Chapter Outline

The chapter outline gives all the headings and subheadings within the text chapter and thus shows you the complete structure, or framework, of the text material. Enough space is left between entries for you to make brief notes.

The chapter outlines will help you preview each chapter, will clarify the relationship among topics and subtopics, and will later be useful for reveiwing.

### Key Terms

This section of key terms provides you with a list of the basic vocabulary that you should learn in each chapter. It is designed to help you focus on the most important terminology—which reflects the most important information and concepts.

The key terms are listed in alphabetical order, and space is provided for you to make short notes of definitions or examples. Note that for each key term, a page number in the text is cited; this is where the definition or explanation is located. Once you have made notes of definitions, examples, or both, the key terms sections will be an excellent reference to review for examinations.

Note that when key terms are used in the "learning objectives" (the next section of each Study Guide chapter), they are set in *italic* at their first appearance.

### Learning Objectives

Each learning objective corresponds to a major principle or concept discussed in the main text. The learning objectives let you know in advance what will be required of you; you should also find that, by making new words and concepts seem familiar, they will make the material easier to grasp.

We have left some space between objectives so that you can take notes as you read the textbook chapter.

Some of the objectives require rote learning of the text material (examples are those which ask you to define, list, describe, or explain). Other objectives focus on higher-level comprehension of abstract conceptual material (examples are those that ask you to compare and contrast or to analyze). You should read all the objectives before you read the text chapter. By doing so, you will give yourself an organizational framework for integrating and understanding the material in the text.

The learning objectives also serve as a yardstick to measure your understanding of the text and will indicate if you need to spend more time studying certain material.

Furthermore, the objectives can be particularly beneficial if your instructor gives essay-type questions or examinations, since essay questions may often resemble these objectives. Writing out "answers" to some of the objectives will give you practice in dealing with essay exams.

### Supplemental Readings

For each chapter in the textbook, we have selected an interesting current article which complements or expands on one or more important concepts. The readings are intended to "bring to life" some of the issues which are presented more theoretically in the text.

Collectively, the readings should have something for everyone, and each reading is a provocative and insightful analysis of an issue reflecting one of the developmental tasks of life.

Two or three general questions follow each reading, to help you assess your understanding of the issues in the article and how they relate to the material in the text.

## Self-Tests

The section of self-tests is a carefully selected group of objective questions—multiple-choice, matching, and completion items—that test your understanding of facts and concepts in the textbook chapter. Working out answers to these questions will help you to integrate the chapter material and prepare for questions you might encounter on examinations.

## Answer Key

Answers are provided for each item in the self-tests. It is a good idea to check off or highlight any questions you missed and spend additional time on that material, referring back to the textbook. To help you restudy the material you find troublesome, we have provided a text page reference for each answer.

---

## STUDYING, TAKING TESTS, AND YOU

Let's face it—if you are using this Study Guide as part of a course, one of your personal objectives is passing examinations. You want to know how to do well on exams and, in particular, how the Study Guide can help you.

There are several different ways to learn anything, and how you study for a test—that is, how you go about learning—can affect your ability to answer test questions. To take a very simple example, you may be able to recognize the names of the two authors of your textbook if you are presented with four pairs of names and asked to choose the correct answer (a multiple-choice question):

1. The authors of your textbook are
   a. Crandell and Bieger
   b. McGraw and Hill
   c. Papalia and Olds
   d. Watson and Skinner

However, you may not be able to recall the authors' names if you are asked to produce them without being given any choices (a completion question):

2. The authors of your textbook are _____ and _____ .

This difference between recognition and recall (a topic discussed in some detail in the text) is only one aspect of studying and learning.

Research shows that there are at least four main obstacles which prevent students from doing as well as they should on tests.

*Obstacle 1:* Some students have difficulty seeing relationships between new concepts and what they already know. Consequently, they do not know how to study effectively.

*Obstacle 2:* Some students do not know how to use supplemental instructional materials (such as this Study Guide) effectively.

*Obstacle 3:* Many students have never developed a successful strategy for preparing for and taking tests, especially objective tests—multiple-choice, matching, completion, and true-false items. (You might say that they are not "test smart.")

*Obstacle 4:* Many students develop test anxiety.

On the following pages, we offer specific strategies that will help you overcome these obstacles.

## USING THE STUDY GUIDE TO LEARN MORE EFFECTIVELY

To improve your overall understanding of the material in the textbook and to help yourself recall that material on tests, follow these steps in the sequence described.

### Step 1:
### Previewing the Chapter

Before reading each chapter in the textbook, read the introduction to the chapter in the Study Guide and preview the key terms.

Next, read and familiarize yourself with the chapter outline and the learning objectives in the Study Guide. This will help you see the scope and direction of the material in the text. The Study Guide serves as an advance organizer (a bridge between old and new learning), enabling you to anticipate important issues, facts, and concepts in the textbook.

This preview should take only a few minutes.

### Step 2:
### Reading the Chapter

*Creating study units.* Read the textbook chapter, but *don't* try to read the entire chapter at one sitting. Research has demonstrated that the capacity for long-term retention increases if we do not try to overload our short-term memory with too much new information at one time.

Therefore, break the chapter into smaller "chunks" or units for study. You can use the chapter outlines in the Study Guide to establish your "chunks" or study units. Preferably, each unit, and thus each learning session, should cover only about 7 to 9 pages of the text.

*Using the key terms and learning objectives.* As you read the textbook chapter, use the space provided in the Study Guide to define each key term briefly and to jot down short notes for each of the learning objectives. The purpose of this approach is to involve you directly with the material during and following your reading of the textbook.

Using the key terms and objectives in this way will make you actively involved in reading, and being an active reader will increase your learning and comprehension of the material.

Merely reading a chapter passively does not mean that you have mastered it. Everything may seem to make sense as you read it; however, if you try to recall the material or summarize the main points, you will frequently find that terms, concepts, and names are not retrievable. On the other hand, by defining key terms and responding to the learning objectives, you will make the text more significant and hence easier to recall on a test (or, for that matter, in appropriate situations in "real life").

### Step 3:
### Reviewing the Chapter
### and Testing Your Mastery

After you have read the chapter—being sure to follow the procedure described in step 2—you should review what you have learned. (Remember to use the chapter outline, key terms, and learning objectives for reviewing.)

Then take the self-tests in the Study Guide. The purpose of the self-tests is to to evaluate your understanding and recall of the material and to reinforce what you have learned.

As we've already noted, an answer key is provided at the end of each chapter in the Study Guide, so that you can check your answers to the self-tests.

Take the self-tests seriously. If you could not answer a question, do not merely look up the correct answer in the key. For each answer in the key, a text page reference is given; use this reference to find the textbook passage that answers the question, and reread that passage. Then reanswer the question. In this way, you will shore up any areas that need additional review and help store the information in long-term memory.

### Step 4:
### Rereading the Chapter

Reread the textbook chapter, and then go through the self-tests again.

As you go through step 4, you should find that the chapter material is more "connected"—and therefore much easier to remember.

## Summary: The Four Steps

In summary, these are the steps we recommend that you follow.

*Step 1: Preview.* Read the introduction to the chapter in the Study Guide, and examine the key terms.

*Step 2: Read.* Break the textbook chapter down into small study units, and read it one unit at a time. As you read, write down in the Study Guide brief definitions of the key terms and brief notes on each of the learning objectives.

*Step 3: Review and test yourself.* Review what you have learned; then take the self-tests in the Study Guide. Check your answers against the answer key and correct your mistakes.

*Step 4: Reread.* Read the textbook chapter again, and then take the self-tests again.

## A Note on Learning and the Senses

Keep in mind that not everyone learns in the same way. For example, some students understand information better when they see it in written form—they learn best from the textbook, the Study Guide, lecture notes and handouts, etc. Other students prefer to hear information; they learn best from listening to lectures, making and listening to tape recordings of lectures, making and listening to recordings of their own notes on the learning objectives and their own definitions of terms, and studying with other students groups where answers can be discussed.

If you need oral assistance in learning, you should be aware that many textbooks have been recorded on tape; check with your library to see if *Human Development* is available. You may also be able to work directly with a tutor on your campus. Some colleges provide "note-takers" for students who need this extra assistance.

Of course, many people learn best by combining seeing and hearing. By simultaneously using the senses which are most helpful to you, you will make the material more memorable and more retrievable at test time.

## PREPARING FOR AND TAKING TESTS

As we noted above, there are at least four factors that can prevent you from doing your best on tests and examinations: (1) ineffective studying, (2) ineffective use of supplemental materials, (3) lack of strategies for taking tests, and (4) inability to overcome test anxiety. Our step-by-step procedure for using *Human Development* textbook and this Study Guide—a procedure which can also be adapted for use with other textbooks and other supplements—will help you overcome the first two of these barriers. Strategies for taking tests and dealing with test anxiety are beyond the scope of this Study Guide, but we can give you some useful, if brief, advice.

### Overcoming Test Anxiety

*Test anxiety* can be defined as a feeling of helplessness before or during a test.

It is important to realize that examinations cause many people to become anxious, and that this is normal. Complete freedom from test anxiety is un-

attainable; and even if it were attainable, it would probably not be desirable. Low to moderate anxiety before a test actually tends to have a positive effect on test performance.

However, if your test anxiety is so high that it prevents you from demonstrating what you have learned, then it becomes a problem and should be addressed. Unfortunately, such anxiety is usually a complex problem, which often cannot be traced to any single cause. Personality traits (such as a tendency to take risks), emotional states (such as a negative outlook and fear of failure), and personal needs and priorities (such as overemphasis on grades) can sabotage your performance on tests.

If you consistently experience test anxiety, we recommend that you make an appointment with someone in the college or university counseling center to discuss the problem and work out a procedure for dealing with it. College counselors are trained to help you assess the cause or causes of your test anxiety and to provide you with strategies for reducing it, and for improving your performance on tests.

## Becoming "Test Smart"

Students who are "test smart" are able to prepare for tests efficiently, and to take advantage of the characteristics of tests.

For example, different tests (such as multiple-choice tests and essay tests) have different properties, which students can be taught to recognize. In fact, your college library or bookstore should be able to provide materials dealing with the nature of tests and "test smarts"; and we can recommend one such reference: a practical, pocket-sized book by Jason Millman, entitled *How to Take Tests* (Cornell Publishing, Cornell University, Ithaca, New York). Some colleges also offer workshops or study sessions on how to take different kinds of tests. Remember that instructors want your test scores to reflect what you have learned. If you do poorly because you do not understand the nature of the test, then the test becomes an obstacle to accurate assessment rather than a tool for assessment. Familiarizing yourself with various kinds of tests will help ensure that your grade will be determined by your learning.

Below, we suggest some strategies that will help you prepare for and take tests, so that an examination will become a genuine opportunity for you to demonstrate what you have learned.

### Intellectual preparation

Preparing for a test has intellectual, emotional, and physical aspects. Let's look first at some strategies for intellectual preparation.

- Attend classes.
- Follow our step-by-step procedure for using *Human Development* and the Study Guide. Remember that this procedure can be adapted for use with other textbooks and supplements.
- Schedule regular study sessions in a specific, quiet place; and set small, reachable goals for each study session.
- Study relevant quizzes and tests that you have already taken.
- Become familiar, in advance, with the purpose and format of the test. Ask your instructor to what types of questions will appear.
- See yourself—realistically—as succeeding on the test.

### Emotional and physical preparation

Now let's look at some strategies for preparing yourself emotionally and physically.

- Appreciate the usefulness of the test.
- Relax.
- Concentrate.
- Get a good night's sleep before the test.
- Eat a good meal before the test.
- Avoid sugars before the test, and consume *no* caffeine.
- Arrive early for the test, and come prepared with all necessary supplies (such as #2 pencil, pens, paper).

### Taking the test: General strategies

*Use time wisely.* Since the time allowable for taking the test is limited, it's important to use that time efficiently.

- Find out how long you have to complete the test.
- Look over the entire test briefly before you start to answer any questions. Find out which items yield the most points.
- Begin to work as rapidly as is possible with some reasonable assurance of accuracy.
- At the outset, omit items that stump you, or just take a guess. If you have enough time when you've completed the rest of the test, remember to return to these items.
- Work immediately, and quickly, on the items which will yield the most points.
- If you become too nervous to work, stop briefly and use some relaxation techniques to calm yourself.
- If you have any time left when you've finished the test (including any difficult items you skipped at the beginning), use it to reconsider and improve your answers. As a rule, however, don't change an answer unless you are absolutely certain that you misread the question initially, or that you missed some important aspect of it. Your first answer is often the correct one.

*Read all directions and questions carefully.* Students often lose points simply because they haven't followed directions, or because they have misinterpreted questions.

- Before you start writing, become familiar with the test directions.
- Pay particular attention to the directions that most influence how you will take the test.
- Ask the examiner for clarification when necessary.

- Keep the test directions in mind while you are answering the questions.
- Be careful to read each question "as is"—not as you might like it to be.
- Pay attention to any vocabulary terms that appear in the questions. If you are allowed to make your own notes on your exam paper, sometimes it helps to circle or highlight vocabulary terms in a question; this can help you pinpoint what the question is asking for.
- If you can write your own notes on on the exam paper, it may be helpful in multiple-choice to cross out answers that you have eliminated as incorrect, and in matching sections to cross off items you've already paired up.

### Taking the test:
### Strategies for specific types of questions

*Multiple-choice items.* The typical multiple-choice format consists of an incomplete sentence with several options for completing it, or a question with several possible answers. (You may have to circle the correct choice, or write its identifying letter or number in an answer space.)

- Read the fragment or question carefully, anticipate the answer, and then look for your anticipated answer among the choices.
- If the choices do not include the answer you anticipated, consider all the alternatives using a process of elimination. It can be helpful to treat the item as a "completion" question, covering all the choices and then uncovering one at a time.
- If, in a four-choice format, you have eliminated two of the choices but are undecided about the remaining two, treat each of the remaining two as a "true-false" question.
- Relate each option to the question.

*Matching items.* The typical matching format consists of two sets of items to be paired off. They might be in side-by-side columns; or one set might be inside a box, as in this Study Guide; or there may be some other setup. (Arrangements for indicating the answers vary. In this Study Guide, for instance, each item in one of the sets is followed by an answer space.)

- As always, read the directions carefully.
- Count the number of items in each set.
- Determine the relationship between the two sets.

- Try the first item. If you can't find its "partner" in the second set, skip to the second item. Keep skipping until you find one matching pair, then go on until you find another pair, and so on.
- When you have matched all the items you know, use a process of elimination for the remaining items. If you are allowed to write your own notes on the exam paper, cross out the items you have already matched.

*Completion items.* The typical completion, or "fill-in," item is a sentence with one or more blanks; you are to make the sentence read correctly by supplying whatever is needed in each blank. (You may be asked to write your answer in the blank itself, or in a separate answer space.)

- Give a general answer if you don't know the specific answer.
- Examine the sentence for grammatical clues. (For example, *a* or *an* preceding a blank tells you that the answer is singular; *these* or *those* tells you that the answer is plural.)

*True-false items.* The typical true-or-false item is a statement which you are to identify as correct or incorrect. (You may have to write *T* or *true*, or *F* or *false*, in an answer space; or check off or circle a *T* or an *F*.)

- Remember the odds (50-50).
- As always, read each item carefully.
- Look for qualifiers (*not, new, recent,* etc.).
- Watch for absolute terms (*always, never, all, none, every*). Items using absolute terms are usually false.
- Watch for conditional terms (*some, few, occasionally, sometimes*). Items using conditional terms are usually true.

*Essay items.* An essay item may be phrased as a question ("Why did Freud believe that ... ?" or as an imperative ("Explain why Freud believed that ... "). You are to write a full answer. Often, your answer will be graded not only for content but also for grammar and for the logic of your presentation. (Space may be provided for each answer; or all the essay items may be on a printed sheet, with answers to be written in an examination booklet or on your own paper.)

- When a test has more than one essay item, read each one carefully.

- If you are allowed to make notes on the exam paper, jot down beside each essay item the relevant points that occur to you.
- If you can make notes on the exam paper, you may also want to highlight or circle parts of the question that indicate exactly what you are being asked to write about.
- Analyze the verbs in the item: *contrast, compare, describe, list, explain,* etc. Circle them for emphasis if that is permitted.
- Organize your answer before you start writing.
- If you are not sure of the best answer, quickly write down all your ideas.
- Follow a format: introduction, body, conclusion.
- If you do not have enough time to write a full essay answer, give your answer in outline form.

- When you have finished an essay item, read it over. Check to be sure that you have followed each of the direction verbs you identified (you may have circled these, as noted above).
- WRITE LEGIBLY.

*"Bubble sheets" and optical scanner sheets.* These are not, of course, types of questions; nevertheless, they are formats that you should know how to deal with. Two hints:

- Before turning in your exam, make sure that you have filled in all the spaces.
- If you skip any items on the test, be sure to complete the remaining items in the correct order.

## IN CONCLUSION

As we mentioned earlier, there are no shortcuts to learning; and there are no shortcuts to good grades. Good grades are the result of hard work. But for serious students who want their grades to reflect the amount of effort they have spent studying, these study tips and guidelines for test-taking should be very helpful.

This Study Guide was designed as an educational tool to help you learn the material in *Human Develop-ment*. Therefore, you should plan to use it as a working document. Mark up the pages: make notes on the chapter outlines, make notes of definitions and examples of the key terms, jot down your thoughts about the learning objectives, and write in your answers to the self-tests.

Doing all this, and following our suggestions, will help you improve your overall memory of the material you are learning.

## ACKNOWLEDGMENTS

Several people have contributed to the development of the Study Guide, and their help is gratefully acknowledged here. Corinne Crandell, Colleen Crandell, and Karen Bieger generously contributed their time and talents in helping us with the important but tedious work necessary to write valid and reliable test questions. We express special thanks to our creative editors at McGraw Hill: to Renee Shively Leonard and Susan Gamer, for doing all the behind-the-scenes things which resulted in making this Study Guide a more readable and more useful learning tool for students; and, finally, to Jane Vaicunas for her continued support of our work.

*Thomas L. Crandell*
*George R. Bieger*

# CHAPTER 1

# ABOUT HUMAN DEVELOPMENT

## INTRODUCTION

**Chapter 1** provides an overview of the field of human development from both theoretical and research perspectives. Several important issues are discussed, including the following:

■ A historical presentation of the study of human development leading to the current life-span view.

■ The influences on human development, ranging from those which are purely individual to those common to specific (cross-cultural) groups.

■ Experimental methods, nonexperimental methods, and data-collection techniques used to discover more about

human nature, as well as the framework of ethical considerations for conducting research on human subjects.

■ The four dominant theories of development—psychoanalytic, mechanistic, organismic, and humanistic—and the role they play in helping to explain, interpret, and predict human behavior and guide future research.

The authors' intent in this textbook is to provide the reader with practical information based on research with human subjects—as much as is currently available—and to portray people as unique individuals with the capacity to change and to influence their own development.

## CHAPTER OUTLINE

**I. HUMAN DEVELOPMENT:
THE SUBJECT AND THE TEXT**

A. WHAT IS HUMAN DEVELOPMENT?

B. HOW THIS BOOK APPROACHES
HUMAN DEVELOPMENT

   1. We Celebrate the Human Being

   2. We Respect All Periods of the Life Span

   3. We Believe in Human Resilience

   4. We Recognize That People Help Shape
     Their Own Development

   5. We Believe That Knowledge Is Useful

**II. HUMAN DEVELOPMENT:
THE STUDY AND ITS HISTORY**

A. ASPECTS OF DEVELOPMENT

   1. Physical Development

   2. Intellectual Development

   3. Personality and Social Development

B. PERIODS OF THE LIFE SPAN

C. INDIVIDUAL DIFFERENCES
IN DEVELOPMENT

D. INFLUENCES ON DEVELOPMENT

   1. Types of Influences: Sources and Effects

     a. Internal and external influences

     b. Normative and nonnormative influences

   2. Contexts of Influences:
     An Ecological Approach

   3. Timing of Influences: Critical Periods

E. HOW THE STUDY OF HUMAN
DEVELOPMENT HAS EVOLVED

   1. Studies of Childhood

   2. Studies of Adolescence, Adulthood,
     and Aging

   3. Life-Span Studies

**III. HUMAN DEVELOPMENT:
RESEARCH METHODS**

A. NONEXPERIMENTAL METHODS

   1. Case Studies

   2. Observation

     a. Naturalistic observation

     b. Laboratory observation

   3. Interviews

   4. Correlational Studies

B. EXPERIMENTAL METHODS

   1. Variables and Groups

   2. Sampling and Assignment

   3. Types of Experiments

     a. Laboratory experiments

     b. Field experiments

     c. Natural experiments

   4. Comparing Experimentation
     with Other Methods

C. METHODS OF DATA COLLECTION

   1. Cross-Sectional and Longitudinal Studies

   2. Sequential Studies

D. ETHICS OF RESEARCH

  1. Ethical Issues

    a. Informed consent

    b. Deception

    c. Self-esteem

    d. Privacy

  2. Ethical Standards

## IV. HUMAN DEVELOPMENT: THEORETICAL PERSPECTIVES

A. THEORIES AND HYPOTHESES

B. PSYCHOANALYTIC PERSPECTIVE

  1. Sigmund Freud: Psychosexual Theory

    a. Freud's stages of psychosexual development

    b. Id, ego, and superego

  2. Erik Erikson: Psychosocial Theory

    a. Erikson's approach

    b. Erikson's eight crises

  3. Critique of Psychoanalytic Theory

C. MECHANISTIC PERSPECTIVE

  1. Behaviorism: Learning through Conditioning

    a. Classical conditioning

    b. Operant conditioning

      (1) Reinforcement and punishment

      (2) Shaping

  2. Social-Learning Theory: Learning through Modeling

  3. Critique of Mechanistic Theory

D. ORGANISMIC PERSPECTIVE

  1. Jean Piaget: Cognitive-Stage Theory

    a. Piaget's cognitive structures

    b. Piaget's principles of cognitive development

  2. Critique of Piaget's Theory

E. HUMANISTIC PERSPECTIVE

  1. Abraham Maslow: Self-Actualization and the Hierarchy of Needs

  2. Critique of Humanistic Theory

## V. A WORD TO STUDENTS

## KEY TERMS

control group (18)

correlational studies (15)

critical period (9)

cross-sectional study (20)

cross-sequential study (20)

data (21)

defense mechanisms (23)

dependent variable (17)

ecological approach (9)

ego (25)

environmental influences (8)

equilibration (33)

experiment (17)

experimental group (17)

extinction (29)

heredity (8)

human development (3)

humanistic perspective (33)

hypothesis (22)

id (25)

independent variable (17)

interview (15)

laboratory observation (14)

longitudinal study (20)

mechanistic perspective (27)

naturalistic observation (14)

neutral stimulus (27)

operant conditioning (28)

organismic perspective (31)

organization (32)

psychoanalytic perspective (23)

psychosexual development (25)

psychosocial-development theory (26)

punishment (28)

qualitative change (3)

quantitative change (3)

random sample (18)

reinforcement (28)

sample (18)

scheme (32)

scientific method (12)

shaping (29)

social-learning theory (30)

superego (25)

theory (21)

unconditioned response (unconditioned reflex) (UCR) (27)

unconditioned stimulus (UCS) (27)

## LEARNING OBJECTIVES

After finishing Chapter 1, you should be able to:

1. Explain what is meant by the study of *human development*.

2. Differentiate between *quantitative* and *qualitative* changes in development.
   a. Give an example of a *quantitative* change.

   b. Give an example of a *qualitative* change.

3. Explain four major steps applied in the study of human development.
   a.

   b.

   c.

   d.

4. List the four major aspects of the self in which growth and change occur.
   a.

b.

c.

d.

5. Name and briefly describe eight periods of development within the life span.
   a.

   b.

   c.

   d.

   e.

   f.

   g.

   h.

6. Define *internal* and *external* influences on development and cite an example of each.
   a. internal

   b. external

7. Differentiate between normative and nonnormative influences on development.
   a. Give an example of a normative age-graded influence.

   b. Give an example of a normative history-graded influence.

   c. Give an example of a nonnormative influence.

8. On the basis of the *ecological approach* to development, briefly describe the four different levels of *environmental* influence.
   a.

   b.

   c.

   d.

9. Explain how cross-cultural research is applied in the study of human development.

10. Define *critical period* and explain how this concept relates to human development.

11. Explain how societal and medical progress in the nineteenth century caused adults to take a new view of childhood.

12. Define *scientific method,* and explain its application to research.

13. Name and describe the five categories of nonexperimental methods for collecting data:
    a.

    b.

    c.

    d.

    e.

14. Define the following terms as they relate to *experimental* research:
    a. *independent variable*

    b. *dependent variable*

    c. *experimental group*

    d. *control group*

    e. *random sample*

15. List the three types of experiments, give an example of each, and cite advantages and disadvantages of each.
    a.

    b.

    c.

16. Describe, compare, and contrast the three methods of data collection.
    a. *cross-sectional* studies

    b. *longitudinal* studies

    c. *cross-sequential* studies

17. In your own words, explain each of the following issues as it relates to the ethics of human research.
    a. informed consent

    b. deception

    c. self-esteem

    d. privacy

    e. ethical standards

18. Define the following research terms.
    a. theory

    b. data

    c. hypothesis

**19.** Briefly describe the goals of *psychoanalytic theory,* and name the physician who is attributed with having originated it.

**20.** Referring to page 24 in the text, describe in your own words each of Erik Erikson's eight psychosocial crises of development and indicate approximately at what ages these occur:
  **a.** basic trust versus basic mistrust

  **b.** autonomy versus shame and doubt

  **c.** initiative versus guilt

  **d.** industry versus inferiority

  **e.** identity versus identify confusion

  **f.** intimacy versus isolation

  **g.** generativity versus stagnation

  **h.** integrity versus despair

**21.** Describe the two major theories comprised by the mechanistic perspective.
  **a.** *behaviorism*

  **b.** *social-learning theory*

**22.** Briefly describe the *organismic perspective* of development and name its major proponent.

**23.** Name and describe Piaget's four stages of cognitive development, and indicate at approximately what age each occurs.
  **a.**

  **b.**

  **c.**

  **d.**

**24.** Explain the major beliefs of the *humanistic perspective,* and name the person who is credited with developing it.

**25.** Briefly describe Maslow's hierarchy of needs that motivate human behavior.

## SUPPLEMENTAL READING

Gerald W. Bracey is a research psychologist and policy analyst for the National Education Association. This article is a reprint from the *Phi Delta Kappan*, May 1990.

## Culture, Science, and the Concept of Child

### Gerald W. Bracey

Not too long ago I told a friend that I was thinking about writing an article charging that all educational research is a lie. This article would not fault the academic obsession with "knowledge production," though that is dreadful enough. Nor would it harp on the limitations of the methods of quantitative research, though they are severe enough. No, the thrust of this article would be that educational research is largely unguided by anything other than implicit ideas of child development or of what it means to be human. Much research seems to be a combination of naive realism and unthinking behaviorism. Certainly if you tried to reconstruct a human being from the features described in the literature of educational research, your construction would be a peculiar-looking creature.

The field of developmental psychology attends, in part, to such concepts as "child." It turns out that the concept of a child, which is influenced by the prevailing ideology of development, is now in flux and has been for some time. At least, those are some of the conclusions I draw from an article by Kathryn Young of Yale University in the February 1990 issue of *Child Development*.

Young notes that women's magazines began to publish articles about child care near the end of the 19th century and that such publications "evolved into a sustained alliance between experts and parents in which pediatricians, psychologists, educators, and child developmentalists have assumed the role of counsel to parents." Two publications, *Parents Magazine* and *Infant Care Manual*, have long histories of communicating information from professionals to parents. Young set out to see what these publications were telling parents between 1955 and 1984.

She analyzed the articles in both publications for topical content (how often certain topics appeared) and thematic content (what was said about certain themes, such as breast-feeding or the role of the mother in development). The 443 articles on infants that were published between 1955 and 1984 fell about evenly into two categories: information from research and theory and information about practical concerns and infant care.

Young also looked at the frequency data on the percentage of articles appearing in each of the three decades covered, 1955–64, 1965–74, and 1975–84. Different topics showed different patterns. Articles on the mother/child relationship accounted for about 10% of the articles in the first two decades, then rose to 20% in the third decade. Articles on feeding, on the other hand, accounted for 25% of all articles between 1955 and 1964, then fell to about 15% for the next two decades.

Articles about working mothers were virtually nonexistent in the first two decades, then rose to about 8% of the articles in the third. Similarly, pieces about infant cognition rose from about 7% in the first two decades to about 15% in the third.

When one looks at what the articles actually said, other trends emerge. Although mother/child interaction continued to be important throughout the three decades, the overarching power and centrality of the maternal role declined. Similarly, articles in the first two decades emphasized the role of the mother as full-time caretaker. An article that appeared in *Parents Magazine* in 1960 said that "a baby needs his mother as vitally as he needs food and air." Only in the Eighties did *Parents Magazine* begin to reassure mothers that out-of-home care for infants is okay and to provide advice about child-care centers. So marked has this trend become that some articles have appeared that reassure mothers that it is also okay to stay at home with the children.

Although the coverage of fathers by *Parents Magazine* did not change much in terms of frequency, the emphasis shifted from the father as someone the mother should include but not expect a lot out of to the view that the father has an integral and unique role to play.

The topic of feeding cycled with the times, emphasizing breast-feeding in the Fifties, advising either method in the Sixties and Seventies, and shifting back to breast-feeding in the Eighties. This shift occurred in spite of what Young calls "attempts of both publications to present a balanced perspective" and in spite of the lack of solid research evidence about the benefits of breast feeding.

Shifting away from themes about child-rearing practice, *Parents Magazine* maintained a notion of infants as active and thinking, presenting Piaget's concepts when they became popular in the late Fifties and early Sixties. *Infant Care*, on the other hand, was slower in shifting from the view of infants as passive receptacles to the view of infants as active learners.

Discussions about communication and temperament also followed the research findings of the periods. Young writes:

> Two trends are noted in what experts tell parents. The first trend is research-driven, as experts have used psychological research of the last 30 years as the basis for the information and advice they present to parents. . . . Equally powerful is a second trend that in certain areas expert advice is more based on the broader social context and changing demographics.

Clearly, our conceptions of children change. The cry, "Women and children first," is of recent origin, even for sinking ships. Our conception is clearly not that of the English in the early stages of the Industrial Revolution, when children worked in factories for 14 hours a day, seven days a week. It has even been argued that, until the 17th century, the concept of childhood did not exist at all. Children were given no special clothes, toys, or attention. They were generally ignored until they were about 7 years old. Then, when it looked as if they might actually live to adulthood, they were treated as adults. As recently as 1979, another Yale psychologist, William Kessen, referred to both children and child psychology as "cultural inventions."

Although it may be disconcerting to people trained to perceive science as the objective pursuit of truth, all socially meaningful constructs, such as the concept of the child, will always be affected by culture, and, yes, by a degree of expediency. I think, though, that those of us in education would do better if our concepts were made more explicit and comprehensive than they currently are. (From Young's article, I don't think that 30 years of *Parents Magazine* painted a comprehensive picture either.)

TIPS FOR READERS OF RESEARCH

Some tips bear repeating. So, in the spirit that there are "lies, damned lies, and statistics," I repeat some advice about looking at statistics in ways other than the ways they are presented to you by various authors and reports.

For example, a recent survey concluded that the two most dangerous cars in America were two Chevrolet creations, the Corvette and the Camaro. This conclusion was drawn from a statistic showing number of deaths per accident. Well, to begin with, one can ask whether this is the best measure of "dangerousness." How about accidents per thousand miles driven? Or the number of recalls by the manufacturer? Clearly, there are other statistics that could be used.

More important, though, does it strike you as reasonable that these full-sized cars would be inherently more dangerous than the tiny Subaru Justy, Ford Festiva, or Toyota Tercel? Me either. The Corvette, of course, is a pure power machine, and one might wish to inquire about the average speed of those Corvettes at the time of all those accidents. A Camaro, on the other hand, is a lot like acne; it affects males more often than females, and most people grow out of it when they reach adulthood. Since it is sadly the case that young males have more accidents than other people, one might want to know the sex and the average age of the drivers in Camaro accidents.

When identifying trends in reporting about infant development, the subject discussed above, the choice of statistical measures may affect our perception of importance. Kathryn Young used percentage of articles appearing in publications over a 30-year period. Seems a reasonable choice. But I note that most of the topical magazines that I subscribe to have grown thicker in recent years. The use of a percentage lets us see the importance of certain topics relative to other topics. The role of fathers, for example, may have gotten significantly more important in terms of the number of articles published, but this would be obscured if numbers were rising in other categories as well.

On the other hand, the length of articles in many publications has diminished as we have become a more factoid-oriented society with an apparently declining attention span for print. As a result, we could be having more articles that say a lot less. Without analyses in addition to the one Young offered, reasonable though it was, we simply cannot tell.

## Questions about the Reading

1. Referring to Chapter 1 in your text, is Young's research experimental or nonexperimental?

2. What do you think is the hypothesis behind Young's research?

3. After reading this article, do you think that studying trends is a valid method for identifying changes in development across the life span?

---

## SELF-TESTS

---

## Multiple-Choice

Circle the letter of the response which best completes or answers each of the following statements and questions.

1. A change in height or weight is referred to as what kind of a change?
   a. qualitative
   b. psychological
   c. quantitative
   d. social

2. What kind of developmental change is illustrated by Alzheimer's disease, which affects memory and other cognitive abilities?
   a. qualitative
   b. process
   c. quantitative
   d. social

3. Research conducted by observing and recording children's behavior after they watch certain television programs is called what kind of research?
   a. implied
   b. cross-sectional
   c. developmental
   d. applied

4. The unique way each person views the world and expresses emotions is considered a result of what kind of development?
   a. physical
   b. personality and social
   c. intellectual
   d. none of the above

5. Which of the following is the term for the first stage of development, when the human organism grows from a single cell to a complex of billions of cells?
   a. infancy
   b. prenatal
   c. postnatal
   d. neonatal

6. The inborn biological endowment that people inherit from their parents is an internal influence known as
   a. cultural influence
   b. inherited response
   c. heredity
   d. external influence

7. Noninherited influences upon development attributed to a person's experiences are called
   a. original influences
   b. environmental influences
   c. genetic influences
   d. genetic responses

8. Most people in the United States retire from paid employment between the ages of 55 and 70. Which of the following terms is used for an event such as retirement that influences development?
   a. common
   b. normative
   c. similar
   d. nonnormative

9. The authors have presented the research in this text with which of the following philosophies in mind?
   a. People actively shape and influence their own lives.
   b. Research can be cited only on work with animal subjects.
   c. Research cannot be presented with practical applications.
   d. People do not seem to have the potential for change.

10. Studying people who are unemployed because of a depressed economy comes directly from the which approach to understanding development?
    a. psychosocial
    b. mechanistic
    c. ecological
    d. psychoanalytic

11. Careful observation, recording of data, testing of alternative hypotheses, and public dissemination of findings and conclusions are phases of which method?
    a. humanistic
    b. correlational
    c. open-ended
    d. scientific

12. Which of the following research techniques is/are considered nonexperimental?
    a. case studies
    b. correlational studies
    c. naturalistic observation
    d. all of the above

13. Which of the following research techniques is/are considered experimental?
    a. case studies
    b. interviews
    c. clinical studies
    d. a research design using a treatment and a control group and controlling for many variables

14. Data can be collected about development through
    a. cross-sectional studies
    b. longitudinal studies
    c. sequential studies
    d. all of the above

15. Which of the following issues deals with the ethics of human research?
    a. sample size
    b. deception
    c. experimental design
    d. extraneous variables

16. The psychoanalytic perspective differs from other theoretical perspectives because it is concerned with
    a. animal rather than human subjects
    b. how the environment controls behavior
    c. how thinking affects behavior
    d. how the unconscious affects behavior

17. A young man whose parents have recently divorced becomes increasingly dependent on them to make his decisions. Freud called this defense
    a. repression
    b. regression
    c. projection
    d. fixation

18. When there is an arrest in a person's development as a result of too little or too much gratification at a given stage, Freudians would call the person
    a. unhealthy
    b. fixated
    c. deprived of pleasure
    d. lacking goals

19. In the psychosocial-development theory formulated by Erik Erikson
    a. behaviors are measured and recorded
    b. study of the id, ego, and superego is paramount
    c. the systems of home, society, religion, etc., are considered the strongest influences on development
    d. personality development is viewed across the life span, in terms of successful or unsuccessful resolution of a "conflict" at each of eight stages of development

20. The study of behavior that tries to identify and isolate environmental factors that make people behave in certain ways without regard to their own will is related to which perspective?
    a. mechanistic
    b. organismic
    c. psychoanalytic
    d. humanistic

21. A baby girl begins to suck when she sees her mother preparing her bottle before a feeding. This sucking response is an example of a/an
    a. unconditioned stimulus
    b. conditioned stimulus
    c. conditioned response
    d. unconditioned response

22. A stimulus which follows a desired behavior and increases the likelihood that the behavior will be repeated is called
    a. a conditioned response
    b. negative conditioning
    c. punishment
    d. reinforcement

23. Whenever Bobby's mother raises her voice, he knows he is about to be sent to his room for misbehaving. Bobby learns to recoil whenever his mother raises her voice. This learning is an example of
    a. operant conditioning
    b. negative reinforcement
    c. classical conditioning
    d. shaping

24. When a particular response is sometimes reinforced and sometimes not (intermittent reinforcement), the result is usually
    a. extinction
    b. more durable behavior
    c. punishment
    d. shaping

25. Reinforcement in the form of praise from the mother when a child learns to speak sounds that are progressively more like words is identified as
    a. extinction
    b. durable behavior
    c. punishment
    d. shaping

26. Behavioral theory is to _____ as social-learning theory is to _____ .
    a. environmental experience; observation and imitation of models
    b. unconscious urges; environmental experience
    c. historical influences; observation and imitation of models
    d. biological factors; environmental experience

27. A young girl spends a great deal of time watching television. Social-learning theorists predict that
    a. her behavior will be molded solely by her environment
    b. she will develop role models from characters on the screen
    c. she will stop playing with her peers
    d. her own characteristics will not influence which television characters she chooses as role models

28. A young boy succeeds in getting a toy by reaching for it with his hands. When it is moved out of his reach, he gets it by climbing onto a nearby stool. What is the term for this?
    a. equilibration
    b. assimilation
    c. shaping
    d. accommodation

29. Which recent perspective, identified with Maslow, suggests that people have a progression of needs to be met?
    a. cognitive
    b. behavioristic
    c. humanistic
    d. psychoanalytic

30. A person who reaches the highest levels of Maslow's hierarchy of needs is considered
    a. self-actualized
    b. externally influenced
    c. more human
    d. self-aware

## Matching:
## Theoretical Perspectives on Development

Match each of the lettered items in the box (in the opposite column) with the appropriate item or items in the list that follows the box.

> B   behaviorism
> C   cognitive theory
> PS  psychosocial theory
> H   humanism
> PA  psychoanalytic theory
> SL  social-learning theory

1. greatly concerned with early childhood (oral, anal, and phallic stages) and fixations __PA__

2. considers environmental factors the major influence on personality development _____

3. approach in which adaptation, assimilation, accommodation, and equilibration are pertinent concepts __PA  C__

4. maintains that people need to learn some mistrust to be prepared for danger __SL__

5. goals include developing a healthy self-concept and striving for self-actualization _____

6. founded on the belief that children learn by observing and imitating models in their environment (such as parents) _____

7. branch of psychology associated with Maslow _____

8. theory originated by John Watson _____

9. idea that each of us has free will and can make choices (to which environment is not the major contributing factor) _____

10. belief that the kinds of behavior people imitate depends on what kinds of behavior exist and are valued in their culture _____

11. concept of id, ego, and superego as parts of our conscious and unconscious _____

12. theory that we use "defense mechanisms" to protect the psyche _____

13. used mainly for quitting smoking; losing weight; removing phobias; producing appropriate behavior in delinquent adolescents and mentally retarded people; etc. _____

14. suggests that an innate tendency to adapt to our environment is the essence of intelligent behavior _____

15. traces personality development across the life span, stressing societal and cultural influences on the ego at each of eight stages involving resolution of a developmental crisis _____

## Matching: Important People

Match each of the lettered names in the box with his, her, or their contribution to developmental psychology in the numbered list below the box.

> a. Philippe Ariès
> b. Albert Bandura
> c. Urie Bronfenbrenner
> d. Erik Erikson
> e. Sigmund Freud
> f. G. Stanley Hall
> g. Abraham Maslow
> h. Bernice Neugarten
> i. Diane Papalia and Sally Wendkos Olds
> j. Ivan Pavlov
> k. Jean Piaget
> l. B. F. Skinner
> m. Louis Terman
> n. John Watson

1. studied much of what we know about children's thinking _____

2. originated psychoanalysis _____

3. first behaviorist to apply classical conditioning in the study of child development _____

4. formulated psychosocial theory _____

5. professor at Stanford and advocate of social-learning theory _____

6. American behaviorist using behavior modification _____

7. studied middle age and adulthood _h_

8. formulated a theory of adolescence _f_

9. developed a hierarchy of needs _____

10. authors of your text _i_

11. studied very intelligent children _____

12. developed principles of classical conditioning using dogs _____

13. conceived an ecological approach to development focusing on four levels of environmental influences _____

14. documented that, historically, children were seen as qualitatively different from adults _A_

## Completion

Supply the term or terms needed to complete each of the following statements.

1. Changes in body, brain, sensory capacities, and motor skills are all part of _____ development.

2. Changes in a variety of mental abilities, such as learning, memory, reasoning, thinking, and use of language, are aspects of _____ development.

3. The range of individual differences increases as people _____ .

4. Influences on development which originate with heredity are called _____ influences.

5. Noninherited influences on development attributed to a person's experiences with the world outside the self are called _____ influences.

6. Life events occurring in a similar way for most people in a given group are referred to as _____ events.

7. According to Bronfenbrenner's ecological approach, to understand individual human development, we must understand each person within the context of multiple _____.

8. A specific time during development when a given event will have its greatest impact is called a _____ period.

9. Whether or not the capacity for learning language is inborn has been examined through _____ research.

10. G. Stanley Hall, a pioneer in the child study movement, was the first psychologist to formulate a theory of _____ , published in 1904.

11. In the 1950s, Neugarten and her associates had begun studying and formulating theories about _____ age.

12. The prevalent idea today is that human development is a _____ process.

13. _____ studies consider a person's life or a single case, recording behavior but not explaining it.

14. In _____ observation, researchers observe and record people's behavior in real-life settings without manipulating the environment.

15. With the _____ method, people are surveyed and asked to state their attitudes or opinions or to relate certain aspects of their life histories.

16. Investigating the relationship between variables or events by applying a mathematical formula is the _____ method.

17. In a controlled experiment, the variable over which the experimenter has direct control is the _____ variable.

18. The _____ group of subjects will be exposed to the experimental manipulation, also known as the *treatment,* but the _____ group will not receive the treatment.

19. A _____ is a set of related statements about data, the information that is obtained through research.

20. Freud said that people unconsciously combat anxiety (over aggressive and sexual conflicts) by distorting reality using _____ mechanisms, such as regression.

21. Although young children at first seek immediate gratification, they eventually develop a _____ which incorporates values and thinking into their personality.

22. Erikson's approach, called *psychosocial theory,* emphasizes the quest for _____ as a major theme in life and traces personality development across the life span.

23. The _____ perspective views human development primarily as a response to external events.

24. The behaviorist credited with being the first to apply stimulus-response theories of learning to the study of child development is _____ .

25. Positive reinforcement, negative reinforcement, and punishment are the basis for _____ conditioning.

26. Reinforcement is most effective when it is _____ .

27. Albert Bandura is a proponent of social-learning theory, which states that children learn by _____ and _____ models (e.g., their parents).

28. Proponents of the organismic perspective argue that although internal and external influences interact, the source of change is _____ , and development occurs in qualitative stages.

29. According to the _____ perspective, people are able to take control of their own lives and influence their own development.

30. Maslow identified a hierarchy of needs; a person who attains the highest level on this hierarchy is described as _____ .

## ANSWERS FOR SELF-TESTS

## Multiple-Choice

1. c (page 3)
2. a (3)
3. d (5)
4. b (6)
5. b (7)
6. c (8)
7. b (8)
8. b (8)
9. a (8–9)
10. c (9)
11. d (10)
12. d (12–15)
13. d (17–20)
14. d (20)
15. b (21)
16. d (23)
17. b (23)

18. b (25)
19. d (26)
20. a (27)
21. c (28)
22. d (28)
23. c (28)
24. b (29)
25. d (29)
26. a (29–30)
27. b (30)
28. d (32)
29. c (33)
30. a (33–34)

## Matching: Theoretical Perspectives

1. PA (pages 24–25)
2. B (27)
3. C (32)
4. PS (26)
5. H (33)
6. SL (30)
7. H (33)
8. B (28)
9. H (33)
10. SL (30)
11. PA (25)
12. PA (23)
13. B (31)
14. C (32)
15. PA (26)

## Matching: Important People

1. k (page 31)
2. e (23)

3. n (28)
4. d (26)
5. b (30)
6. l (28)
7. h (12)
8. f (11)
9. g (33)
10. i (2)
11. m (12)
12. j (27)
13. c (9)
14. a (10)

## Completion

1. physical (page 6)
2. intellectual (6)
3. age (*or* grow older) (6)
4. internal; biological; genetic (8)
5. external or environmental (8)
6. normative (8)
7. environments or systems (9)
8. critical (9)
9. cross-cultural (10)
10. adolescence (11)
11. middle (12)
12. lifelong or life-span (12)
13. case (12)
14. naturalistic (14)
15. interview (15)
16. correlational (15)
17. independent (17)
18. experimental; control (17)
19. theory (21)
20. defense (23)

21. superego (25)

22. identity (26)

23. mechanistic (27)

24. John Watson (28)

25. operant or instrumental (29)

26. immediate (29)

27. observing and imitating (30)

28. internal (31)

29. humanistic (33)

30. self-actualized (33–34)

# CHAPTER 2

# CONCEPTION THROUGH BIRTH

## INTRODUCTION

Chapter 1 examined the subject of human development and discussed several research methods and theoretical perspectives that are used in the study of various aspects of human development. **Chapter 2** discusses what the most current research has found about the beginning of human development, the period from conception until birth. Several issues are covered, including:

■ One of the most perplexing questions in the study of human development: whether human nature is primarily inherited or learned.

■ Fertilization and the basic genetic principles that describe the mechanisms of heredity.

■ Stages of prenatal development before birth, including germinal, embryonic, and fetal.

■ Methods of assessing development before birth, such as amniocentesis, chorionic villus sampling, blood sampling, and umbilical sampling.

■ The stages of the birth process and various settings for childbirth available today.

The chapter also discusses the interaction between heredity and environmental influences on the developing organism.

## CHAPTER OUTLINE

**I. FERTILIZATION**

A.  HOW DOES FERTILIZATION TAKE PLACE?

B.  WHAT CAUSES MULTIPLE BIRTHS?

C.  WHAT DETERMINES SEX?

**II. HEREDITY AND ENVIRONMENT**

A.  WHAT IS THE ROLE OF HEREDITY?

   1.  Mechanisms of Heredity:
      Genes and Chromosomes

   2.  Patterns of Genetic Transmission

     a.  Mendel's laws

     b.  Dominant and recessive inheritance

     c.  Sex-linked inheritance and other forms

   3.  Genetic and Chromosomal Abnormalities

     a.  Defects transmitted by
        dominant inheritance

     b.  Defects transmitted by
        recessive inheritance

     c.  Defects transmitted by
        sex-linked inheritance

     d.  Chromosomal abnormalities

   4.  Genetic Counseling

B.  HOW DO HEREDITY AND ENVIRONMENT
    INTERACT?

   1.  "Nature versus Nurture":
      Hereditary and Environmental Factors

     a.  Hereditary and environmental influences
        on traits

     b.  Maturation

   2.  Studying the Relative Effects
      of Heredity and Environment

   3.  Some Characteristics Influenced
      by Heredity and Environment

     a.  Physical and physiological traits

     b.  Intelligence

     c.  Personality

   4.  Some Disorders Influenced
      by Heredity and Environment

     a.  Alcoholism

     b.  Schizophrenia

     c.  Infantile autism

     d.  Depression

   5.  The Importance of the Environment

**III. PRENATAL DEVELOPMENT**

A.  STAGES OF PRENATAL DEVELOPMENT

   1.  Germinal Stage (Fertilization to
      about 2 Weeks)

   2.  Embryonic Stage (2 to 8–12 Weeks)

   3.  Fetal Stage (8–12 Weeks to Birth)

B.  THE PRENATAL ENVIRONMENT

   1.  Maternal Factors

     a.  Prenatal nourishment

       (1)  Why is prenatal nutrition important?

       (2)  What should pregnant women eat?

b. Maternal drug intake

    (1) Medical drugs

    (2) Alcohol

    (3) Marijuana

    (4) Nicotine

    (5) Opiates

    (6) Cocaine

    (7) Caffeine

c. Other maternal factors

    (1) Illness

    (2) Incompatibility of blood types

    (3) Medical x-rays

    (4) Environmental hazards

2. Paternal Factors: Environmental Influences Transmitted by the Father

## IV. BIRTH

### A. STAGES OF CHILDBIRTH

### B. METHODS OF CHILDBIRTH

1. Medicated Delivery

2. Natural and Prepared Childbirth

3. Cesarean Delivery

4. Medical Monitoring

### C. SETTINGS FOR CHILDBIRTH

---

## KEY TERMS

alleles (page 44)

amniocentesis (54)

autosomes (42)

cesarean delivery (72)

chorionic villus sampling (CVS) (54)

chromosomes (43)

concordant (56)

depression (60)

dizygotic twins (41)

DNA (deoxyribonucleic acid) (43)

dominant inheritance (44)

Down syndrome (51)

electronic fetal monitoring (73)

embryonic stage (64)

fertilization (40)

fetal alcohol syndrome (FAS) (67)

fetal stage (65)

gametes (40)

gene (43)

genetic counseling (53)

genetics (43)

genotype (45)

germinal stage (64)

heredity (43)

heterozygous (44)

homozygous (44)

independent segregation (44)

infantile autism (59)

karyotype (53)

maternal blood test (54)

maturation (56)

medicated delivery (71)

monozygotic twins (41)

multifactorial inheritance (45)

multiple alleles (45)

natural childbirth (72)

ovulation (40)

personality (58)

phenotype (45)

prepared childbirth (72)

recessive inheritance (44)

schizophrenia (59)

sex chromosomes (42)

sex-linked inheritance (45)

spontaneous abortion (65)

temperament (58)

teratogenic (65)

ultrasound (54)

zygote (40)

---

## LEARNING OBJECTIVES

---

After finishing Chapter 2, you should be able to:

1. Describe the following processes.
   a. *ovulation*

   b. *fertilization*

2. Describe the two mechanisms which produce multiple births.
   a.

   b.

3. Describe the mechanism that determines a baby's sex.

4. Explain how *heredity* is determined at fertilization.

5. Explain the principles that govern the transmission of inherited traits.

6. Explain briefly how hereditary traits are transmitted—as separate units or as a group. Name the scientist responsible for this finding.

7. Describe briefly what is meant by *dominant, recessive,* and *sex-linked* inheritance.
   a. dominant



   b. recessive



   c. sex-linked

8. Differentiate between *phenotype* and *genotype*.

9. List some of the birth defects which are caused by *genetic* and *chromosomal* abnormalities.

10. Describe the methods for prenatal diagnosis of birth defects.

11. Explain how hereditary and environmental factors interact to influence human nature.

12. Define *maturation,* and explain how it can be affected by environmental forces.

13. Describe the various methods for studying the relative effects of *heredity* and environment.

14. Explain how certain characteristics and disorders are influenced by both heredity and environment.

15. Describe the three stages of prenatal development.
    a.


    b.


    c.

16. Describe and explain some of the maternal factors that influence prenatal development.

c.

17. Describe and explain some of the paternal factors that influence prenatal development.

19. Name and explain the various methods of childbirth.

18. List and describe the three stages of childbirth.
a.


b.

20. List some alternative settings for childbirth.

---

## SUPPLEMENTAL READING

This article is reprinted from *Time* Magazine, Special Issue, Fall 1990.

## Do the Unborn Have Rights?

**Richard Lacayo**

That Lynn Bremer is an attorney with a good job was not enough to keep her from developing a cocaine habit. The fact that she was pregnant was not enough to make her drop it. So when her daughter tested positive at birth for the presence of drugs in her urine, health officials in Muskegon County, Michigan, took the child into temporary custody. But, to Bremer's astonishment, there was more. The county prosecutor stepped in to charge her with a felony: delivery of drugs to her newborn child. The means of delivery? Her umbilical cord.

After Bremer completed a drug treatment program, she regained her daughter, who is apparently healthy. But the criminal charges remain. "I could lose her," says Bremer. "I could go to prison, and she could grow up with who knows who." Prosecutor Tony Tague is unmoved. He says the threat of prison is sometimes the only way to get pregnant addicts to seek treatment. "Someone must stand up for the rights of the children."

Similar cases involving prenatal drug delivery have cropped up in nine states across the country. Like the abortion issue, they raise serious questions about a woman's right to privacy and the obligations of the state and the individual toward the unborn. At the center of these cases lies a controversial legal concept: fetal rights. This notion also underlies one of the most important cases before the Supreme Court during its current term. At issue are "fetal-protection policies" used by many companies to forbid fertile female employees from taking jobs that might expose them to substances that could harm an unborn child. Fetal-rights advocates say such policies are needed to protect the unborn. Critics say they are an intrusion into the lives of women and a false comfort for a society that fails to offer adequate prenatal care for all women or workplace safety for all workers.

Courts in the U.S. have recognized that third parties—for instance, a drunk driver who injures a pregnant woman—can be sued for doing harm to a fetus. More recent is the notion that expectant mothers can be held criminally responsible for problems suffered by their fetuses. Even pregnant women who are resigned to the legalisms pervading American life might wince to learn that the child forming inside them is also a budding legal entity, possessing rights that may put it at odds with its mother even before it emerges into the world. But the idea has gathered support with the growing spectacle of drug-damaged newborns. Maternity wards around the country ring with the high-pitched "cat cries" of crack babies, who may face lifelong handicaps as a result of their mothers' drug abuse.

With some researchers estimating that each year as many as 375,000 newborns in the U.S. could suffer harm from their mothers' prenatal abuse of illegal drugs, district attorneys are tempted by what looks like the quick fix of pregnancy prosecution. "You have the right to an abortion. You have the right to have a baby," says Charles Molony Condon, prosecutor for the Charleston, North Carolina, area. "You don't have the right to have a baby deformed by cocaine." Courts have given a mostly skeptical reception to the attempt to apply existing drug laws in such a novel fashion, but eight states and Congress are considering legislation that would explicitly criminalize drug use and alcohol abuse by pregnant women that result in harm to the child.

Critics of such measures say that a true effort on behalf of unborn children would focus on the needs of expectant mothers rather than punishing bad behavior after the fact. Few drug treatment programs, for instance, accept pregnant addicts. A study of New York City drug-abuse programs found that 87% turned away pregnant crack users. Says Sidney Schnoll, a psychiatrist at the Medical College of Virginia: "We seem more willing to place the kid in a neonatal intensive-care unit for $1,500 or $2,000 a day, rather than put $1,500 into better prenatal care."

Some legal experts also warn that prenatal drug-use prosecutions could open the way to punishing women for many other kinds of behavior during pregnancy. What about drinking? Smoking? Taking prescription drugs? Or working too hard? "Are we going to be policing people's wine closets?" asks Stanford University law-school professor Deborah Rhode. Other legal scholars insist that such "slippery slope" arguments are exaggerated; laws commonly distinguish between reckless behavior and acceptable risk.

Still, the efforts to protect the rights of the fetus have far-reaching implications, and not just for pregnant women. The UAW et al. v. Johnson Controls case, now facing the Supreme Court, provides a dramatic example. In 1982 Johnson Controls, a Milwaukee-based company that is one of the nation's largest car-battery manufacturers, decided to forbid its fertile women employees to hold jobs that would expose them to lead levels potentially damaging to a fetus. High doses of lead—higher than any permitted by law in the workplace—have been linked to miscarriages and fetal death. Even lower levels, however, can result in learning problems and diminished growth for exposed babies. "This decision was not taken lightly," says Denise Zutz, director of corporate communications for Johnson Controls. "We were concerned about the risks to children." The company was also seeking to avoid later lawsuits by any children who might be harmed in the womb.

That was not much comfort to Shirley Jean Mackey, who worked at one of the company's plants in Atlanta. A mother of one who had no immediate plans to get pregnant, she was forced to move from a job she liked, bundling lead plates, to another she hated, punching holes in hundreds of battery containers. "Each hole I punched, it was somebody's head," says Mackey. "That's just the way I felt." Along with the United Auto Workers, which represents many of Johnson Controls' employees, she is one of eight workers bringing suit against the company. They charge that its policy violates the 1964 Civil Rights Act, which bars employment discrimination on the basis of sex, pregnancy, or related medical conditions unless the practice in question directly relates to the worker's ability to do the job.

So far, two lower federal courts have ruled in favor of the company. But a California court went the other way, calling the policy "blatant" discrimination and adding, "If the Supreme Court rules for Johnson Controls, then by some estimates up to 20 million jobs, many of them well paid, could eventually be closed to women." Gulf Oil, B. F. Goodrich, Du Pont and Eastman Kodak are just some of the companies that have instituted fetal-protection policies since a federal court upheld such measures in 1984. Johnson Controls estimates that more than half its production jobs are barred to fertile women.

To some people, fetal-protection policies are merely a way to avoid making the workplace safe for men and women equally. Feminists also dismiss them as discrimination masquerading as compassion, a disguised way of keeping women out of more lucrative men's jobs. Critics of the fetal-protection policies also point out that toxic substances in the workplace may damage genes in the male sperm. "A man or woman working in a plant should be told the dangers and make up their own minds," says Molly Yard, president of the National Organization for Women.

Ironically, it was the Supreme Court's decision creating a right to abortion in Roe v. Wade that also provided some of the legal underpinning for fetal rights. The same ruling recognized a government interest in protecting the fetus during the last trimester of pregnancy. But while judges had a hand in creating fetal rights, courts will never be able to ensure real protection to an unborn child. That will have to come from mothers who take responsibility for the lives they carry within them—and a nation willing to provide the fetus with real prenatal care. For now, it seems more willing to provide a lawyer.

(Reported by Barbara Cornell/New York.)

## Questions about the Reading

1. After having read Chapter 2, what would you says are some of the reasons for supporting protection of fetuses?

2. What is this article saying about the role of the environment in fetal development?

---

## SELF-TESTS

---

## Multiple-Choice

Circle the letter of the response which best completes or answers each of the following statements and questions.

1. The single cell that is formed when an ovum is fertilized is called a/an
   a. zygote
   b. embryo
   c. gamete
   d. fetus

2. The term *dizygotic twins* identifies
   a. twins who develop from one-cell division
   b. identical twins
   c. twins created by different ova and different sperm, who may be the same sex or different sexes
   d. twins who are always of the same sex

3. The chromosomal combination that results in a female is
   a. YY
   b. YX
   c. XX
   d. XY

4. *Heredity* is defined as
   a. two gametes uniting to form a zygote
   b. the study of sex chromosomes
   c. a process of cell division
   d. inborn factors inherited from our parents that affect our development

5. The sex of a child depends entirely upon the
   a. sex chromosome of the father
   b. sex chromosome of the mother
   c. autosomes of both parents
   d. autosomes of the mother

6. An underlying, invisible genetic pattern that causes certain traits to be expressed is called
   a. a phenotype
   b. a genotype
   c. recessive inheritance
   d. dominant inheritance

7. Which of the following statements about chromosomal defects is the most accurate?
   a. All chromosomal defects are inherited.
   b. Accidental chromosomal abnormalities are not likely to recur in the same family.
   c. Down syndrome is the least common chromosomal disorder.
   d. All people with chromosomal abnormalities are severely retarded.

8. A couple might seek genetic counseling if
   a. one handicapped child has already been born
   b. there is a family history of hereditary illness
   c. one partner has a condition suspected to be inherited
   d. all of the above

9. A 40-year-old woman expresses concern to her obstetrician regarding the health of her developing fetus; she fears the baby may have Down syndrome. The obstetrician would probably suggest testing by using
   a. amniocentesis
   b. a fetoscope
   c. ultrasound
   d. IQ scores

10. The prenatal diagnostic technique which creates a picture of the uterus, the developing fetus, and placenta and is used to detect multiple pregnancies and major abnormalities is
    a. chorionic villus sampling
    b. umbilical cord assessment
    c. ultrasound
    d. amniocentesis

11. The prenatal diagnostic technique which analyzes a sample of the tissue from the membrane around the embryo is called
    a. chorionic villus sampling
    b. umbilical cord assessment
    c. ultrasound
    d. amniocentesis

12. Umbilical cord assessment can allow a doctor to
    a. test for metabolic disorders and immunodeficiencies
    b. take samples of the fetus's blood
    c. examine liver function and heart failure
    d. all of the above

13. Jamie was adopted as an infant. During adolescence, his IQ score was found to be extremely high. Which factor is most closely correlated with Jamie's intelligence?
    a. his adopted parents' IQ
    b. his biological mother's IQ
    c. his adoptive siblings' IQ
    d. none of the above is associated at all with his intelligence

14. A young pregnant woman consumes large amounts of alcohol. Her developing baby will be most vulnerable to alcohol-induced birth defects during which stage of prenatal development?
    a. gamete
    b. embryonic
    c. germinal
    d. fetal

15. The term for the stage of prenatal development during which the organism is implanted in the wall of the uterus is
    a. germinal
    b. embryonic
    c. fetal
    d. gamete

16. The stage of prenatal development during which the organism develops the major body systems (respiratory, alimentary, nervous) is
    a. germinal
    b. embryonic
    c. fetal
    d. gamete

17. In which stage of development is a spontaneous abortion (miscarriage) most likely to occur?
    a. germinal
    b. embryonic
    c. fetal
    d. gamete

18. Which of the following statements about the placenta is the most accurate?
    a. The placenta is a barrier between mother and fetus.
    b. The placenta shields the fetus from the toxins in the mother's body.
    c. The placenta filters out hazards before they reach the fetus.
    d. Virtually everything the mother takes in is passed to the fetus.

19. The method of childbirth in which the baby is removed surgically from the mother's uterus is called
    a. prepared childbirth
    b. cesarean delivery
    c. natural childbirth
    d. medicated delivery

20. Which of the following statements is most accurate?
    a. It is now known that the father cannot transmit environmentally caused defects.
    b. It is best to do continuous, routine electronic fetal monitoring when a pregnancy seems uncomplicated.
    c. Proportionately more babies die at or soon after birth in the United States compared with a number of western European countries.
    d. The mortality rate in the United States has declined over the past several decades, in terms of world rankings.

## Matching

Match each lettered item in the box with the appropriate description in the numbered list below the box.

a. autosomes
b. monozygotic
c. fertilization
d. gametes
e. phenotype
f. karyotype
g. autism
h. maturation
i. teratogenic
j. homozygous
k. heredity
l. Mendel
m. genes
n. 6
o. 23

1. an observable trait  _e_
2. inborn factors affecting development  _k_
3. laid foundation for understanding inheritance in 1860s  _l_
4. unfolding of age-related behaviors _____ _h_
5. nonsex chromosomes  _A_
6. producing birth defects _____ _i_
7. a single egg and a single sperm  _D_
8. percent of babies born yearly in the United States with handicaps  _n_
9. zygote receives this many chromosomes from the mother and  same number from the father  _o_
10. fusion of sperm cell and ovum  _c_
11. enlarged photos of chromosome structure analyzed for abnormalities _____ _f_
12. term used when both alleles are the same for a given characteristic  _j_
13. rare developmental disorder involving inability to communicate with or respond to other people; a baby with this disorder may be apathetic or oblivious to other people  _g_
14. twins formed from one ovum  _b_
15. made of DNA and determine inherited characteristics  _a_  _m_

## Completion

Supply the term or terms needed to complete each of the following statements.

1. The release of an egg cell by the ovaries, about once a month, is called _____ .

2. An ovum (woman's egg) can be fertilized about _____ hours after release from the ovary about midcycle. Thus, there is a "window" of about _____ hours during each menstrual cycle when sexual intercourse can result in fertilization.

3. _____ carry the genes that determine inherited characteristics.

4. Genes that govern alternative expressions of a particular characteristic are called _____ .

5. In _____ inheritance, certain recessive genes, carried on the sex chromosomes, are transmitted differently to make males and females.

6. _____ is a person's overall pattern of character, behavioral, temperamental, emotional, and mental traits, some of which are believed to be inherited.

7. A major body of recent research suggests that shyness and boldness are _____ characteristics, are related to various physiological functions, and tend to stay with people throughout life.

8. During the germinal stage of development, the blastocyst is developing into the nurturing and protective organs called the _____ , _____ , and _____ .

9. Today, we know that various _____ factors can affect a male's sperm and the children he conceives.

10. A combination of slowed prenatal and postnatal growth, disorders of the central nervous system, and body malformations attributable to maternal alcohol use during pregnancy is labeled _____ .

11. "An apathetic, lethargic baby who in early childhood will have trouble loving his or her mother, making friends, and playing normally"—this describes a child whose mother probably used _____ during pregnancy.

12. Childbirth, which takes place in three stages, usually begins after about _____ days of gestation.

13. The _____ method of childbirth instructs women in anatomy to remove fear of the unknown and trains them to vary their patterns of breathing to match the strength of contractions and to concentrate on sensations other than contractions.

14. _____ is an assessment technique that provides valuable information during high-risk deliveries.

15. While the specific services a pregnant woman in western Europe would receive would vary depending upon which country she lived in, the woman would most likely receive _____ prenatal and postnatal care as well as _____ maternity leave from work.

## ANSWERS FOR SELF-TESTS

### Multiple-Choice

1. a (page 40)
2. c (41)
3. c (42)
4. d (43)
5. a (43)
6. b (45)
7. b (51)
8. d (53)
9. a (54)
10. c (54)
11. a (54)
12. d (55)
13. b (57)
14. b (64)
15. a (64)
16. b (64)
17. b (65)
18. d (66)
19. b (72)
20. c (75)

### Matching

1. e (page 45)
2. k (43)
3. l (44)
4. h (56)
5. a (42)
6. i (65)
7. d (40)
8. n (48)
9. o (43)
10. c (44)
11. f (53)
12. j (44)
13. g (59)
14. b (41)
15. m (43)

### Completion

1. ovulation (page 40)
2. 24, 48 (41)
3. chromosomes (43)

4.  alleles (44)

5.  sex-linked (45)

6.  personality (58)

7.  inborn *(or* genetic, *or* inherited) (60)

8.  placenta; umbilical cord; amniotic sac (64)

9.  environmental (65)

10.  FAS, fetal alcohol syndrome (67)

11.  cocaine *(or* crack) (68)

12.  266 (70)

13.  Lamaze *(or* natural, *or* prepared) (72)

14.  electronic fetal monitoring (73)

15.  paid, paid (75)

# CHAPTER 3

# PHYSICAL DEVELOPMENT IN INFANCY AND TODDLERHOOD

## INTRODUCTION

In **Chapter 3** we learn that the first year of life is usually one of rapid physical growth, more so than any other time in the child's life, with stabilized regulation of all major systems of the body.

■ At birth, immediate medical and behavioral assessment is crucial to determine a baby's health status. Low-birthweight babies are at a higher risk of potential complications; several recommendations are made for preventing or overcoming the physiological and psychological problems of these babies.

■ The cerebral cortex of the brain especially becomes enriched with neural connections, allowing for more flexible, higher-level motor and intellectual functioning.

The importance of proper nutrition, nurturance, and stimulation during this year cannot be overemphasized.

■ A neonate's initial reflex behaviors will disappear during the first year or so, being replaced by deliberate behaviors. More recent research examines the importance of early sensory stimulation for all newborns. Three principles of infants' development are explained: head to toe, inner to outer, and simple to complex.

■ Infants' variations in daily cycles of sleep, wakefulness, and activity are thoroughly described.

■ The interaction of heredity and environment as it affects the timing of milestones of motor development is discussed, along with a multicultural view of motor development.

# CHAPTER OUTLINE

## I. THE NEONATE

A. PHYSICAL CHARACTERISTICS

B. BODY SYSTEMS

1. Circulatory System

2. Respiratory System

3. Gastrointestinal System

4. Temperature Regulation

C. THE BRAIN AND REFLEX BEHAVIOR

1. Growth and Development of the Brain

2. A Newborn's Reflexes

D. THE NEWBORN'S HEALTH

1. Medical and Behavioral Screening

   a. Immediate medical assessment: The Apgar scale

   b. Neonatal screening for medical conditions

   c. Assessing responses: The Brazelton scale

2. Effects of Birth Trauma

3. Low Birthweight and Infant Mortality

   a. Types of low birthweight

   b. Risk factors in low birthweight

   c. Consequences of low birthweight

   d. Treatment of low birthweight

4. Sudden Infant Death Syndrome (SIDS)

## II. DEVELOPMENT DURING THE FIRST 3 YEARS OF LIFE

A. PRINCIPLES OF DEVELOPMENT

1. Top-to-Bottom Development

2. Inner-to-Outer Development

3. Simple-to-Complex Development

B. STATES: THE BODY'S CYCLES

C. GROWTH AND NOURISHMENT

1. Influences on Growth

2. Breastfeeding

3. Bottle Feeding

4. Cow's Milk and Solid Foods

D. THE SENSES

1. Touch

2. Taste

3. Smell

4. Hearing

5. Sight

E. MOTOR DEVELOPMENT

1. Milestones of Motor Development

   a. Head control

   b. Hand control

   c. Locomotion

2. Environmental Influences on Motor Development

3. Can Motor Development Be Speeded Up?

F. HOW DIFFERENT ARE BOYS AND GIRLS?

## KEY TERMS

anoxia (page 82)

Apgar scale (85)

birth trauma (88)

Brazelton Neonatal Behavioral Assessment Scale (88)

cephalocaudal principle (94)

cerebral cortex (83)

Denver Developmental Screening Test (102)

habituation (100)

infant mortality rate (88)

lanugo (81)

low birthweight (88)

meconium (82)

neonatal period (80)

neonate (81)

physiologic jaundice (82)

preterm (premature) babies (90)

proximodistal principle (94)

reflex behaviors (85)

small-for-date babies (90)

states (95)

sudden infant death syndrome (SIDS) (93)

vernix caseosa (81)

visual cliff (101)

visual preferences (101)

## LEARNING OBJECTIVES

After finishing Chapter 3, you should be able to:

1. Describe some common physical characteristics of the *neonate*.

2. Name three examples of a neonate's primitive *reflexes*, and explain them briefly.
   a.


   b.

c.


3. Compare the consequences, for a baby, of an enriched environment versus a deprived environment.


4. Describe the differences between the *Apgar scale* and the *Brazelton scale*.

5. The authors have given considerable information about the relationship between *low birthweight* and health complications. Explain several factors which can contribute to low birthweight.

6. In your own words, define *SIDS* and explain two hypotheses about what may cause it.

7. Briefly describe the following three principles about babies' growth and development.
   a. top-to-bottom development

   b. inner-to-outer development

   c. simple-to-complex development

8. List and briefly describe the five *states* of infants.
   a.

   b.

   c.

   d.

   e.

9. Describe what the normal infant's capacities seem to be in each of the following sensory systems.
   a. touch

   b. taste

   c. smell

   d. hearing

   e. sight

10. Bearing in mind that there is no "average" baby, list several milestones of motor development for all children.

11. Describe some environmental and hereditary influences during a baby's first year of development.

12. Explain a few differences and similarities between baby boys and girls.

## SUPPLEMENTAL READING

This article is reprinted from *Newsweek*, October 29, 1990.

## Brother Sun, Sister Moon

### Sharon Begley

How can siblings, who share 50 percent of their genes and the same home, be so different? First-time parents believe fervently in the power of nurturing: how they raise their child will strongly sculpt her personality, temperament, behavior and talents. But when the second child arrives, and they look from one sibling, maniacally flinging books off a shelf, to the other, silently crayoning and ducking the missiles without protest, they wonder, "We didn't treat them *that* differently, did we?" That's when parents become instant converts to the idea that nature—heredity—is all.

Psychologists, too, have vacillated between proclaiming nature or nurture the strongest force shaping human development. Now, a book by two Pennsylvania State University professors of human development tries to stop this pendulum. In *Separate Lives: Why Siblings Are So Different* (Basic Books, $19.95, 210 pages), Judy Dunn and Robert Plomin point to an overlooked factor: children growing up in the same home do not share the same "environment."

The logic of their argument is impeccable. Siblings are only 50 percent similar genetically (they share half their genes, which are estimated to account for about half the difference in individuals' IQs and 30 percent of personality differences). Put the other way, siblings are 50 percent *different* genetically. But they are more than 50 percent different as measured by tests of personality, attitude, belief and temperament, Dunn and Plomin point out. So unique biological inheritances cannot account for all the dissimilarity. That leaves environment. And since most siblings share the same parents, class and all the other measures that psychologists trot out to explain how kids turn out the way they do, it can only be the *differences* in that environment—real or perceived—that make children so diverse. Siblings' similarities, say the authors, "can be completely explained by heredity"—nature. "Sibling differences . . . emerge for reasons of nurture as well as nature."

This is a revolutionary concept, the idea that children can—and often do—experience the same factors differently and that this idiosyncratic response nudges their characters down different roads. It means that if children share some environmental factor, such as parental permissiveness, what is important in explaining their separate personalities is the various ways they respond to that shared factor. A child who is shy by nature will react very differently to having a social butterfly for a mother than does his outgoing sister. In studies of thousands of children in Sweden, England and Colorado, siblings were indeed found to frequently respond to the same event (a parent's absence, a burglarized home) and interpret the same behavior (a mother's social preening) in totally disparate ways.

The origin of sibling differences—what makes one Carter brother the cartoonish pusher of "Billy Beer" and the other the architect of the Camp David accords—must lie, then, in how such *apparently* shared influences shape siblings differently. If shared experiences per se were important, then siblings would turn out more similar to each other than they are to children in other, nonalike families. They do not. The theory thus casts doubt on such sacred cows as the importance of class to IQ, of paternal permissiveness to personality. Such factors are experienced so differently by siblings that they are more likely to differentiate children, not make them similar.

Consider the "shared" environment of, for example, an affectionate mother. She is very loving to her children when they are 1, but less so as they grow into independent 3-year-olds. The 3-year-old, Dunn and Plomin found, pays more attention to her brother's being smothered with kisses than to the memory of being cuddled herself at his age. Even worse, treating one child better than another, in a misguided attempt to give her an edge in life, actually hurts the spurned child without helping the favorite become better adjusted. Children who feel that their parents show more love to a sibling generally grow up with a lower sense of self-competence and self-worth.

### ADORED ELDER

The mere presence of another child has a powerful effect. The firstborn may have a childhood of unrelenting irritation from one who demands attention, whines and runs to Mommy at any provocation. The younger suffers an unrequited desire to play with the adored elder and tries desperately to keep up. These are starkly different "environments."

The results of the study do not lend themselves to easy how-tos for parents, and it is hard to let go of the hope that by reading to kids at bedtime and spending other "quality time" parents can shape their children. One message that's hard to dismiss is how acutely children suffer from even the slightest differences in treatment by father and mother. The consequences of that are almost always negative, so parents would do well to minimize those differences. But if children are shaped by differences in the shared environment, and if parents minimize those differences, does that imply that parents will have no effect on their off-spring? Sort of. "As parents we tend to believe that we have enormous influences on . . . our children," says psychologist Sandra Scarr of the University of Virginia. "Actually, if we are reasonable, loving, but not perfect parents, children will grow up to be themselves—all different but OK." For parents reeling under constant warnings and how-tos, that's the most reassuring news of all.

## Questions about the Reading

1. Cite a few examples of environmental influences on your own development.

2. Cite a few examples of what you believe to be hereditary influences on your own development.

3. From your own personal experience, which do you believe has a greater impact on development—heredity or environment?

---

## SELF-TESTS

---

## Multiple-Choice

Circle the letter of the response which best completes or answers each of the following statements and questions.

1. During the first 4 weeks of life after birth—a time of transition from support by the mother's body to independent existence—an infant is called a/an
   a. gamete
   b. neonate
   c. primate
   d. embryo

2. Which of the following statements about newborns is correct?
   a. It is rare for a newborn to have jaundice.
   b. Not all of a newborn's skull bones are completely fused at birth.
   c. In their first few days after birth, newborns usually gain up to 10 percent of their body weight.
   d. Size at birth is not related to size during childhood.

3. Shortly after birth, about half of all newborn babies develop a condition resulting from immature liver function that is called
   a. physiological jaundice
   b. oxygen deprivation
   c. corticalization
   d. anoxia

4. As the baby matures, in what area of the brain do cells increase their complexity of connections the most?
   a. cerebellum
   b. hypothalamus
   c. cerebral cortex
   d. subcortical areas

5. *Moro, tonic, rooting,* and *grasping* are all terms related to what part of an infant's development?
   a. sensory
   b. intellectual
   c. physical
   d. reflex

6. In a study which compared rats and other animals raised in an "enriched" environment with counterparts raised in isolated cages, it was found that those raised in the "enriched" environment had
   a. thicker cortical layers
   b. higher neurochemical activity
   c. more connective cells
   d. all of the above

7. Which of the following statements about motor development is the most accurate?
   a. With regard to motor development, there is very little difference between different cultures.
   b. Cultural differences in motor development are completely independent of genetic differences among peoples.
   c. Both environment and heredity play a role in determining motor development.
   d. All infants respond with identical reflex behaviors to external stimuli.

8. Which of the following factors is *not* assessed by the Apgar test?
   a. reflex irritability
   b. skin texture
   c. muscle tone
   d. breathing

9. The major factor in infant mortality is
   a. birth trauma
   b. a deprived environment
   c. apnea
   d. low birthweight

10. Low-birthweight babies born before the thirty-seventh week of gestation are
    a. premature
    b. embryos
    c. small for date
    d. fetuses

11. Which of the following women is statistically *least* likely to give birth to an underweight infant?
    a. Annette: she is black, 16 years old, and unmarried; this is her first child; she was underweight before pregnancy and has gained 12 pounds during the pregnancy; she smokes.
    b. Brenda: she is black, 39 years old, and married; she has had two previous miscarriages; she has high blood pressure; she drinks.
    c. Christine: she is white, 29 years old, and married; this is her second child; she has gained 22 pounds during this pregnancy.
    d. Dorothy: she is white, 41 years old, and unmarried; this is her fifth child; she has diabetes; she smokes.

12. The unexpected death of an apparently healthy infant during the first year of life is called
    a. low birthweight
    b. cephalocaudal impairment
    c. SIDS
    d. proximodistal failure

13. During his first months of life, Jamie is an alert baby who cries often and shows a variety of responses to his environment. Katie, however, is a much less vigorous newborn; she is quiet and rarely active. Which of the following might we infer?
    a. By age 10, Jamie will be more developed physically, emotionally, and intellectually.
    b. By age 10, Katie will be more developed physically, emotionally, and intellectually.
    c. Both infants will develop similarly.
    d. During infancy, Katie's parents created an environment with a great deal of stimulation.

14. What is usually considered the "best food" for babies?
    a. mother's milk
    b. goat's milk
    c. soy milk
    d. milk-based formula

15. Which sensory system appears to develop earliest?
    a. touch
    b. vision
    c. taste
    d. smell

16. A 4-month-old baby boy is repeatedly exposed to a recording of a young woman's voice whenever he sucks on his pacifier. Eventually, the infant stops responding to this auditory stimulus. Habituation experiments indicate that when a new voice is introduced on the recording, the baby will
    a. still not respond to the recording
    b. be unable to distinguish between the two different voices
    c. becomes upset and begin to cry
    d. show revived interest and begin to suck hard on the pacifier

17. Babies' visual preference seems to be for
    a. straight lines
    b. familiar sights
    c. simple patterns
    d. pictures of faces

18. A child who fails to exhibit a skill at an age when 90 percent of all children ordinarily exhibit it is considered
    a. intellectually delayed
    b. low-birthweight
    c. physically delayed
    d. developmentally delayed

19. After about 3 months, babies are generally able to
    a. sit by themselves
    b. drink from a cup
    c. giggle and laugh
    d. roll over front to back

20. Sarah's baby boy has begun to show striking changes; he is fearful of new situations, imitates complex behaviors, and appears most secure around Sarah and her husband. These changes seem to occur in the second half of the baby's first year of life and are initiated by
    a. precise hand control
    b. the new ability to crawl
    c. visual preferences
    d. the ability to walk

21. Delays in motor development can result from an environment deficient in
    a. nutrition
    b. physical freedom
    c. attention from adults
    d. all of the above

22. Which of the following is a conclusive statement about early toilet training?
    a. It is quite successful and easy to achieve.
    b. It is very difficult to achieve.
    c. Elimination is originally voluntary.
    d. Maturation must occur before training can be effective.

23. Normal physical growth and development
    a. proceed uniquely for each individual
    b. proceed in a preordained sequence
    c. depend only on environmental factors
    d. depend only on genetic factors

24. What is the general conclusion about using infant "walkers"?
    a. They are highly related to injuries in infants.
    b. They encourage early walking.
    c. They are usually safe.
    d. They definitely make for happy babies.

25. Which of the following statements about physical differences between boys and girls is true?
    a. Boys are usually smaller.
    b. Boys are more vulnerable throughout life.
    c. Infant boys and girls are dramatically different.
    d. Boys are definitely more active.

## Matching

In the box below are several numbers. Match each number with the appropriate description in the list following the box.

```
1
2
3
4
5 1/2
7
16
25
40
60
```

1. average number of years at which a baby's eyesight approaches adult acuity ___ 3
2. number of weeks in the neonatal period ___
3. number of weeks of normal full-term gestation ___ 40
4. number of pounds at birth below which an infant is classified as low-birthweight ___ 5 1/2
5. number of hours the average neonate sleeps each day ___ 16
6. number of minutes after birth when an infant who has not yet begun to breathe may be in danger ___ 2
7. approximate percentage of the adult brain weight that a newborn's brain weighs ___ 25
8. minimum score attained by 90 percent of normal infants on the Apgar scale ___ 7
9. approximate percentage of newborn boys upon which routine nonritual circumcision is currently performed ___ 60
10. age in years after which children need a varied diet, drawn from all major food groups ___ 1

## Completion

Supply the term or terms needed to complete each of the following statements.

1. For approximately the first 4 weeks of life, a newborn infant is called a/an _____ .

2. A newborn's skin is usually quite pale and may have an oily covering referred to as _____ to protect the baby against infection.

3. Some neonates are born with fuzzy prenatal hair called _____ , which usually falls off within a few days.

4. Waste matter formed in the fetal intestinal tract and excreted during the first 2 days or so after birth is _____ .

5. _____ is the medical term for oxygen deprivation at birth.

6. A child's motor development is influenced by both genetic and _____ differences among peoples.

7. The _____ Neonatal Behavioral Assessment Scale is a neurological and behavioral test used to measure the way neonates respond to their environment.

8. According to the _____ principle, development proceeds from the head to the lower parts of the body.

9. According to the _____ principle, development proceeds from the central parts of the body to the outer parts.

10. Periods of sleep, wakefulness, and activity for an infant are known as _____ .

11. Recent studies support the theory that obesity has a strong _____ basis.

12. _____ occurs when a baby becomes used to a stimulus and stops responding to it.

13. Gibson and Walk learned through their _____ experiment that babies perceive depth from a very early age.

14. Because experiments have shown that babies have the ability to distinguish between sights and the ability to select what they view, we can identify some of their visual _____ .

15. The _____ Test was designed to identify children who are not developing normally.

---

## ANSWERS FOR SELF-TESTS

---

### Multiple-Choice

1. b (page 80)
2. b (81)
3. a (82)
4. c (83)
5. d (84)
6. d (85)
7. c (85)
8. b (87)
9. d (89)
10. a (90)
11. c (91, 92)
12. c (93)
13. a (96)
14. a (98)
15. a (99)
16. d (100)
17. d (101)
18. d (102)
19. d (103)
20. b (103)
21. d (105)
22. d (105)
23. b (105)
24. a (106)
25. b (106)

### Matching

1. 3 (page 101)
2. 4 (80)
3. 40 (90)
4. 5 1/2 (88)
5. 16 (96)
6. 2 (82)
7. 25 (83, 85)
8. 7 (85)
9. 60 (100)
10. 1 (98)

## Completion

1. neonate (page 80)

2. vernix caseosa (81)

3. lanugo (81)

4. meconium (82)

5. anoxia (82)

6. cultural (86)

7. Brazelton (88)

8. cephalocaudal (94)

9. proximodistal (94)

10. states (95)

11. genetic (99)

12. habituation (100)

13. visual cliff (101)

14. preferences (101)

15. Denver Developmental Screening (102)

# INTELLECTUAL DEVELOPMENT IN INFANCY AND TODDLERHOOD

## INTRODUCTION

Chapter 3 discussed the physical development of the baby from birth through toddlerhood. **Chapter 4** continues the examination of that early stage of life but shifts the focus to intellectual development. Contrary to earlier beliefs, the infant is capable of significant learning and not only responds to the environment but works actively to alter it.

■ This chapter explores the intellectual capabilities of the newborn and examines the processes by which the developing infant begins to interact with the environment in order to render it meaningful.

■ Three different approaches to studying intellectual development will be described: the psychometric, Piagetian, and information-processing approaches.

■ The major intellectual accomplishment of infancy—the development of language—will be examined from the standpoints of learning theory and nativism.

■ The chapter concludes with a discussion of the child's emerging sense of competence and how it is acquired and develops relative to parents' child-rearing styles.

## CHAPTER OUTLINE

**I. HOW INFANTS LEARN**

A. LEARNING AND MATURATION

B. WAYS OF LEARNING

1. Habituation

2. Conditioning

   a. Classical conditioning

   b. Operant conditioning

   c. Combinations of classical and operant conditioning

C. LEARNING AND MEMORY

**II. STUDYING INTELLECTUAL DEVELOPMENT: THREE APPROACHES**

A. PSYCHOMETRIC APPROACH: INTELLIGENCE TESTS

1. What Do Intelligence Tests Measure?

2. What Do Scores on Intelligence Tests Mean?

3. Why Is It Difficult to Measure Infants' and Toddlers' Intelligence?

4. What Is Developmental Testing?

5. Can Children's Scores on Intelligence Tests Be Improved?

B. PIAGETIAN APPROACH: COGNITIVE STAGES

1. Piaget's Sensorimotor Stage (Birth to About 2 Years)

   a. Cognitive concepts of the sensorimotor stage

   b. Substages of the sensorimotor stage

      (1) Substage 1: Use of reflexes (birth to 1 month)

      (2) Substage 2: Primary circular reactions and acquired adaptations (1 to 4 months)

      (3) Substage 3: Secondary circular reactions (4 to 8 months)

      (4) Substage 4: Coordination of secondary schemes (8 to 12 months)

      (5) Substage 5: Tertiary circular reactions (12 to 18 months)

      (6) Substage 6: Beginning of thought—mental combinations (18 to 24 months)

   c. Research based on the sensorimotor stage

2. Piaget's Timing: When Do Children Actually Attain Various Abilities?

   a. Object permanence

   b. Invisible imitation

   c. Deferred imitation

   d. Number concepts

   e. Conservation

C. INFORMATION-PROCESSING APPROACH: PERCEPTIONS AND SYMBOLS

1. Information Processing during Infancy as a Predictor of Intelligence

2. Influences on Information Processing and Cognitive Development

## III. DEVELOPMENT OF LANGUAGE

A. THEORIES OF LANGUAGE ACQUISITION

   1. Learning Theory

   2. Nativism

B. STAGES IN LANGUAGE DEVELOPMENT

   1. Prespeech

   2. First Words

      a. Growth of vocabulary

      b. Symbolic gesturing

      c. Language and cognition in the first-word stage

   3. First Sentences

   4. Early Syntax

C. CHARACTERISTICS OF EARLY SPEECH

D. INFLUENCES ON LANGUAGE ACQUISITION

   1. Heredity

   2. Environment

   3. Delayed Language Development

## IV. DEVELOPMENT OF COMPETENCE

A. THE HARVARD PRESCHOOL PROJECT

   1. What Influences Competence?

   2. How Can Parents Enhance Children's Competence?

   3. Can Training Help Parents Improve Children's Competence?

B. HOME: THE HOME OBSERVATION FOR MEASUREMENT OF THE ENVIRONMENT

## KEY TERMS

acquired adaptations (page 122)

Bayley Scales of Infant Development (119)

causality (121)

circular reactions (122)

classical conditioning (114)

cognitive development (120)

conditioned response (114)

conditioned stimulus (114)

deferred imitation (126)

habituation (113)

holophrase (132)

information-processing approach (126)

intelligence quotient (IQ) tests (117)

intelligent behavior (117)

invisible imitation (125)

language acquisition device (LAD) (130)

learning (112)

learning theory (130)

linguistic speech (132)

maturation (112)

nativism (130)

neutral stimulus (114)

novelty preference (128)

object permanence (120)

operant (instrumental) conditioning (115)

Piagetian approach (120)

prelinguistic speech (131)

primary circular reaction (122)

psychometric approach (117)

reinforcement (115)

reliable (117)

representational ability (121)

schemes (122)

secondary circular reactions (122)

sensorimotor stage (120)

standardized norms (117)

tertiary circular reactions (124)

unconditioned response (114)

unconditioned stimulus (114)

valid (117)

visible imitation (125)

visual-recognition memory (127)

weight conservation (126)

## LEARNING OBJECTIVES

After finishing Chapter 4, you should be able to:

**1.** Distinguish between *learning* and *maturation*.

**2.** Explain *habituation*.

**3.** Define the following terms associated with *classical conditioning:*
a. *unconditioned stimulus*

b. *unconditioned response*

c. *neutral stimulus*

d. *conditioned stimulus*

e. *conditioned response*

**4.** Give an example of *operant conditioning* and an example of a reinforcer.

5. Describe how *classical conditioning* and *operant conditioning* can combine to produce complex learning.

6. Briefly describe, compare, and contrast the three approaches to studying intellectual development.
   a. *psychometric*

   b. *Piagetian*

   c. *information-processing*

7. Explain the following basic concepts of the psychometric approach.
   a. *IQ*

   b. *standardized norms*

   c. *validity*

   d. *reliability*

8. Describe some problems involved in trying to measure intelligence in infants and toddlers.

9. Explain *cognitive development* in Piaget's *sensorimotor stage,* and define the following terms in his theory.
   a. *object permanence*

   b. *causality*

   c. *representational ability*

   d. *circular reactions*

   e. *schemes*

10. List the six substages of the sensorimotor period.
    a.

    b.

    c.

    d.

    e.

    f.

11. Describe infants' intellectual development according to the information-processing approach.

12. Explain how information processing in infancy is related to intelligence.

13. Briefly relate the cultural difference between the Chinese and American approaches to child development that Professor Gardner found in his study in China in 1989.

14. Describe the development of *prelinguistic speech*.

15. Compare and contrast *learning theory* and *nativism* as approaches to *language acquisition*.

16. List and briefly describe the five stages of linguistic development.
    a.

    b.

    c.

d.

e.

17. Describe some of the factors that influence acquisition of language.

18. Give three suggestions for talking with babies at different stages of language development:
    a.

    b.

    c.

19. Briefly explain what influences competence, and give a few suggestions for enhancing a child's competence.

20. Describe some findings of studies using the HOME inventory.

## SUPPLEMENTAL READING

Leah Levinger, Ph.D., is a clinical child psychologist and a professor at Bank Street College. Jo Adler writes about child development ("Jo Adler" is the pen name of Josie Oppenheim). This article is reprinted from *Good Housekeeping*, September 1990.

## How Children Learn

### Leah Levinger, with Jo Adler

No two children learn and develop in exactly the same way. Each has an individual style and pace. Even though all children go through the same stages of development, it's not possible to know exactly at what point your child should be crawling, tying shoelaces, or reading *Moby Dick.*

But parents, aware that the adult world is highly competitive, often compare children of the same age. This approach can be misleading. The best way to help your child reach maximum potential is to understand and respect individual growing time.

Let's take a look at some of the ways children differ in how they learn.

### WHAT AFFECTS LEARNING?

**Temperament.** Recent research shows that children are born with certain distinct characteristics or temperaments that generally remain with them throughout life. Some children adapt easily to new situations right from birth; others need repeated exposure to people and surroundings before they feel comfortable. A "slow to warm-up" child may ultimately have a greater grasp of a subject than a child who catches on quickly; he just needs added time to get used to the new learning situation.

**Concentration.** Some children concentrate on one task so intently that they have no time for anything else. For example, 14-month-old Adam isn't speaking yet but is walking and trying to climb the stairs. Using his hands for balance, he makes his way up the full flight. The minute his mother brings him down, he tries again, crawling up six or eight times in a row. He intends to master efficient stair navigation no matter what it takes. While perfecting his skill, he lets speech take a backseat. He'll get to it in good time, but right now he's busy practicing on the stairs.

**Skipping a Step.** At 11 months, Brian could say a few words like "hot," which he used for anything that might hurt him, and "dog," which referred to the cat as well. At 16 months

he was combining some words and at 20 months speaking in sentences. Brian's parents were very pleased with his progress because he seemed to be right on schedule.

But Brian's sister, Julie, caused parental concern. At three, though she responded to verbal directions, she barely uttered a word and seemed way behind others in her age-group. Then, just after her third birthday, she amazed her mother by announcing at lunch, "This lemonade is too sour!" Julie simply skipped a substage of learning. While other children experimented with each step in acquiring speech, Julie figured out how to speak but kept this new knowledge to herself. When everything clicked, she was ready to converse.

Sometimes a conflict takes priority in a child's life and learning tasks are ignored for a while. For example, when a new baby enters the home, a young child's interest and affection for the newcomer may conflict with fear of being displaced. Sorting through these feelings requires a special learning process of its own and demands just as much concentration as learning to read or ride a bike.

### HOW PARENTS CAN HELP

Now let's see what parents can do—and not do—to help children learn and develop.

**On the Move.** At seven or eight months, a child is developmentally able to begin crawling, and that's what most children do. But not all. Some first sit up and "row" themselves across the room. Parents of "rowers" often wait eagerly for that magic moment when their child crawls. But that moment may never be. Instead, one day, usually between nine and 16 months, their child stands up and is ready to walk.

Kids also have different methods of learning to walk. One holds on, falls down, crawls part of the way, tries and tries again. Another won't make a move until both feet are planted firmly on the ground. Parents need do little more than provide a safe learning area and then observe how their baby masters locomotion.

**Can We Talk?** Speaking for most children begins somewhere between four to eight months with nonsensical language or babbling. Babies are innately capable of the entire range of sounds possible in human speech. Through babbling, they get ready to speak their native language by imitating its specific sounds. In fact, a baby's babbling has an accent; you can usually tell whether she is from France, Maryland, or Brooklyn by listening to her inflection. Parents can help their children with language by babbling back to their infants and by speaking, singing, and reciting rhymes.

This verbal communication should continue through early childhood to set the groundwork for speech and later for reading.

When children begin to speak in earnest, many have trouble with certain sounds, such as "th," "r," or a sharp "s" sound. Some parents rush these kids to speech therapists, but it's wiser to wait; most outgrow this "baby talk" by first or second grade. Some children all but master the "th" sound only to find themselves back where they started after the first visit from the tooth fairy.

Young children need time to master correct pronunciation and grammar. It's wiser not to stop a child in the middle of a sentence when she says "dat" instead of "that" or "mouses" instead of "mice." Interrupting a child's continuity of thought may cause her to forget what she was saying and become uncomfortable about expressing her ideas.

How is a child to learn to speak properly if not corrected? Most children eventually correct themselves by being around adults who speak well. If a child does become self-conscious or is repeatedly teased about a speech problem by other children or adults outside the home, it may be best to set aside a special time for some exercises. A pediatrician will suggest exercises geared to specific problems or make a referral to someone who can. Be sure to keep the exercise sessions separate from ordinary daily conversation.

**ABCs and More.** Reading is a form of magic. Those who possess its key have the power to transform simple strokes on a page into something quite fantastic—a story, an idea, an answer to a question, or instructions for a special toy. Such possibilities make finding the secret code very appealing. Studies show that children should not begin structured reading lessons until they are six or seven. But there is much a parent can do to enhance a child's feeling for language without formal teaching. Here are some tips:

*Provide a verbal environment.* A child's vocabulary increases if adults don't talk down. One teacher of five year olds uses words like "claustrophobia" and "decorum" to the children's delight. They can be understood as easily as "too close" or "behavior" and offer a wider range of experience.

*Be alert to a child's method of learning.* Some children learn to read by recognizing the visual pattern of words. Others guess the right word from the context. Still others decode by breaking words into sight and sound. If you assume your child is learning to read in the same way you did, you may miss opportunities to help.

*Encourage children to be creative with language.* Young children make up their own spellings, reinvent letters, and write in scribbles only they can understand. This is a meaningful step in learning. A child develops best at this stage if parents accept and enjoy this early foray into the adult world. Tender feelings can be hurt with remarks that a crayoned sentence is only "scribbles" or that a backwards letter is "silly."

*Participate.* Parents can easily create an atmosphere filled with the fun of reading. In the car, have children help with road signs. "Slow" and "Stop" are easy words. Most early readers enjoy figuring out words on cereal boxes, street signs, and billboards. And, of course, the more you read to a child, the better.

**How Children Think.** As children grow, the way they understand the world grows with them. Before about 10 months, a child believes that if something disappears from sight it no longer exists. But gradually, he learns to look for a ball that has rolled under the couch or a coin hidden in someone's hand. By between 12 and 16 months, children are able to make use of symbols. Language is one such set of symbols. A bar of soap floating in the bathtub becomes the symbol for a boat. While fantasy play continues into early school years, it slowly gives way to a perception of the world based on facts. "How does it work?" is a typical question at this period. This is a time for games with complex rules like baseball and Monopoly and for learning how events really evolve.

At around 12, children begin to think abstractly, to generalize, and to relate different ideas. They become interested in forces that cannot be seen, such as gravity, and moral principles, such as justice.

Michael Jellinek, M.D., chief of child psychology at Massachusetts General Hospital, says, "Children move at their own pace from stage to stage. Getting to a stage early has no particular significance or value. In fact, rushing a child into more advanced kinds of thinking is likely to turn him away from learning."

What can parents do to maximize a child's intellectual potential? "Just involve your child in normal life events, such as playing with toys, reading the newspaper, and having discussions," Dr. Jellinek advises. "If parents provide these opportunities for interaction, nature and learning will take care of themselves."

## Questions about the Reading

1. Would you agree or disagree with a critic who argued that supersuccess is probably more a function of differences in inherited ability than differences in parenting? Why?

2. According to learning theory, children learn language through reinforcement. What types of reinforcers can parents provide to help their young children learn to talk?

## SELF-TESTS

### Multiple-Choice

Circle the letter of the response which best completes or answers each of the following statements and questions.

1. Which of the following statements about newborns' capacities is the most accurate?
   a. Babies are blind at birth.
   b. Babies are born with the ability to learn.
   c. Newborn babies are unable to feel pain.
   d. Newborn babies do not have fully developed brains.

2. "A relatively permanent change in behavior that results from experience" is a good definition for
   a. maturation
   b. habituation
   c. learning
   d. development

3. Which of the following most correctly states the relationship between maturation and learning?
   a. Learning cannot take place without maturation.
   b. Maturation cannot take place without learning.
   c. Learning and maturation are not related.
   d. Maturation and learning are indistinguishable from each other.

4. The process of getting used to a stimulus is known as
   a. maturation
   b. habituation
   c. learning
   d. development

5. Anna was used to her father's taking pictures with a camera and flashbulb. One day she actually blinked *before* the flashbulb went off. Anna now associated her blinking with the camera. Anna's learned behavior is an example of
   a. classical conditioning
   b. spontaneous learning
   c. operant learning
   d. incidental learning

6. If the flashbulb's going off is called the *unconditioned stimulus,* then Anna's blinking her eyes is the
   a. neutral response
   b. spontaneous response
   c. unconditioned response
   d. incidental response

7. In one study, 2-day-old infants were reinforced by hearing music as long as they sucked on a dry nipple. The babies would prolong their sucking as long as the music continued. This is an example of
   a. classical conditioning
   b. operant (instrumental) conditioning
   c. incidental learning
   d. a neutral stimulus

8. Which approach to studying intellectual development emphasizes the quantity of intelligence as measured by intelligence tests?
   a. Piagetian
   b. quantitative
   c. information-processing
   d. psychometric

9. Which approach to studying intellectual development emphasizes the quality of intellectual functioning?
   a. Piagetian
   b. quantitative
   c. information-processing
   d. psychometric

10. Which approach to studying intellectual development analyzes the processes underlying intelligent behavior?
    a. Piagetian
    b. quantitative
    c. information-processing
    d. psychometric

11. Test developers must try to devise tests that measure what they claim to measure; we call this criterion
    a. validity
    b. reliability
    c. standardization
    d. a norm

12. A test that is reasonably consistent from one time to another in the measurements it yields is said to be
    a. valid
    b. standardized
    c. reliable
    d. normed

13. In recent years, people in general have been performing at higher levels on the Stanford-Binet IQ test, probably as a result of
    a. better-educated parents
    b. exposure to educational television programs
    c. experiences in preschool and prekindergarten programs
    d. all of the above

14. Bayley's Scales of Infant Development, used with children from 2 months to 2 1/2 years old, is *not* used to
    a. measure abilities such as perception, memory, learning, and verbal communication
    b. predict later intelligence
    c. measure gross motor skills and fine motor skills
    d. look at emotional development, social behavior, and persistence

15. From 1970 to 1975, Parent-Child Development Centers tested the hypothesis that the performance of low-income children on intelligence tests can be improved by influencing parents' attitudes and behavior during the child's first 3 years of life. This study found which of the following?
    a. Mothers in the experimental group encouraged their children to think and talk and gave their children praise.
    b. Mothers in the experimental group gave their children more play materials and more flexible routines.
    c. Mothers in the control group were less emotionally supportive and more interfering than those in the experimental group.
    d. all of the above

16. What is the first stage of cognitive development, according to Piaget?
    a. representational
    b. sensorimotor
    c. reflexive
    d. circular reactions

17. Learning how to reproduce a pleasurable or interesting occurrence that was originally discovered by chance is called
    a. causality
    b. representational ability
    c. circular reaction
    d. object permanence

18. More recent research on Piagetian theories has found which of the following?
    a. Young infants may fail to search for hidden objects because they weren't capable physically to perform actions to find an object.
    b. Visible imitation using body parts the baby cannot see has occurred as early as within a day of birth.
    c. Babies aged 14 months could accurately imitate an action seen as much as one 1 week earlier.
    d. all of the above

19. Which approach sees people as manipulators of perceptions and symbols and focuses on individual differences in intelligent behavior?
    a. Piagetian
    b. information-processing
    c. psychometric
    d. each of the above

20. Researchers gauge the efficiency of infants' information processing by
    a. measuring variations in attention
    b. measuring how quickly babies habituate to familiar stimuli
    c. measuring how much time the babies spend looking at new and old stimuli
    d. all of the above

21. In Professor Gardner's investigation of early childhood education and creativity in China in 1989, which of the following did he find?
    a. American parents encourage more exploratory, independent behavior than Chinese parents do.
    b. Chinese parents encourage more exploratory, independent behavior than American parents do.
    c. Chinese parents do not believe in guiding their children's behavior in order to diminish the children's frustration.
    d. American parents believe in guiding their children's behavior in order to diminish the children's frustration.

22. Which of these statements about language acquisition is the most accurate?
    a. Children learn language without reinforcement.
    b. Children who grew up in institutions babble more because there are more adults to listen to.
    c. Human beings seem to have an inborn capacity for acquiring language and learn to talk as naturally as they learn to walk.
    d. Human beings do not seem to have an inborn capacity for acquiring language; language is learned only through reinforcement.

23. When we observe a child about 14 to 15 months old gesturing and using nonverbal signals to represent specific objects, events, desires, and conditions, we know that
    a. television or day care has been a major influence
    b. the child is acquiring the fundamentals of syntax
    c. even before children can talk, they understand that objects and concepts have names
    d. the parents have usually taught the child these gestures

24. A major factor in determining how quickly and how well a baby learns to speak is
    a. watching and listening to television
    b. one-to-one conversation with adults that paraphrases and expands on the baby's interests
    c. a limited use of "motherese"
    d. discouragment by parents of the baby's babbling

25. When researchers compared HOME scores with children's scores on the Stanford-Binet intelligence test, the single most important factor in predicting high IQ was found to be
    a. how early the child had begun to talk
    b. high socioeconomic status
    c. the mother's ability to create and structure an environment that fostered learning
    d. the quality and quantity of the father's involvement with his child

## Matching

Match each of the lettered items in the box with the appropriate description in the numbered list that follows the box.

---

a. maturation
b. fears
c. intelligent behavior
d. IQ tests
e. cognitive development
f. object permanence
g. nativism
h. left hemisphere
i. Chomsky
j. prelinguistic speech

---

1. is goal-oriented and adaptive _____
2. growth in thought processes _____
3. part of the brain with which language is associated _____
4. psychometric indicator of relative intellectual functioning _____
5. proposed the concept of a language acquisition device (LAD) in the human brain _____
6. unfolding of patterns of behavior in a biologically age-related sequence _____
7. cooing, babbling, accidental imitation, and deliberate imitation _____
8. these can be learned through association _____
9. realization that an object or person continues to exist even when out of sight _____
10. belief that human beings have an inborn capacity for language _____

## Completion

Supply the term or terms needed to complete each of the following statements.

1. The visual cliff experiments demonstrated that learning must be preceded by _____ the biologically determined readiness to master new abilities.

2. A large, representative sample of children of the same age who took a test while it was in the process of preparation produces scores called the standardized _____ .

3. Comparing a baby's ability with the ability typical of infants of the same age is the basis for _____ testing.

4. While intelligence tests are often presumed to measure innate ability, what they actually measure is _____ and _____ .

5. The recognition that certain events cause other events was referred to as _____ by Piaget.

6. Piaget claimed that children at the sensorimotor stage have difficulty grasping concepts such as causality because of their limited _____ .

7. Ahmed enjoys shaking a rattle to hear the noise it makes. Piaget would call this _____ reactions.

8. If Noah steps on a rubber duck, then presses on it, and then sits on it, he is practicing _____ reactions.

9. At around 18 months of age, children become capable of _____ thought, making mental representations and thinking about actions before taking them.

10. Recent research involving studies with hidden objects suggests that _____ may actually appear in children much earlier than Piaget theorized.

11. According to the _____ view, children learn language through reinforcement; but according to _____ , human beings have an inborn capacity for acquiring language.

12. When their speech becomes more complex, so that they use tenses, endings, articles, subjects, verbs, etc.—usually sometime between the ages of 20 and 30 months—children are acquiring the fundamentals of _____ .

13. In order for children to learn to speak and communicate, they need both _____ and _____ ; hearing speech on television is not enough.

14. When speaking to a baby, if you pitch your voice high, use short words and sentences, speak slowly, ask questions, and repeat your words, you are speaking what is called _____ .

15. The Harvard Preschool Project study of 400 preschoolers in 1965 found that _____ level was unimportant, but the child's caretaker's _____ becomes much more important.

## ANSWERS FOR SELF-TESTS

### Multiple-Choice

1. b (page 112)
2. c (112)
3. a (113)
4. b (113)
5. a (114)
6. c (114)
7. b (115)
8. d (117)
9. a (117, 120)
10. c (117)
11. a (117)
12. c (117)
13. d (118)
14. b (119)
15. d (119)
16. b (120)
17. c (122)
18. d (125, 126)
19. b (126)
20. d (127)
21. a (129)

22. c (130)

23. c (133)

24. b (134, 135)

25. c (138)

## Matching

1. c (page 117)

2. e (120)

3. h (130)

4. d (118)

5. i (130)

6. a (112)

7. j (131)

8. b (115)

9. f (120)

10. j (130)

## Completion

1. maturation (page 112)

2. norms (117)

3. developmental (118)

4. achievement; performance (118)

5. causality (121)

6. representational ability (121)

7. secondary circular (122)

8. tertiary circular (124)

9. symbolic (124)

10. object permanence (125)

11. learning theory; nativism (130)

12. syntax (133)

13. practice; interaction (134)

14. motherese (136)

15. socioeconomic; personality (137)

# CHAPTER 5

# PERSONALITY AND SOCIAL DEVELOPMENT IN INFANCY AND TODDLERHOOD

## INTRODUCTION

**Chapter 5** compares Freud's psychosexual theory and Erikson's psychosocial theory with current studies of babies' emotional development and temperamental differences, growth of self-awareness and self-control, gender differences in personality, patterns of attachment to a primary caregiver, relationships with siblings and other children, and individual differences in sociability.

■ Freud's psychosexual theory and Erikson's psychosocial theory provide two different views about toddlers' personality development which have prompted research on relationships between babies and their mothers and fathers and other caretakers, and their relationships with siblings and other babies.

■ Freud's theories about healthy personality development are based on having a physical need met (such as oral gratification), whereas Erikson's theories are based on successful balancing of a critical pair of opposing views of the world (such as trust versus mistrust).

■ The degree to which parents feel comfortable with their child affects their feelings toward that child, and many factors can contribute toward their feelings—including the child's own temperament and degree of sociability.

■ Consequences of high-quality parental care or, on the other hand, of neglect and abuse are also covered in this chapter.

## CHAPTER OUTLINE

### I. THEORETICAL APPROACHES TO EARLY PERSONALITY DEVELOPMENT

A. PSYCHOSEXUAL THEORY: SIGMUND FREUD

    1. Freud's Oral Stage (Birth to 12–18 Months)

    2. Freud's Anal Stage (12–18 Months to 3 Years)

B. PSYCHOSOCIAL THEORY: ERIK ERIKSON

    1. Erikson's Crisis 1: Basic Trust versus Basic Mistrust (Birth to 12–18 Months)

    2. Erikson's Crisis 2: Autonomy versus Shame and Doubt (12–18 Months to 3 Years)

C. EVALUATING THE THEORIES

### II. EMOTIONS: THE FOUNDATION OF PERSONALITY

A. HOW INFANTS' EMOTIONS ARE STUDIED

B. HOW EMOTIONS DEVELOP: THE EMERGING SENSE OF SELF

C. HOW INFANTS SHOW THEIR EMOTIONS

    1. Crying

    2. Smiling

    3. Laughing

D. HOW EMOTIONS ARE COMMUNICATED BETWEEN INFANTS AND ADULTS

    1. Mutual-Regulation Model

    2. Social Referencing

### III. DIFFERENCES IN PERSONALITY DEVELOPMENT

A. EMOTIONAL DIFFERENCES

B. TEMPERAMENTAL DIFFERENCES

    1. Components of Temperament

    2. Three Patterns of Temperament

    3. Influences on Temperament

    4. Effects of Temperament on Adjustment: "Goodness of Fit"

C. GENDER DIFFERENCES

### IV. THE FAMILY AND PERSONALITY DEVELOPMENT

A. THE MOTHER'S ROLE

    1. The Mother-Infant Bond

        a. Is there a critical period for mother-infant bonding?

        b. What do babies need from their mothers?

    2. Attachment: A Reciprocal Connection

        a. Studying attachment

        b. Patterns of attachment

        c. How attachment is established

            (1) What the mother does

            (2) What the baby does

        d. Changes in attachment

        e. Long-term effects of attachment

        f. Effects of other caregivers

        g. Critique of attachment research

B.  THE FATHER'S ROLE

    1.  Bonds and Attachment between Fathers and Infants

    2.  How Do Fathers Act with Their Infants?

    3.  What Is the Significance of the Father-Infant Relationship?

C.  STRANGER ANXIETY AND SEPARATION ANXIETY

D.  DISTURBANCES IN FAMILY RELATIONSHIPS

    1.  Loss of Parents

       a.  Institutionalization

       b.  Hospitalization

    2.  Child Abuse and Neglect

       a.  Causes of abuse and neglect

          (1)  Abusers and neglecters

          (2)  Victims

          (3)  Families

          (4)  Communities

          (5)  Cultures

       b.  Long-term effects of abuse and neglect

       c.  Combating abuse and neglect

       d.  Preventing sexual abuse

## V.  RELATIONSHIPS WITH OTHER CHILDREN

A.  SIBLINGS

    1.  How Children React to the Arrival of a New Baby

    2.  How Siblings Interact

B.  SOCIABILITY

---

## KEY TERMS

ambivalent (resistant) (page 159)

anal stage (146)

attachment (158)

autonomy (147)

autonomy versus shame and doubt (147)

avoidant (159)

basic trust versus basic mistrust (146)

battered child syndrome (166)

child abuse (166)

depression (152)

emotions (148)

imprinting (156)

mother-infant bond (157)

negativism (144)

neglect (166)

nonorganic failure to thrive (166)

oral stage (145)

securely attached (158)

self-awareness (149)

self-control (147)

self-recognition (149)

self-regulation (147)

separation anxiety (164)

sexual abuse (166)

social referencing (151)

socialization (156)

strange situation (158)

stranger anxiety (164)

temperament (153)

## LEARNING OBJECTIVES

After finishing Chapter 5, you should be able to:

1. Name the two significant theories of early personality development and the person who conceived of each.
   a.

   b.

2. Briefly describe how personality is formed according to the psychosexual theory and what the goal of healthy personality development is.

3. Briefly describe how personality is formed and what the goal of healthy personality development is, according to psychosocial theory.

4. Explain what the *oral stage* is, and give approximate ages.

5. Explain what the *anal stage* is, and give approximate ages.

6. Define the following psychosocial terms as they relate to early personality development.
   a. crisis

   b. *basic trust versus basic mistrust*

   c. *autonomy versus shame and doubt*

   d. virtue of hope

   e. virtue of will

7. Explain two criticisms of the psychosexual and psychosocial theories.

8. Name five of the *emotions* that researchers believe babies are able to show.
   a.

   b.

   c.

   d.

   e.

9. List the three ways that babies are able to show their emotions.
   a.

   b.

   c.

10. Explain how a mother's *depression* affects her baby.

11. Briefly describe the range of emotional differences in babies.

12. In your own words, briefly explain what is meant by the following terms pertaining to a baby's *temperament*.
   a. easy child

   b. difficult child

   c. slow-to-warm-up child

   d. goodness of fit

13. Describe how, in a research study on gender differences, strangers tended to react to a supposedly male baby and a supposedly female baby.

14. Describe what babies need from their mothers.

15. Describe recent research findings about nonmaternal care for a child whose mother is working.

16. Describe are recent findings about fathers' interaction with young children.

17. Describe recent findings about siblings' interaction with young children.

18. Distinguish between *stranger anxiety* and *separation anxiety*.

19. Briefly describe how babies may react to the following changes in their lives.
    a. parents' divorce, or death of a parent

    b. institutionalization

    c. hospitalization

20. List some of the causes of *child abuse* and *child neglect*.

---

## SUPPLEMENTAL READING

---

Michele Block Morse is a free-lance writer who lives with her husband and two daughters in Westchester County, New York. This article is a reprint from *Parents*, July 1990.

### Fitting into the Family

#### Michele Block Morse

Elizabeth Mullen [parents' and children's names are pseudonyms] is basically an upbeat person—the type who assumes that the glass is half full, not half empty. She's low-key, rarely gets angry, and makes friends easily. When Mullen became pregnant, she assumed her child would turn out to be as good-natured as she is.

Instead, she got Jimmy.

Cranky and irritable from the day he was born, Jimmy grew into a hesitant toddler who wouldn't try anything new and who embarrassed his mother with his clinginess. His behavior bewildered Mullen, who found herself contemplating, sometimes in anger, whether her son had been born into the wrong family. "It wasn't the way it was supposed to be," she says, thinking back on her son's troubled first years. "I figured I was doing something wrong."

It was a classic case of bad chemistry that could easily have degenerated into full-scale family warfare. Instead, nine-year-old Jimmy and his mother are getting along fine today. "He's still afraid of new things—convinced that whatever it is, it's going to be too hot or too cold, it's going to break, or it's going to be boring," says Mullen. But after struggling with her own expectations, she has learned to accept the more difficult aspects of Jimmy's personality. "I understand now that it wasn't anything I did—that this is simply his temperament," says Mullen.

## EXPECTATIONS VERSUS REALITY

Mullen and other parents have discovered that it's not always easy to accept your child for who he is. After all, most parents harbor particular hopes and expectations for their children, and it can be rough when the finished product is decidedly different—or worse, decidedly difficult. Since parents are often blamed for any imperfection in their offspring, many feel guilty for somehow causing the problem behavior.

However, many child-rearing experts believe parents have been unjustly accused. Research has shown that from the first day of life, babies display specific, innate differences in temperament. Important personality traits, such as energy level, mood, and attention span, are inborn, destined to influence how a child interacts with his family and friends. And according to some experts, equally built-in are "sensory thresholds"—physical sensitivities that can cause one child to balk at wearing new clothes, another to refuse food that smells "funny." "It's the luck of the draw what kind of temperament your child will have," maintains Antoinette Saunders, Ph.D., founder of the Capable Kid Organization, in Evanston, Illinois.

Saunders says that for many parents, understanding that their kids are born with fairly constant character traits enables them to give their children the respect and tolerance they need to function well within the family and with others.

For Elizabeth Mullen, improving the family chemistry meant learning to let her son work out some of his problems on his own. For instance, it bothered Elizabeth that in first grade, Jimmy couldn't make friends easily because he was sometimes abrasive and overaggressive. Rather than punish or nag him, though, Mullen bided her time. "Eventually Jimmy admitted he was lonely and asked me for help. I let him talk about it, holding back the urge to criticize him. When we discussed how you make friends, I explained that if he grabbed other kids' toys or pushed someone too hard, it made it more difficult for others to get along with him. When Jimmy made up his mind to change, he worked very hard at it," says Mullen. It took close to a year, but her son finally made several close friends.

Happily, parents and kids needn't have identical temperaments or talents in order to achieve what specialists like to call a "good fit." How comfortably a family meshes depends on the parents' willingness to accommodate the innate behavioral style of their child, maintains Stella Chess, M.D., professor of child psychiatry at New York University Medical Center, in New York City, and a pioneer in the field of children's temperament.

This does not mean a parent must put up with unacceptable behavior, says Chess. But as you struggle to curb your child's unpleasant tendencies, it helps to remember that in a very real sense, sometimes a child genuinely "can't help it."

For example, a six-year-old child who throws a major temper tantrum whenever it's time to stop playing and come to the dinner table isn't necessarily being deliberately naughty, Chess says. Rather, she may have a tendency to get deeply involved in whatever she's doing, and her tears and screams of protest stem from her inability to suddenly shift gears to another activity. Chess suggests that rather than wait for the next tantrum to occur and then punish the child, the parents should take preventive action by warning their daughter when it's close to dinnertime so that she has an opportunity to finish what she's doing.

Similarly, a second-grader who insists on wearing the same faded shirt day after day may not mean to be uncooperative. According to Saunders, many kids are irritated by certain fabrics because they have a low threshold for sensory stimuli. Rather than forcing the child to wear an uncomfortable piece of clothing, parents might simply try washing his other shirts several times to soften the material.

The kind of parental adjustment needed to achieve a "good fit" can start virtually at birth, says renowned pediatrician T. Berry Brazelton, M.D., author of *Infants and Mothers* (Delacorte/Dell), which chronicles infants' divergent developmental paths. Even newborns display distinct personalities that, experts say, have a profound impact on the parent-child relationship.

For example, Karyn and Henry White's baby, Alison, ate well, slept easily, and fussed only when she was hungry. However, by the time Alison reached two months, her parents felt anxious over what they perceived to be their baby's unresponsiveness. Although Alison would smile occasionally, she seemed to be irritated by her parents' attempts to excite her and would even turn her head away when her father shook a rattle or waved a colorful toy at her.

When parents have a difficult time making a connection with their child, it can create a great deal of anxiety. But the relationship is not irreparable. "It takes a parent pulling back and saying, 'Am I having trouble reaching this baby because of my own personality and goals? How can I reorganize and pick up my baby's cues better?'" Brazelton says.

Through trial and error, the Whites learned that Alison preferred gentle stimuli. A quiet lullaby before bedtime became a favorite ritual, and Henry loved to see Alison gazing intently at his face as he sang softly.

## SENDING THE WRONG MESSAGE

Unfortunately, some parents find it difficult to adjust their expectations, and the fact that they cannot change their child into what they would like him to be becomes a lifelong source of frustration. Worse, a child who thinks his parents don't really like him isn't going to grow up liking himself. "To feel rejected by your own family," warns Saunders, "is the cornerstone of poor self-esteem. Such a child inevitably senses the disappointment behind his parents' disapproval. Often, the message from the parents is, 'You don't fit into this family, what's wrong with you?'" she explains.

Of course, children aren't really born into the wrong family. But if a child's personality becomes a source of irritation and resentment, experts urge parents to make allowances for their child's nonconformity in order to prevent feelings of estrangement. Stanley Turecki, M.D., author of

*The Difficult Child* (Bantam) and physician-in-charge at The Difficult Child Center in New York City, counseled one mother who fought constantly with her preschooler about the child's desire to wear brightly colored, mismatched clothing. "This was a relatively minor thing that another parent might just let go," explains Turecki, but for this mother, who was sensitive about her child's appearance and angered by her stubbornness, the issue took on major proportions. After some resistance, he says, the mother finally agreed that giving her daughter confidence in her own judgment was, in the long run, more important than what others thought of the girl's offbeat outfits.

Major differences in activity levels can also throw off family chemistry and make for a poor fit. Martin and Mary were a quiet, precise couple in their forties who had a highly energetic and excitable toddler. They were continually threatening and punishing their rambunctious child, without much success. "They didn't understand that their son wasn't 'bad,' just naturally high-spirited, and he couldn't calm himself to fit into their decorous home environment," says Turecki.

Turecki's advice for the couple was straightforward and simple. Compromise. Deciding which behavioral conflicts were truly important to resolve and letting the rest go would make the couple much more effective in disciplining their child, suggested Turecki. As a first step, the parents stopped trying to stifle the child's excessive energy by punishing him; instead, they set up a special playroom in the house where he could run around and let off steam. But the child was also told that if he woke up at 6 a.m., he must amuse himself until his parents were awake, too. Once his parents stopped demanding that he always be neat and quiet, the toddler became much better at settling down when it was really important to behave himself.

The tensions between a child and her parents can also be exacerbated when other siblings do fit Mom and Dad's style. Chess worked with a couple who were both actors. "They were in a profession in which a show of emotion was highly regarded. The two younger kids occasionally threw tantrums, and the parents had no trouble coping with their outbursts, but the parents could not understand their oldest child, who rarely screamed or shouted," Chess recalls. "I pointed out that the child did have strong emotions but showed them in ways like persistence to obtain what she wanted, not by jumping up and down." Once her parents learned how to read their daughter's feelings better, they no longer felt as if she didn't belong in the family.

SEEING YOURSELF IN YOUR CHILD

As difficult as personality conflicts can be, family chemistry can easily combust when a child reminds a parent too much of herself. Lisa Stanford remembers being painfully shy as a child. When her daughter, Rebecca, gave every indication of being just as timid, Stanford was determined to make her more outgoing, in the hopes that she wouldn't experience the misery her mother once did. It didn't work. "The more I pushed Rebecca, the tighter she clung to me," Stanford remembers. "If we visited one of her playmates, she wouldn't leave my side. I thought, 'What did I do wrong?' I resented Rebecca's reluctance to assert herself."

Finally, a discussion with Rebecca's day-care provider convinced Stanford to change her approach. The caregiver suggested that if Rebecca wasn't pressured to be more outgoing, she would likely come out of her shell. It took some effort on Stanford's part, but eventually, she says, "I could just let Rebecca be herself, for better or worse." So when a selective nursery school refused Rebecca's plea that her mother stay in the room during the interview, she withdrew their application. "This obviously was the wrong place for Rebecca," she says, and the Stanfords found a more nurturing program. Ironically, when the first school saw the results of the intelligence test they had given Rebecca, they actually asked the Stanford's to resubmit their application, but they refused.

Becoming their child's advocates rather than her critics has helped the Stanfords get along better with her and also has alleviated the pressure that Lisa Stanford had placed on herself to change her daughter. Recently when Rebecca refused to leave her mother's side during a friend's birthday party, Stanford recalls, "I thought, 'It's okay, this is hard for Rebecca.' Even though everybody was looking at us, it was fine. . . . There's still a part of me that wishes Rebecca was more outgoing, but that's because it would make her life easier, not because it would make me look better."

Like Lisa Stanford, Elizabeth Mullen has also pulled back from trying to change her son's habitual resistance to experiencing new things. "I used to tell him that if he was going to complain, we wouldn't go," says Mullen. "Now I take a more neutral approach and say, 'Let's go swimming. I think it's going to be fun. But if the water's too cold, we'll just sit by the pool.' And most of the time, Jimmy really does enjoy himself. His grandmother still tries to convince him to be more optimistic, but that just makes it worse. It's not that he really doesn't want to go—he just needs to talk about his anxieties along the way."

"When you stand back and focus your attention on the underlying causes of major behavior conflicts," observes Turecki, "three things happen: Your expectations tend to fall into place; you become more tolerant; and you regain authority." Ultimately, many parents find that once they are able to work with their child's temperament effectively, they naturally feel more positive about their child's personality—and about themselves as well.

## Questions about the Reading

1. Have you ever had a major conflict with one or both of your parents? If so, do you think you can now explain why?

2. Can you sum up what your parenting philosophy is or what you think it will be?

## SELF-TESTS

## Multiple-Choice

Circle the letter of the response which best completes or answers each of the following statements and questions.

1. If you were the parent of a 2-year-old child, what might be a signal that your child was beginning to make the shift from the dependence of infancy to the independence of childhood?
   a. clinging behavior
   b. saying "No"
   c. playing by himself or herself
   d. playing with others

2. Who developed a theory that personality is decisively formed in the first few years of life, as children deal with conflicts between their biological, sexually related urges and the requirements of society?
   a. Maslow
   b. Erikson
   c. Harlow
   d. Freud

3. Freud held that if certain needs are not met in each of the stages of personality development, a person will continue to try to meet those needs throughout life; his term for this is
   a. fixation
   b. pleasure principle
   c. pleasure deprivation
   d. reality principle

4. Erikson maintained in his psychosocial theory that at each stage of development, there is a
   a. fixation
   b. crisis to be resolved
   c. goal to be reached
   d. need for pleasure

5. According to Erikson's theory, what lays the groundwork for the child's developing sense of worth?
   a. the father's attitude
   b. the role of siblings
   c. the mother's (caretaker's) sensitive care
   d. gratification of oral needs

6. If a child's emerging personality is to develop in a healthy way, what sort of control is needed?
   a. neither too much nor too little control from adults
   b. control by the mother
   c. control by the father
   d. control by the child

7. José is a toddler whose developing sense of control over his world takes the form of tantrums and refusals. The term for this is
   a. negativism
   b. developmental crisis
   c. growing up
   d. fixation

8. The most powerful way that babies can express their needs is by
   a. crying
   b. smiling
   c. being colicky
   d. laughing

9. Which of the following statements about a baby's developing emotional "language" is *false*?
   a. The emergence of various emotions seems to be governed by the biological clock of the brain's maturity.
   b. The most powerful way that babies can express their needs is by crying in a variety of patterns.
   c. Babies gain confidence when they realize that they get a response to their crying or smiling.
   d. Babies who cry a lot and need more attention from a caregiver are more likely to have a positive relationship with the caregiver.

10. Anna's crying is consistently responded to with tender, soothing care; research indicates that, consequently, Anna will
    a. continue to cry as much
    b. cry even more
    c. stop crying completely
    d. actually cry less

11. How does a mother's depression affect her baby?
    a. The baby will most likely learn to be unresponsive and sad.
    b. The baby will probably grow slowly and perform poorly on cognitive measures.
    c. The baby is more likely to have accidents and present behavioral problems into adolescence.
    d. all of the above.

12. There appears to be a biological component to personality development, since young infants' emotional responses seem to reflect patterns or traits that
    a. are hard to recognize
    b. persist as they get older
    c. are not likely to be consistent
    d. are identical to parents

13. Which type of child is more likely to develop behavior problems?
    a. slow-to-warm-up
    b. difficult
    c. easy
    d. none of the above; there is no connection between these types and behavior problems

14. The key to adjustment of temperament between parents and children appears to be
    a. parenthood classes
    b. ample support
    c. goodness of fit
    d. the age of the parents

15. In dealing with behavior problems, it is important for parents
    a. to be permissive
    b. not to try to mold the child's personality
    c. to be authoritarian
    d. to be punitive

16. A main finding in a study where adults played with boy and girl babies without knowing the babies' actual gender was that
    a. "boys" were encouraged to play actively
    b. "girls" were encouraged to play actively
    c. adults talked more to "boys"
    d. there were no differences in the way adults behaved

17. Research has shown that your parents' feelings about you and their actions toward you were influenced by
    a. your gender and temperament
    b. your health
    c. whether you were the oldest, youngest, or middle child
    d. all of the above

18. Harlow's experiment with infant monkeys, a "wire" mother, and a "cloth" mother seems to imply that
    a. animals seek their mothers only to be fed
    b. animals seek their mothers to be touched and held as well as fed
    c. animals can learn nurturant behavior instinctively without observing and imitating
    d. animals can thrive without bodily contact

19. An essential element of personality development is
    a. becoming attached to siblings
    b. developing sibling rivalry
    c. becoming attached to a mother figure or primary caretaker
    d. becoming resistant to the primary caretaker

20. In comparison with other industrialized countries, especially those in western Europe, the United States
    a. has established a national policy for parental leave which protects mothers' and fathers' jobs
    b. has established a national policy for child care and compiles figures on the number of children in day care
    c. is lagging behind in policies regarding child care and parental leave
    d. none of the above

21. In our culture, fathers tend to do which of the following with their babies?
    a. play with them
    b. care for them
    c. ignore them
    d. be gentle with them

22. A recent study found that when fathers show a sensitive and caring attitude toward their children, the children
    a. talked more
    b. showed more effective problem-solving abilities
    c. were very active
    d. expressed a wide variety of emotions

23. If a child must be hospitalized, the stress can be reduced if
    a. the parents can stay overnight with the child
    b. the child meets his or her caregivers and and keeps the same caregivers
    c. family members visit daily
    d. all of the above

24. Which of the following applies to abused, battered, and neglected children?
    a. They are resilient, especially if they have a supportive family member to whom they can form an attachment.
    b. They tend to be sexually maladjusted and often become victims of rape or sexual assault later in their lives.
    c. They have low self-esteem and have difficulty trusting others.
    d. all of the above

25. Which of the following is an important suggestion based on research in child development?
    a. Confine your baby so that he or she will feel more secure.
    b. Don't respond quickly to a baby's cries; that will only spoil the child.
    c. Don't give a baby toys in his or her crib, because this is dangerous.
    d. Provide interesting things for a baby to see and to do and be patient with your baby.

## Matching: Temperament and Attachment

Match each of the lettered terms in the box with the appropriate description in the numbered list following the box.

---

a. activity level
b. regularity
c. approach or withdrawal
d. adaptability
e. threshold of responsiveness
f. intensity of reaction
g. quality of mood
h. distractibility
i. attention span; persistence
j. easy child
k. difficult child
l. slow-to-warm-up child
m. securely attached child
n. avoidant child
o. ambivalent child

---

1. generally happy child _____
2. predictability of cycles _____
3. how energetically a child responds _____
4. child with mild but hesitant temperament _____
6. how much stimulation is needed to evoke a response _____
8. how much a person moves _____
9. response to a new stimulus _____
10. predominant behavior _____
11. cooperative child who likes exploring and uses mother as a "base" _____
12. how long a child pursues an activity _____
13. child with irritable temperament and intense response to new situations _____
14. how easily a stimulus interferes with behavior _____
15. child who is anxious and hard to comfort _____
16. child who dislikes being held and tends to be angry _____
17. how easily a response can be modified in a desired direction _____

## Completion

Supply the term or terms needed to complete each of the following statements.

1. Feeding is the main source of sensual gratification, or pleasure, which is achieved by stimulation of the mouth, lips, and tongue in Freud's _____ stage.

2. The chief source of gratification during the _____ stage shifts from the mouth to the anus and rectum.

3. Erikson proposed that the first stage of personality development (birth to 12–18 months) is resolution of the critical pair of opposites of _____ versus _____ .

4. The successful balancing of the first crisis will result in the virtue of _____ , according to Erikson's theory.

5. Erikson's second crisis (12–18 months to 3 years) is called _____ versus _____ , and the virtue of _____ emerges from it.

6. An important step toward self-control and autonomy for the child, according to Erikson, is _____ training.

7. Subjective feelings such as sadness, joy, and fear, which arise in response to situations and experiences, are labeled _____ .

8. When babies realize that they are separate from other things in their environment, they are developing the sense of self- _____ ; and when babies begin to recognize their own image, at approximately 18 months, this is called self- _____ .

9. By expressing their feelings, babies begin to gain a sense of _____ over their world.

10. One of the ways that a baby can discharge tensions is by _____ , which also reflects cognitive development and emotional growth and expression.

11. A characteristic style of approaching and reacting to people and situations is known as our _____ .

12. Generally speaking, gender differences cannot be described clearly until after the age of _____ .

13. How children learn the behaviors their culture deems appropriate is called the process of _____ .

14. An instinctive type of learning in which an animal learns to recognize and trust a particular individual after a single encounter is called _____ .

15. The mother's feeling of close, caring connection with her newborn is called _____ .

16. Many fathers form close bonds with their babies soon after birth, and this paternal reaction has been called _____ .

17. _____ anxiety occurs when a new person is around a baby at least 8 months old, and _____ anxiety occurs when a familiar caregiver tries to leave the child.

18. A battered or neglected child can also develop a complication called _____ where the child fails to grow or gain weight, even though the child is receiving nutrition.

19. More than _____ percent of all child abuse occurs at home.

20. Two cultural factors that seem to lead to child abuse are _____ and _____ .

## ANSWERS FOR SELF-TESTS

### Multiple-Choice

1. b (page 144)
2. d (145)
3. a (145)
4. b (146)
5. c (146)
6. a (147)
7. a (148)
8. a (150)
9. d (149, 150)
10. d (150)
11. d (152)
12. b (153)
13. d (154)
14. c (155)
15. b (155)
16. a (155)
17. d (155)
18. b (158)
19. c (160)

**20.** c (162)

**21.** a (164)

**22.** b (164)

**23.** d (166)

**24.** d (167)

**25.** d (171)

## Matching

**1.** j (page 153)

**2.** b (153)

**3.** f (153)

**4.** l (153)

**5.** e (153)

**6.** a (153)

**7.** c (153)

**8.** g (153)

**9.** m (159)

**10.** i (158)

**11.** k (153)

**12.** h (153)

**13.** o (158)

**14.** n (159)

**15.** d (153)

## Completion

**1.** oral (page 145)

**2.** anal (146)

**3.** trust; mistrust (146)

**4.** hope (146)

**5.** autonomy; shame and doubt; will (147)

**6.** toilet *(or* language) (147)

**7.** emotions (148)

**8.** awareness, recognition (149)

**9.** control (150)

**10.** laughing (151)

**11.** temperament (153)

**12.** 2 (155)

**13.** socialization (156)

**14.** imprinting (156)

**15.** mother-infant bonding (157)

**16.** engrossment (163)

**17.** stranger; separation (164)

**18.** nonorganic failure to thrive (166)

**19.** 90 percent (167)

**20.** violent crime; physical punishment (168)

# 6

# PHYSICAL AND INTELLECTUAL DEVELOPMENT IN EARLY CHILDHOOD

## INTRODUCTION

The discussion of physical and intellectual development in early childhood in **Chapter 6** begins a pattern that will continue through most of the remainder of the textbook. Each period of development (early childhood, adolescence, etc.) will be discussed in two chapters: the first will deal with physical and intellectual development during that period, and the second with personality and social development during that same period.

■ Chapter 6 begins by describing the physical growth and change of children aged 3 to 6 and discusses how growth and motor development require adequate nutrition and health care.

■ Children's sleep patterns and sleep disturbances, and how they change during early childhood, are discussed in this chapter. Bed-wetting and its causes are also discussed.

■ In the area of intellectual development, Chapter 6 describes how memory, speech, and intelligence develop and function during early childhood. It focuses on Piaget's preoperational stage of cognitive development, and modifies his theories with recent research.

■ Recent research on the effects of the quality of day care, preschool, prekindergarten, and kindergarten programs are also presented and evaluated, with new research from three different cultures.

# CHAPTER OUTLINE

## PHYSICAL DEVELOPMENT

### I. PHYSICAL GROWTH AND CHANGE

A. HEIGHT, WEIGHT, AND APPEARANCE

B. STRUCTURAL AND SYSTEMIC CHANGES

C. NUTRITION

### II. HEALTH

A. HEALTH PROBLEMS IN EARLY CHILDHOOD

    1. Minor Illnesses

    2. Major Illnesses

    3. Accidental Injuries

B. INFLUENCES ON HEALTH

    1. Exposure

    2. Stress

    3. Poverty

    4. Homelessness

### III. MOTOR SKILLS

A. LARGE-MUSCLE COORDINATION

B. SMALL-MUSCLE AND EYE-HAND COORDINATION

### IV. SLEEP: PATTERNS AND PROBLEMS

A. Normal Sleep Patterns

B. Sleep Disturbances

C. Bed-Wetting

## INTELLECTUAL DEVELOPMENT

### V. ASPECTS OF INTELLECTUAL DEVELOPMENT

A. DEVELOPMENT OF MEMORY: INFORMATION PROCESSING

    1. Types of Memory: Recognition and Recall

    2. Influences on Children's Memory

        a. "Mastery motivation" and study activities

        b. General knowledge

        c. Unusual activities and new experiences

        d. Social interactions

B. COGNITIVE DEVELOPMENT: PIAGET'S PREOPERATIONAL STAGE

    1. The Symbolic Function

    2. Achievements of Preoperational Thought

        a. Understanding of functions

        b. Understanding of identities

    3. Limitations of Preoperational Thought

        a. Centration

        b. Irreversibility

        c. Focus on states rather than on transformations

        d. Transductive reasoning

        e. Egocentrism

## KEY TERMS

animism (page 193)

centrate (190)

conservation (190)

decenter (190)

deferred imitation (189)

egocentrism (191)

enuresis (186)

irreversibility (190)

preoperational stage (189)

private speech (197)

Project Head Start (203)

recall (187)

recognition (187)

scaffolding (198)

social speech (196)

Stanford-Binet Intelligence Scale (197)

symbol (187)

symbolic function (189)

symbolic play (190)

transduction (191)

transitional objects (185)

Wechsler Preschool and Primary Scale
of Intelligence (WPPSI-R) (197)

zone of proximal development (ZPD) (198)

## LEARNING OBJECTIVES

After finishing Chapter 6, you should be able to:

1. Describe changes during early childhood in the following areas.
   a. height

   b. weight

   c. muscular

   d. structural

2. Explain the vital influence of nutrition on children's health.

3. List some of the common childhood illnesses and other factors that influence health.

4. Describe how poverty affects young children, and explain what recommendations are made to improve the situation for children most at risk.

5. Describe some of the serious concerns about children who are growing up homeless.

6. Describe eye-hand coordination and some of the characteristic motor skills, both large- and small-muscle, that are present or develop in early childhood.
   a. eye-hand coordination

   b. motor skills

7. Describe patterns of sleep and some common sleep disturbances in early childhood.

   **b.** *symbolic play*

   **c.** *deferred imitation*

8. Explain some biological and environmental facts about bed-wetting, and list some of the approaches used to deal with it.

   **d.** *transduction*

9. Explain how memory is developed and operates in early childhood, and define the following terms.
   **a.** mastery motivation

12. Explain the term *egocentrism*, and give an example of how an egocentric child looks at the world.

   **b.** *recognition*

13. Discuss the issues involved in the question, Can *cognitive* abilities be accelerated?

   **c.** *recall*

   **d.** general knowledge

14. Describe the development and use of language in early childhood.

10. Describe children's thinking processes during the *preoperational stage* of cognitive development.

15. Explain the cognitive benefits a child derives from speaking to others and from speaking to himself or herself.

11. Define the following concepts associated with preoperational thinking.
   **a.** *symbol*

**16.** Describe the purpose of measuring young children's intelligence, and name and describe the three major psychometric intelligence inventories mentioned in the text.

   **a.** purpose—

   **b.** inventory—

   **c.** inventory—

   **d.** inventory—

**17.** Describe how both parents influence children's intellectual development.

**18.** Describe the characteristics and benefits of good day care.

**19.** Describe the findings of a study by Tobin, Wu, and Davidson (1989) comparing and contrasting preschools in the United States, Japan, and China.

**20.** Describe what kindergarten is like in American schools today.

---

## SUPPLEMENTAL READING

---

Rob Waters is a San Francisco-based freelance writer. This article is a reprint from *Parenting*, October 1991.

### Young and Old Alike

**Rob Waters**

The door to the lounge pops open and a dozen children charge into the room. They dive underneath a parachute, the sides of which are being held by 12 senior citizens seated in a circle of folding chairs and wheelchairs. A foam ball is tossed onto the parachute, and the kids bat it from below. It bounces around the blue and white nylon, gently caroming off wrinkled hands. A 62-year-old man named Don Mycek, sporting a Jimmy Durante schnoz and loud plaid pants, ducks beneath the parachute and is immediately besieged by small, squealing bodies. "I'm being surrounded!" Don bellows, as the wide-eyed kids continue to pile on. After a few minutes, Don tires and heads back to his seat, dragging two little boys locked in a tight grip around his legs.

In the next room, four-year-old David is intrigued. There is something about Julia Pevarnek, white-haired and 83, that draws his attention. He comes over to her wheelchair and takes a closer look. "Where's your other foot?" he asks. Julia tries to ignore him, but he inquires again and then peeks beneath the blanket draped discreetly across her lap. He repeats his question and Julia, a bit dismayed, doesn't know what to say. "What do I tell him?" she asks a nearby aide. "The truth," the attendant replies. Julia turns toward David. "It got sick," she says simply, "and now it's gone." That mystery solved, they go on to discuss his next question: the function of the shiny brake lever on the side of her wheelchair.

Julia and David, like Don and the young parachute-ball players, were born more than half a century apart. They spend their days down the hallway from each other at Oakwood Hospital Day Care Services in Dearborn, Michigan, coming together a few times a week to talk and play games. David's home base is the Penguin Room, where he romps and stomps with his fellow preschoolers. At the other end of the building, Julia passes the time with other seniors (or "older adults" as they are called here), talking and playing cards. On Mondays, Wednesdays, and Fridays, the Penguins mingle with the older adults. They sing songs, they inspect visiting fire trucks, they help each other paint. And while they may not know it, they're part of an imaginative new trend in American daycare: "intergenerational" programs that bring young and old together.

With the senior population swelling steadily and the number of working mothers continuing to climb, experts are predicting a daycare crisis: By the year 2000, they say, half of the nation's work force will depend on childcare, elder care, or both. This burgeoning demand for both childcare and daycare for older adults has sparked two ingenious solutions: one, as at Oakwood, in which children and frail seniors are cared for together; the other, in which active seniors, working as staff members, help look after the kids.

The first model, intergenerational daycare, is relatively new, but its popularity is growing steadily. Last year, for instance, the Stride Rite Corporation, a Massachusetts shoemaker, launched an $800,000 state-of-the art intergenerational daycare center on the fourth floor of its corporate headquarters. Hospitals have shown a particular interest in this approach because it allows them to combine a much-sought-after employee benefit—childcare—with a badly needed community service—elder care.

Kim Helfgott, who is conducting a major national survey for the Washington, D.C.-based group Generations United, estimates that some 250 of these two-pronged daycare centers now dot the United States (a figure that has nearly doubled in the past few years). She anticipates that corporations, developers of office buildings, and even neighborhood malls will soon be looking into intergenerational daycare.

But while some seniors are dependent and in need of daycare, the vast majority are healthy people with time on their hands and a strong desire to remain both productive and social. Childcare centers across the country, hard-pressed to attract qualified younger teachers at the low salaries common to the field, are beginning to use these seniors as providers of daytime care. And this is giving rise to the second model, intergenerational *child*care.

Yet the case for bringing young and old together goes beyond statistical trends and bottom-line needs. It is also a potent approach to tackling a uniquely American problem: the age-segregated nature of our society, in which children may live across the country from their grandparents, and increasing numbers of old people dwell in isolated retirement communities. With the extended family largely a relic of the past, contact between generations, if it happens at all, must now be consciously orchestrated. Which is precisely what the intergenerational daycare and childcare centers across the country have set out to do.

The thought of their then three-year-old daughter playing and learning in the company of senior citizens was enormously appealing to Tom and Laurie Bigelow of Dearborn, Michigan. Since Christie has only one grandparent, a very active 65-year-old grandmother, the Bigelows were eager for her to have more contact with older adults, particularly men, so that she would have a grandfather figure. "I wanted my daughter to experience the kind of special moments that I shared with my grandfather when I was young, the stories, the little games," says Laurie. And not long after Christie enrolled in Oakwood's intergenerational program, she struck up a friendship with Paul Vella, a 60-year-old ex-maintenance worker. According to her mother, Christie is always excited to see Paul, and the pair spend much of their time together playing and talking about Paul's grandchildren.

For others, like Julia Pevarnek, intergenerational daycare offers a refuge from the prospect of intense loneliness. A regular at Oakwood since May of 1990, Pevarnek entered the program not long after her release from a local hospital, where she spent four traumatic months undergoing amputation procedures on her leg. Her son Mike was told three times that she had only a few days to live, but she pulled through, recovering just in time to attend his wedding.

The Oakwood program is "a godsend" for Mike and his new wife, who had Julia move in with them after her hospitalization. "If she wasn't in this program, my life—and my mother's life—would have been very difficult," Mike says. "Like all people, she needs companionship, someone to talk to. Without that she would feel very much alone."

At first, though, Mike and his mother wondered whether placing her into care with utterly dependent toddlers would undermine her dignity. "But from the beginning my mother realized that we couldn't afford a private nurse, and this was the way it had to be," he says. After nine months at Oakwood, Julia's health improved and she moved into her own apartment, but she still visits the center because, in her son's words, "it gives her the social outlet she needs to feel good about herself. And she's crazy about the kids."

The program where Christie and Julia now spend their days was started by Oakwood Hospital in 1983 as an adult daycare center for frail or dependent seniors. Facing demands from its own employees to provide childcare, the hospital transformed the program two years later into its current intergenerational configuration, becoming one of the first in the country to do so. Employees pay $83 a week for preschoolers and $101 for infants, while the cost for seniors, who need not be related to employees, is $5 per hour.

To ensure that both age groups benefit—and don't cramp each other's style—Oakwood's staff carefully plans their joint activities and limits the duration to 30 minutes; more than that, they find, is taxing for the seniors. As one noted expert says, "You can only have 3-year-olds cannonball running into 83-year-old osteoporotic legs for so long."

The staff is also especially attentive to the parents of young daycare charges who often worry that the older adults, with their visible ailments and their medical contraptions (from prosthetic limbs to oxygen tanks), will frighten the kids. And once in a while these fears are realized. Laurie Bigelow remembers one occasion when Cristie came home in tears because she had been scared by the older woman sitting next to her.

"The kids usually want to know why an older adult looks different," says Teri Brown, Oakwood's childcare manager.

So when the staff introduces the new children and new seniors to each other, they gingerly, but truthfully, explain why one man is sitting in a wheelchair, why another is always falling asleep. Sometimes, Brown says, a child will ask why a particular senior is missing. "We explain that they're not feeling well and now live in a nursing home, or we say, 'He died and doesn't come here any more.'" And, adds Brown, "a ride in a wheelchair goes a long way toward making kids more comfortable with the older adults." Now a confirmed intergenerational enthusiast, Laurie Bigelow believes that "through the center my daughter not only learned to respect seniors, but that it's part of life to get older and to get sick, that these things do happen."

In South San Francisco, California, 2,000 miles away from Christie, Julia, and the Oakwood center, 68-year-old Rena Weinert faced her own battle with impending loneliness. "When my youngsters had grown and gone off to college," she recalls, "I didn't want to stay home and spend my days alone." She responded to a job opening at a local daycare center, and eight years later she's still going strong, working two days a week as a teacher's aide.

Today, Weinert is teaching "opposites," so while the children finish their afternoon nap, she selects an appropriate book to read to them. When the lights come on in the classroom, Weinert and her colleague, 63-year-old Rose Olsen, roam up and down the rows of little bodies gently rousing them from their slumber. The kids scurry into a half circle around Weinert, who reads to them about the adventures of Baby Dino, a dinosaur, and Dennis, a cave-dweller. "Inside the cave it's dark and cold," Weinert says. "How is it outside?" "It's warm!" shouted the children.

Weinert is the oldest staff member at the Leo Ryan intergenerational Child Development Center; with the exception of the program director, all of the teachers and teachers' aides are over 50. Now in its 11th year, the facility is one of the oldest intergenerational childcare centers in the country. It was started by the California-based Elvirita Lewis Foundation, whose president, Steve Brummel, is a leading advocate of hiring seniors as childcare workers. "There's magic that happens between old and young," Brummel says. "Younger workers aren't always there for the kids in the same way; they don't have the same familiarity with children that seniors do."

And as Brummel sees it, seniors have another distinct advantage over young daycare teachers: They're often willing to work for fewer benefits, thus aiding childcare centers, which are usually strapped for funds. "Most older people aren't looking for a career ladder or health insurance," he says. "They're looking for involvement with life." Offering seniors fewer benefits is not exploitative, Brummel argues, because they frequently have pensions or other sources of income. And the financial supplement frequently enables seniors to stay on the job longer, which helps centers cope with one of their most formidable problems: staff turnover. "Any child development expert will tell you that what children need most is stability and consistency," says Brummel. "When younger workers leave, no matter how good

they are, that need isn't being met, and it's very hard on the kids."

Experts in the field agree that there is a strong link between staff turnover and quality daycare. But Caro Pemberton, former associate director of the Oakland, California-based Child Care Employee Project, bristles at the notion of hiring seniors at less cost to the centers is the answer to the childcare crisis. Calling the average childcare wage of $5.35 per hour "abysmally low" and the general lack of benefits "horrifying," Pemberton asserts that "the country's childcare system is breaking down, in part because the labor force is saying, I can't work for this wage; I need to make a living." Giving a few individual seniors a slimmer benefits package is short-sighted, she says. "To solve the childcare staffing shortage, we need to place a new value on the work that childcare teachers are doing."

After a rousing game of intergenerational parachute ball at the Dearborn, Michigan, center, Paul Vella, one arm in a sling, and Don Mycek are ready to sing. They lead the older adults in a thickly-accented and off-key rendition of "Five Foot Two, Eyes of Blue." The children, feeling left out by this nostalgia, answer with "The Alphabet Song." Then a teacher leads the whole group through a finale of "Going on a Bear Hunt," and the kids say their good-byes, giving big hugs to their beaming older friends.

An equally playful scene is unfolding just outside a classroom at the Leo Ryan Center in California. Kids are zooming down slides, cruising on tricycles, and showing off on the jungle gym. "Look at me!" Sasha screams, as she hangs upside down by her legs. In the midst of all this activity, 62-year-old Josefina Nalundasan stands serenely at the foot of the slide, occupied with three giggling little girls. "When I play with the kids," says the teacher's aide, "I forget I'm getting old."

In this age-segregated society that rarely lets its seniors do more than view life from the sidelines, this is no small victory. Few, after all, would have predicted that frail elders and rambunctious youngsters could not only sit in the same room together but actually enjoy it. With the yawning generation gap, the proliferation of senior citizens, and the growing childcare crisis all begging for solutions, a roomful of old and young playing and laughing together is proof positive that this kind of creative thinking can lead the way.

## Questions about the Reading

1. Do you believe that establishing and certifying high-quality day care centers for "intergenerations" should become a priority of government? Of business? Of both? Why or why not?

2. Are there any businesses in your own community that offer intergenerational day care for employees?

## SELF-TESTS

### Multiple-Choice

Circle the letter of the response which best completes or answers each of the following statements and questions.

1.  Which of the following statements is most correct regarding children's body composition during early childhood?
    a.  Per pound of body weight, boys tend to have more fatty tissue; girls tend to have more muscle.
    b.  Per pound of body weight, boys tend to have more muscle; girls tend to have more fatty tissue.
    c.  Both boys and girls tend to be chubby, with more fatty tissue than muscle per pound of body weight.
    d.  Both boys and girls tend to develop noticeable "definition," with more muscle than fatty tissue per pound of body weight.

2.  All of the following descriptions are true of physical growth and development during early childhood *except* one.  Which one?
    a.  The primary teeth continue to emerge, and the first permanent teeth begin to emerge simultaneously.
    b.  Bones become harder, giving children a firmer shape.
    c.  Both large-muscle and small-muscle motor skills increase.
    d.  Increased circulatory and respiratory capacities give the child more physical stamina.

3.  Because of the slowing growth rate, children in early childhood
    a.  are less affected by nutritional deficits
    b.  have difficulty meeting their basic nutritional requirements
    c.  often need vitamin and mineral supplements in their diets
    d.  often have less appetite

4.  Which of the following statements about childhood illness is *not* accurate?
    a.  Suffering minor illness helps children to be more sympathetic toward ill siblings and peers.
    b.  Many children believe that sickness is a result of bad behavior.
    c.  After recuperation from a minor illness, most children's self-esteem is lowered, and they feel less competent.
    d.  Exposure to common childhood illnesses can strengthen a child's immunity.

5.  Bobby is a 6-year-old who was born with AIDS (acquired immune deficiency syndrome).  Which of the following can we infer?
    a.  Bobby's classmates are at a very high risk of contracting AIDS.
    b.  Bobby's family will receive a great deal of emotional support from the community.
    c.  Bobby will behave normally and suffer developmental delays only during the final stages of the disease.
    d.  With minor precautions, Bobby will not transmit the disease to family members.

6.  Which of the following is the most accurate statement about health during childhood?
    a.  Events which produce stress in a family tend to adversely affect the health of children in those families.
    b.  Children in small families are sick more often than children in large families.
    c.  Because of welfare and health care programs for the poor, there is no relationship between poverty and children's health.
    d.  The highly developed immune system in early childhood reduces the risk of illness due to exposure to other children.

7.  Karen's 4-year-old daughter has frequent temper tantrums at bedtime.  To help alleviate this, Karen and her husband should
    a.  punish their daughter by taking away her favorite toy
    b.  send their daughter to bed an hour earlier than the time when she usually falls asleep
    c.  let their daughter sleep in their bed with them
    d.  establish a routine of bedtime stories and activities

8. Enuresis, repeated urination in clothing or in bed,
   a. tends to run in families
   b. is most common among children who were toilet-trained before the age of 18 months
   c. is a serious childhood problem
   d. is more common among girls than boys

9. A young boy is introduced to a number of relatives he has not previously met. Later, when he correctly identifies his Aunt Jane, he is demonstrating
   a. recognition
   b. reencounter
   c. recall
   d. symbolic play

10. Sensorimotor stage is to _____ as preoperational stage is to _____ .
    a. learning by sensing and doing; learning by thinking symbolically
    b. learning by reflecting on actions; learning by acting alone
    c. learning by thinking symbolically; learning by recall
    d. learning by recall; learning by recognition

11. Johnny sees a movie about the "teenage mutant ninja turtles." Within a week, he is imitating their martial arts. This imitation of an observed action after time has passed is known as
    a. latent modeling
    b. post hoc reenactment
    c. deferred imitation
    d. representational modeling

12. In symbolic play, children will
    a. discuss their mental symbols with each other
    b. make jokes in which there is a play on words
    c. mentally rehearse a game that they have played earlier
    d. make an object stand for something else

13. Joey, a 5-year-old in the preoperational stage, fills two identical pails with sand. His brother then pours the sand from one pail into a taller, thinner pail. According to Piaget, which of the following is true?
    a. After conceptualizing pouring the sand into the original pail from the taller one, Joey will understand that the two differently shaped pails contain the same amount of sand.
    b. Joey will perceive either the taller or the wider pail as containing more sand because one of them looks "bigger."
    c. Joey will focus simultaneously on the height and the width of the pails and realize that the amount of sand in the two differently shaped pails is the same.
    d. none of the above

14. According to Piaget, which of the following statements is *least* accurate?
    a. Egocentrism explains why young children often talk to themselves.
    b. Most young children lack the ability to see things from another's point of view.
    c. Preoperational children understand that an operation can go two ways.
    d. Preoperational children cannot think simultaneously about many aspects of a situation.

15. Which of the following scenarios best exemplifies Piaget's principle of transduction?
    a. Johnny knows many people who ate too much food and got sick. Johnny eats too much food, and so he thinks he may get sick.
    b. Susie ate too much candy, and her mother became angry with her. Susie's brothers ate too much candy, and they also were punished. Therefore, Susie understands that eating too much candy is bad.
    c. Eric got into an argument with his little sister and broke one of her toys. The next day Eric had a stomachache. Eric believes that if he misbehaves again, he will feel sick again.
    d. Jenny's parents buy her nice presents on her birthday. Her friends also get nice presents on their birthdays. Jenny understands that people should get presents on their birthday.

16. Which of the following is a characteristic of the speech of children over the age of 3?
    a. telegraphic speech
    b. single-word utterances
    c. simple, active, declarative sentences
    d. plurals and use of past tense

17. Jenny, a 6-year-old, talks aloud to herself in school. From Vygotsky's research on private speech, which of the following can we infer?
    a. Jenny is antisocial and unable to communicate with her peers.
    b. Jenny uses private speech in order to think better, not because of social inadequacy.
    c. Jenny's development of language is delayed.
    d. Jenny will continue to talk aloud to herself throughout grade school.

18. How does the "zone of proximal development" (ZPD) approach help researchers assess children's intelligence?
    a. It enables researchers to measure the extent to which children can learn solely on their own.
    b. It enables researchers to measure and test children's abilities only in completed areas of development.
    c. It enables researchers to measure what children can learn with minimal tutoring, focusing on both completed areas of development and areas still in the process of development.
    d. It enables researchers to measure what children can learn after rigorous tutoring, focusing solely on areas still in the process of development.

19. The temporary support that parents give a child to help him or her complete a task is called
    a. conservation
    b. scaffolding
    c. preoperational thought
    d. animism

20. Which of the following statements is the most accurate regarding a father's influence on his children's intelligence?
    a. A father will tend to influence sons more than his daughters.
    b. A strict, authoritarian father is most likely to have an intellectually developed child.
    c. A father's absence has no effect on his children's cognitive development.
    d. A father who is nurturing and approving will probably not be imitated by his son.

21. Which of the following children would benefit most from a good day care program?
    a. Sally: 3 years old, white, upper-class family, mother does not work
    b. Jimmy: 2 1/2 years old, black, middle-class family, father works full time, mother works part time
    c. Kristen: 3 years old, white lower-class family, parents divorced, mother collects welfare
    d. Joey: 2 years old, black, middle-class family, mother works full time, father works at home

22. A good preschool for young children
    a. emphasizes basically the same values in all cultures
    b. emphasizes academic skills more strongly than social and emotional skills
    c. focuses solely on strengthening social and emotional skills
    d. helps foster social and academic skills, as well as strengthening self-confidence

23. Which of the following is a finding of the recent study of preschools in three different cultures?
    a. Chinese preschools stress academics more than American preschools do.
    b. The United States stresses learning basic skills like concentration and getting along with the group.
    c. The Japanese emphasize play experiences and creativity.
    d. none of the above

24. Educators have performed several studies showing the "age effect." This research indicates that
    a. the youngest children in a class tend to do worse than the oldest
    b. the youngest children in a class are usually more disruptive than older children
    c. social interactions are more developed among the older children in a class
    d. body size is related to young children's academic ability

25. Jimmy will soon be entering kindergarten. In which program should his parents enroll him?
    a. a kindergarten program with an emphasis on cognitive and academic skills
    b. a kindergarten program which expands social interactions and stresses learning when children are self-motivated
    c. a kindergarten program that exposes children to many community activities
    d. an all-day kindergarten

## Matching

Match each of the lettered items in the box with the most appropriate description in the numbered list that follows the box.

a. egocentrism
b. recognition
c. transduction
d. symbolic play
e. animism
f. recall
g. social speech
h. decenter
i. symbol
j. preoperational
k. reversibility
l. centrate
m. transitional objects
n. conservation
p. private speech

1. cognitive stage of 3- to 6-year olds _____
2. talking to oneself _____
3. moving from one particular to another without taking the general into account _____
4. identifying something encountered before _____
5. focus on a single aspect of a situation _____
6. speech to establish or maintain communication _____
7. realization that operations can go both ways _____
8. making an object stand for something else _____
9. realize that amount can be constant even if shape changes _____
10. attributing life to nonliving things _____
11. seeing things from one perspective only _____
12. reproducing knowledge from memory _____
13. aids in progression from dependence of infancy to independence of later childhood _____
14. think of several aspects at once _____
15. mental representation of a sensation _____

## Completion

Supply the term or terms needed to complete each of the following statements.

1. A toy or an animal that a child holds at bedtime is referred to as a _____ .
2. Failure to understand that an operation can go both ways is known as _____ .
3. _____ reasoning goes from the general to the particular.
4. _____ reasoning goes from the particular to the general.
5. _____ reasoning, typical of preoperational children, goes from one particular to another particular, not taking the general into account.
6. The inability to see something from another's point of view is known as _____ .
7. A young child who is overregularizing the rule for forming the past tense of verbs is likely to say _____ as the past of the verb *run*.
8. Research has shown that programs designed to teach specific cognitive abilities seem to work best when the child is already _____ the concept.
9. Speech that is used to establish and maintain communication with other people is referred to as _____ .
10. Talking aloud to oneself, with no intent to communicate with others, is referred to as _____ .
11. Because they are made up largely of _____ items, intelligence tests for use with young children (ages 3 to 5) provide more stable scores than tests for toddlers.
12. Daughters of working mothers tend to be more _____ than daughters of mothers who are at home.
13. The _____ curriculum is child-centered and based on respect for the child's natural abilities.
14. _____ , begun in 1965 as part of the "war on poverty," is the best-known compensatory preschool program in the United States.
15. During the 1970s and 1980s, the kindergarten curriculum became more like that of _____ .

## ANSWERS FOR SELF-TESTS

### Multiple-Choice

1. b (pages 178, 179)
2. a (179)
3. d (179)
4. c (180)
5. d (181)
6. a (182)
7. d (186)
8. a (186)
9. c (187)
10. a (189)
11. c (189)
12. d (190)
13. b (190)
14. c (190, 191)
15. c (191)
16. d (195)
17. b (197)
18. c (198)
19. b (198)
20. a (199)
21. c (201)
22. d (202, 203)
23. a (204)
24. a (206)
25. b (206)

### Matching

1. j (page 189)
2. p (197)
3. c (191)
4. b (187)
5. l (190)
6. g (196)
7. h (190)
8. d (190)
9. n (190)
10. e (193)
11. a (191)
12. f (187)
13. m (185)
14. h (190)
15. i (189)

### Completion

1. transitional object (185)
2. irreversibility (page 190)
3. deductive (191)
4. inductive (191)
5. transductive (191)
6. egocentrism (191)
7. runned (195)

8. on the verge of acquiring (195)
9. social speech (196)
10. private speech (197)
11. verbal (197)

12. independent (199)
13. Montessori (203)
14. Project Head Start (203)
15. first grade (205)

# CHAPTER 7

# PERSONALITY AND SOCIAL DEVELOPMENT IN EARLY CHILDHOOD

## INTRODUCTION

**Chapter 7** presents several theories about personality development in early childhood to help us understand how young children begin to perceive their place in the world around them. Many factors can influence a child's development in this stage—fears, friends, parenting styles, siblings, etc.

■ The theoretical frameworks include Freud's psychoanalytic approach, Erikson's social-learning theory, the cognitive-developmental model, and gender-schema theory.

■ Gender differences, gender roles, and gender stereotyping are discussed in detail, from both the biological and the environmental perspectives.

■ Development of aggressive (or passive) tendencies is explained, along with a section devoted to the detrimental effects of televised violence and a practical section on guiding children in watching television.

■ Childhood fears and the formation of friendships are covered in detail in Chapter 7, with some practical guidelines for helping young children develop friendships.

■ Parents' influence on the development of prosocial (or altruistic) behavior—or the lack of it—is covered in detail, with the father's and the mother's roles examined separately. Parenting styles—authoritarian, permissive, and authoritative—are presented, with some practical suggestions on effective parenting.

■ Research on siblings' influence—or the lack of it—is also covered in detail; the discussion includes findings of a study on China's policies toward the one-child family.

## CHAPTER OUTLINE

**I. PERSONALITY IN EARLY CHILDHOOD: THEORETICAL APPROACHES**

A.  PSYCHOANALYTIC THEORIES: BIOLOGY, SOCIETY, AND CULTURE

  1.  Psychosexual Theory: Freud's Phallic Stage

    a.  Oedipus complex

    b.  Electra complex

    c.  Development of the superego

  2.  Psychosocial Theory: Erikson's Crisis 3— Initiative versus Guilt

  3.  Evaluating the Psychoanalytic Theories

B.  SOCIAL-LEARNING THEORY: OBSERVING AND IMITATING MODELS

  1.  Identification

  2.  Evaluating Social-Learning Theory

C.  COGNITIVE-DEVELOPMENTAL THEORY: MENTAL PROCESSES

  1.  Gender Identity and Gender Constancy

  2.  Evaluating Cognitive-Developmental Theory

D.  GENDER-SCHEMA THEORY: A "COGNITIVE-SOCIAL" APPROACH

  1.  Gender Schemata and Gender Roles

  2.  Evaluating Gender-Schema Theory

**II. ASPECTS AND ISSUES OF PERSONALITY DEVELOPMENT**

A.  GENDER

  1.  Gender Differences—and Similarities

  2.  Attitudes toward Gender Differences

    a.  Gender roles, gender-typing, and gender stereotypes

    b.  Androgyny: A new view of gender

  3.  Roots of Gender Differences

    a.  Biology

    b.  Culture

    c.  Socialization

      (1)  How parents treat sons and daughters

      (2)  Influence of television

B.  FEARS

  1.  What Do Children Fear, and Why?

  2.  Preventing and Dealing with Fears

C.  AGGRESSION

  1.  Stages of Aggression: Rise and Decline

  2.  Triggers of Aggression

    a.  Reinforcement

    b.  Frustration and imitation

    c.  Televised violence

  3.  Reducing Aggression

D.  ALTRUISM: PROSOCIAL BEHAVIOR

  1.  Influences on Prosocial Behavior

  2.  Encouraging Prosocial Behavior

E.  CHILD-REARING PRACTICES

    1.  Parents' Use of Reinforcement
       and Punishment

       a.  Reinforcement

       b.  Ineffective punishment:
           "Rewarding" with punishment

       c.  Effective punishment:
           When does punishment work?

    2.  Parents' Styles and Children's Competence:
       Baumrind's Research

       a.  Three parenting styles

       b.  Authoritative child rearing

    3.  Parents' Love and Maturity

F.  RELATING TO OTHER CHILDREN

    1.  The Only Child

    2.  Brothers and Sisters

    3.  First Friends

       a.  Behavior patterns and
           choice of playmates and friends

       b.  Parents and popularity

G.  PLAY

    1.  Importance of Play

    2.  Perspectives on Play

       a.  Social and nonsocial play

       b.  Cognitive play

       c.  Imaginative play

    3.  Influences on Play: Parents and Day Care

---

## KEY TERMS

aggressive behavior (page 222)

androgynous (218)

authoritarian parents (228)

authoritative parents (228)

behavior modification (227)

castration anxiety (212)

cognitive play (234)

Electra complex (212)

gender (211)

gender constancy (gender conservation) (214)

gender differences (216)

gender identity (214)

gender roles (217)

gender schema (215)

gender stereotypes (217)

gender-schema theory (215)

gender-typing (217)

identification (211)

imaginative play (236)

initiative versus guilt (212)

Oedipus complex (211)

penis envy (212)

permissive parents (228)

phallic stage (211)

prosocial behavior (225)

sex differences (216)

social play (234)

superego (212)

## LEARNING OBJECTIVES

After finishing Chapter 7, you should be able to:

1. Briefly explain Freud's phallic *stage,* specifically comparing the *Oedipus complex* with the *Electra complex.*

2. Describe what Freud meant by the development of the *superego* during the phallic stage.

3. Explain Erikson's third psychosocial crisis, *initiative versus guilt,* and its resolution.

4. Describe and evaluate the social-learning theory of personality development.

5. Briefly explain and evaluate Kohlberg's cognitive-developmental theory of *gender differences* and behavior.

6. Describe and evaluate the *gender-schema theory* of gender development, defining the term *gender schema.*

7. List some *gender differences* and some similarities between boys and girls.

8. Explain some factors that might contribute to *gender stereotyping.*

9. Define *androgyny* as it relates to gender.

10. Explain what research tells us about the following influences on gender differences.
    a. biological influences

    b. cultural influences

    c. socialization

11. List some common childhood fears, and explain why young children seem prone to develop fears.

12. Explain why *aggression* seems to appear in early childhood.

13. Explain what research tells us about violence on television and the relationship between children's behavior and the programs they watch.

14. List some suggestions for reducing children's violence and aggression.

15. Define *altruism* (or *prosocial behavior)* and explain some influences that encourage it.

16. Briefly describe the following, and explain how they affect a child's personality development.
   a. reinforcement

   b. punishment

17. Identify the three styles of parenting identified by Baumrind and briefly describe typical behavior patterns of children raised primarily according to each style
   a.

   b.

   c.

18. Referring to Box 7-3, "Window on the World," describe the findings from the studies of raising only children in China.

19. Explain the research pertaining to relationships between siblings.

20. Explain how play benefits children at this stage of development, and differentiate between *cognitive play* and *imaginative play.*

## SUPPLEMENTAL READING

Carla Cantor is a free-lance writer living in New Jersey who specializes in issues concerning health and the family. This article is a reprint from *Working Mother*, June 1991.

## The Father Factor

### Carla Cantor

My three-year-old daughter is angry with me. It's Friday, the one day I take off from work during the week to be with her. But my editor has called with last-minute revisions that must be finished before the end of the day. I have to break the date my daughter and I had for the park and leave her with the babysitter. "I can't wait until Daddy gets home," my daughter says, her eyes challenging me as I make my move toward my office upstairs.

I, too, can't wait until her father gets home. He'll open the door and joy will fill the room. They'll tussle on the floor and she'll giggle. They'll play with her tricycle outside. He'll shower her with attention, which, at the moment, I'm unable to give; her momentary rejection and my guilt will be resolved by his presence.

My daughter and her father are close. And, according to the experts, theirs is an important connection; after years of ignoring a father's influence, many researchers are examining a role that has long stood in the shadow of motherhood.

"There is no question that when a father's relationship with his children is warm, children grow up more secure, not only in the world but within themselves," says Kyle D. Pruett, M.D., a clinical professor of psychiatry at the Yale University Child Study Center.

### MOMS AND DADS DIFFER

Just as a newborn begins to form a bond with his mother a few hours after birth, so too does he develop an immediate—although different—attachment to his father. Right from the beginning, Pruett explains, "the infant experiences his father as someone very different from his mother—in appearance, size, scent, texture, sound and overall presence."

That's because fathers and mothers interact very differently with their babies. Fathers tend to be playful and physical, initiating unusual, exciting forms of rough-and-tumble play, says Norma Radin, Ph.D., a professor of social work at the University of Michigan, who has conducted research on father-child relationships. Dad's fun-loving approach complements Mom's more verbal, soothing style. According to Radin, mothers spend more time holding their infants and talking to them in a gentle, low-keyed manner. "Mom will shake a rattle and coo, while Dad is more apt to tickle or lift the baby up in the air," she says.

Pediatrician and author T. Berry Brazelton has observed that by the time an infant is three weeks old he has different responses to his father and mother. When his father approaches, the baby will hunch his shoulders and lift his eyebrows as though in anticipation of playtime. He seems to expect more nurturing activities, such as feeding or nuzzling, from his mother. At three weeks, if a baby hears his mother's voice behind him, he will begin to root, his face will soften, and his legs and arms will move in a slow, smooth fashion. If his father's voice is substituted, says Brazelton, the baby's movements "will first stop in anticipation, and when they do start again, they will be jerky." These distinct patterns of responses and rhythms "lock each parent to the baby in a special way."

The different qualities Mom and Dad bring to parenting provide a healthy balance for a child: a diversity of stimulation and a range of experience that shapes individuality later in life. "A child who is highly involved with both parents has a rich, emotional palette from which to draw," says James A. Levine, director of The Fatherhood Project at the Families and Work Institute in New York. But there is more; research also tells us that fathers themselves bestow special benefits on their children.

### SENSE OF INDEPENDENCE

Fathers help children forge an identity outside the powerful intimacy of the mother-child relationship. During those early weeks, when it is Mom who's usually at home, Dad takes on the role of "the most significant other" in a baby's life. "It is through the father that the baby first learns about comings and goings, transitions, separations and non-mother nurturing," observes Pruett in his book *The Nurturing Father* (Warner Books). What this teaches the child is "how to develop a mental image of something longed for and trusted though not always present."

When the "terrible twos" arrive, toddlers frequently pursue the father as an "exciting new source of adventure," Pruett says. Through rough-and-tumble play with Dad, the child learns to take risks and solve physical problems, which fosters his sense of mastery over the outside world. This readies him for further challenges—"I can do it myself." So he turns again to the father, who is more likely than the mother to encourage the child to explore the outer levels of his competence and withstand frustration. Pruett offers the example of a child who falls off his tricycle. "A mother will rush over with hugs and reassurance," he says. "A father is less quick to move in and comfort. He will make the child get right back on."

## SOCIABILITY

Children of loving, attentive dads tend to be outgoing and develop strong friendships. Studies show that infants securely attached to both parents demonstrate a greater interest in unfamiliar adults than infants who have powerful attachments only to their mothers. And babies who spend a great deal of time with their dads are more sociable: They vocalize more, seem more eager to be picked up and show a greater love of play.

It seems that a father's physical, rough-and-tumble approach to play contributes not only to independence, but to a child's social development. Children who roughhouse with their dads at home tend to make friends easily and be popular at school, according to Kevin MacDonald, Ph.D., an associate professor of psychology at California State University at Long Beach who has researched the impact of this form of play.

Roughhousing also teaches kids how far they can go in their play. "They learn that pulling hair, kicking, biting and other forms of aggression are off-limits—knowledge that will serve them well on the playground," MacDonald says. In contrast to popular kids, children who are rejected by their classmates tend to come from homes in which the fathers' roughhousing is either insensitive or too aggressive. Shy and introverted kids often come from homes where there is little or no roughhousing.

David, an economist now in his 30s, recalls the difficulty he had in grade school and high school making friends of the same sex. "My dad and I were never buddies. We never hung out, never threw a ball around or wrestled. Most of our conversations centered on my schoolwork and his career as a lawyer," he says. It wasn't until college that David realized he had carried the "stiff and awkward" feeling of his connection with his father into other male relationships.

## CONFIDENCE AND FLEXIBILITY

Children who spend a great deal of time with their dads adapt well to new situations. Psychiatrist Pruett, who studied families in which fathers are primarily responsible for their children's care, found that children of highly involved fathers experience less anxiety when confronted with new or unusual circumstances, such as nursery school or summer camp. They don't get as rattled when routines are broken, he says, because they have learned "there is more than one way to skin a cat." For example, if a child only knows the way his mother puts him to bed, he's going to have a harder time putting himself to bed than will the child who knows that another method works.

In a study by Carolyn Pape Cowan and Philip Cowan, psychologists at the University of California at Berkeley, three-year-old children whose fathers worked more than 40 hours a week outside the home showed more anxiety than children whose fathers worked shorter hours. The children of fathers who worked long hours were also less warm and

less adept at playroom tasks, such as classifying objects and role-playing.

## INTELLECTUAL DEVELOPMENT

Participatory fathers enhance their children's motivation and ability to achieve. Norma Radin, who studied the effect of fathers by observing preschoolers in traditional families, found that sons of sensitive, affectionate fathers score higher on intelligence tests and do better at school than children of colder, authoritarian fathers. There is also evidence that girls do better in math when dads are more available.

One theory as to why this is has to do with what social scientists call "modeling behavior." Put simply, children are more likely to copy the behavior of a nurturing parent than a rejecting one. Therefore, says Radin, a child who wants to be like his father will internalize his behavior and thinking strategies—the way Dad solves problems, his vocabulary, his efforts to attain a goal.

The child's higher achievement also may reflect the benefits of having extensive attention from two highly involved parents instead of one. A father who spends a lot of time with his kids introduces them to a world of objects, activities and people outside the mother's sphere, Radin says. This expands a child's horizons and stimulates his thinking processes.

## COMPASSIONATE BEHAVIOR

Children of nurturing fathers are more likely to become empathic adults, capable of sharing the emotions and feelings of others. A Harvard University study tracked the lives of 75 boys and girls as they developed over 25 years. The researchers were surprised to find that a child's relationship to the father seemed more important than the mother-child bond in learning compassion.

The study showed that the more time a child spent with his father, the more empathic he became as an adult. "One reason may be that dads who play games with their children and engage in caretaking activities are likely to be empathic and caring themselves; the kids pick it up," says Joel Weinberger, Ph.D., an assistant professor of psychology at Adelphi University in Garden City, New York, and coauthor of the study. "It may also be that in our society it is the mother who is supposed to be sensitive and nurturing, so when the father is too, it makes a big impression on the child."

Fathers who model empathic behavior for their children play an important role in breaking sexual stereotypes, especially for sons, says Mark Barnett, Ph.D., a psychology professor at Kansas State University. Sons are likely to look toward their fathers for appropriate behavior; daughters look to their mothers, he says. "If a father is sensitive and caring, a son will see it's acceptable for him to be too."

## THE SPECIAL IMPACT ON DAUGHTERS

Several studies have suggested that daughters who are encouraged by their fathers to be athletic and competitive are more likely to be higher achievers. If a father involves his daughter in traditional male activities—fixing the car, making home repairs or pitching a softball—he's helping her develop self-confidence and giving her a broader definition of what it means to be female. "A daughter who can compete with her dad on the softball field can probably compete in the boardroom," says Joseph Pleck, Ph.D., a psychology professor at Wheaton College in Norton, Massachusetts, who coauthored a study of the results of fathers' involvement on sons and daughters.

It seems a father has a special role when it comes to a daughter. "He affirms her sex-role orientation in a way that the maternal role doesn't affirm the son's," says Radin. Fathers who are aloof, uninvolved or hostile tend to have daughters who are insecure in their role as a woman. It is not uncommon for them to experience problems in forming relationships with men later in life.

While it's beneficial for a father to help his daughter see herself as attractive and feminine, he must also promote her desire to master obstacles. He mustn't be overly protective. Coddling his daughter may encourage her to be helpless. "A daughter needs fatherly love and support, but she also needs a father who challenges her," Radin says.

Carmela, a 32-year-old fashion consultant, describes her "strict but loving" father as her role model. "It was Dad who taught me to ride a bicycle, pitch a baseball, balance a checkbook and drive," she says. Though he was a man of few words, there was one special conversation she recalls during a "wild and crazy" period she went through after high school. She was floundering in part-time jobs, not using her potential. He said: "Carmela, you're smart, beautiful and creative. This is your time, your world. Find your way and I'll do anything to help you." Eventually, she came to terms with her career and graduated from the Fashion Institute of Technology in New York City. "My dad, with six kids and a struggling construction business, helped every one of us, more than financially," says Carmella. "He encouraged us, but never pushed. He gave us a kind of center, the part of him I carry with me."

## THE BENEFITS ARE MUTUAL

A close relationship with their children brings something to fathers as well. In his book *Working Wives, Working Husbands* (Sage Publications), Joseph Pleck analyzed data from two national surveys and found that the more time a father invests in his children, the happier and more integrated his own life will be.

Other research, coauthored by Pleck, also shows that the more men nourish their children socially and emotionally, the more caring and giving the fathers tend to be when they reach middle age. For instance, they are more likely to take younger co-workers under their wing or volunteer time to charitable organizations, Pleck says. These habits afford men a richer and more fulfilling life.

Dad's involvement with child care also usually means less stress for Mom—reducing her work load and emotional burden as well as promoting her career, according to The Fatherhood Project's James Levine. This sharing in the child care department also relieves women of guilt, according to a *Working Mother* survey reported in the May 1991 issue. Dad's engagement makes both parents feel more fulfilled and enhances their marriage. And that's important: Studies show that a stable, harmonious marital relationship is one of the greatest gifts parents can bestow on their kids. Paternal involvement contributes to parents' feeling that they are competent caretakers. Mothers and fathers get a helpmate, and children get the benefit of two caring, supportive parents.

## LIFE WITHOUT FATHER

For the one million children involved in divorce every year, life is tough. But it isn't divorce alone that is so disruptive of a child's well-being—it is the loss of contact with a father.

A father's absence—whether physical or emotional—can devastate a child's sense of himself. "It's an enormous blow," says Judith Wallerstein, Ph.D., the author of *Second Chances: Men, Women, and Children a Decade After Divorce* (Ticknor and Fields). "Children blame themselves for being unlovable." Kids who have little or no relationship with their dads may develop emotional and behavioral problems, including aggression, poor performance in school and difficulties in establishing relationships.

For many, the problems surface in midadolescence. "Boys often have a hard time taking the first step into manhood without some sense of the father saying, 'I have confidence in you. You're important.' They fear not being loved," Wallerstein says. "Girls are afraid of being abandoned."

What the mother does can make the difference, Wallerstein says. The period right after divorce is the most crucial time. Here are some guidelines:

*Ease the strain of visitation.* Visits are difficult for parents because "they have so many emotional echoes," Wallerstein says. But they also set the tone for the father-child relationship. Unless a father is abusive or emotionally hurtful, realize his importance to your son or daughter. Separate your feelings about your ex from your concern for the child. That may mean listening to your child's excitement about the visit, keeping logistics simple, making transitions easier or not sticking around too much.

*Give your ex-husband a chance.* If Dad isn't visiting regularly, don't conclude he doesn't love his child. He may feel he has been displaced by a stepfather or lover, or that his child doesn't need him anymore. Don't turn on him in anger, or criticize him in front of the child. First, ask yourself whether your behavior is keeping him away. Next, try to talk to him sympathetically to find out if something is bothering him. Let him know how important he is to his child.

*What about a deadbeat dad?* There are, of course, fathers who drop out of their children's lives despite the mother's best efforts. If that happens, you need to share your child's sorrow so he doesn't feel alone. Be sympathetic to his longing and don't try to convey that his father isn't worth missing or loving. But also make it clear that the way the father is acting is not the way all men behave. Finally, try to help your child arrive at an explanation for his daddy's absence. A child must understand that it is not he who is flawed or unlovable.

*Try to offset the negative effects.* But don't attempt to make up for the deficit by yourself. Mothers need other voices to transmit values to their children and help them grow. Make use of the resources in the family, school and community. Try to help your child develop a relationship with a man who makes him feel valued—perhaps a grandfather, uncle, minister, coach or teacher. Of course,

mentors are not always easy to find and cultivating them involves some effort. "Grandpa doesn't live around the corner anymore," Wallerstein says. But do your best to ensure these relationships are rich and continuous.

## Questions about the Reading

1. How do mothers and fathers interact differently with their children?

2. What does research indicate about the "special" relationship between fathers and daughters?

3. Do the findings in this article agree with the findings about the father's influence described in the textbook? If not, in what area or areas do they differ?

---

## SELF-TESTS

---

## Multiple-Choice

Circle the letter of the response which best completes or answers each of following statements and questions.

1. Awareness of one's maleness or femaleness is called
   a. values clarification
   b. gender identity
   c. "goodness of fit"
   d. altruism

2. The process through which children adopt their parents' beliefs, attitudes, and values is referred to as
   a. identification
   b. gender identity
   c. values clarification
   d. altruism

3. Freud's psychosexual theory proposes that identification results from
   a. social success
   b. imitating the parent of the opposite sex
   c. repression or abandonment of the wish to possess the parent of the opposite sex
   d. becoming aggressive toward the opposite-sex parent

4. Proponents of social-learning theory believe that children's identity is formed by
   a. observing a model
   b. acting like a model
   c. wanting to be like a model
   d. all of the above

5. Who is more likely to encourage "masculine" and "feminine" behavior from children?
   a. father
   b. mother
   c. neither a nor b; mother and father are equally likely to do this
   d. none of the above; no studies have been done on this question

6. Which psychologist believes in cognitive-developmental theory—i.e., that children actively think about how they fit into the male or female role?
   a. Freud
   b. Kohlberg
   c. Erikson
   d. Bem

7. John is a preschooler who believes that wearing a dress and makeup will transform him into a girl. John has not yet developed
   a. gender discrimination
   b. gender constancy
   c. identification
   d. gender schema

8. In the United States, girls usually learn that it is important to be sympathetic and empathic, while boys learn to be
   a. capable at parenting
   b. quite verbal
   c. good at sports
   d. strong and aggressive

9. It appears that in our society, children acquire gender-typing at approximately what age?
   a. birth to 1 year
   b. age 2
   c. 3 to 6 years
   d. adolescence

10. What influences gender differences?
    a. biological and genetic factors
    b. cultural factors
    c. the media
    d. all of the above

11. According to Bem, which of the following is *least* likely to aid parents in protecting children against blatant gender stereotypes?
    a. emphasizing sex and anatomy as the main distinctions between males and females
    b. providing their son with a variety of toys to play with, ranging from trucks to dolls
    c. having both parents participate in changing their children's diapers
    d. exposing children to men and women in strictly traditional occupations

12. Philip is a 6-year-old whose father abandoned his mother before Philip's birth. It is likely that Philip will
    a. become very aggressive and independent, as a result of his mother's strong emphasis on gender-typing
    b. develop more exaggerated gender stereotypes than a child raised in a two-parent family
    c. be less gender-stereotyped, as a result of his father's absence
    d. develop the same attitudes toward gender-typing as if he were being raised in a two-parent family

13. Social-learning theorists would predict that children who watch television a great deal will become
    a. more gender-typed
    b. more empathic
    c. less gender-typed
    d. androgynous

14. Girls tend to be more fearful than boys, possibly because
    a. fear is an inherited tendency
    b. girls really have more fears
    c. girls are encouraged to be more dependent and boys are discouraged from admitting fears
    d. parents are more likely to accept boys' fears

15. Samantha, a 4-year-old, often grabs toys away from her playmates. Instrumental aggression such as this indicates which of the following?
    a. Samantha is a competent youngster, and her behavior is a natural part of social development.
    b. Samantha's parents are overly strict and domineering.
    c. Samantha has been raised in the absence of her father.
    d. Samantha will become increasingly aggressive with time and have great difficulty establishing friendships.

16. One preschooler prefers to watch *Sesame Street* while a second prefers to watch more violent television shows like *Teenage Mutant Ninja Turtles*. We can reasonably predict that
    a. the first child will be less social than the second
    b. the first child will show concern more rapidly if a sibling or friend is injured
    c. the second child will be less aggressive toward a sibling
    d. the first child is more likely than the second to be spanked by parents

17. Sarah is a generous, warm child and very sensitive to the needs of others. What can we reasonably infer from this?
    a. Sarah's family is financially well off.
    b. Sarah lacks self-confidence and thus lacks any aggressive tendencies.
    c. Sarah has been raised solely by her mother and thus has not been influenced by the male characteristics of a father.
    d. Sarah's parents encourage her to empathize with others and place little emphasis on values like obedience and making money.

18. An important aspect of raising an altruistic child seems to be
    a. the child's friends
    b. empathic television programs
    c. moral lessons learned in school and church
    d. examples and limits that parents set for their child

19. One of the facts we know about reinforcement is that
    a. preschool teachers have been able to reduce girls' aggressive behavior
    b. punishment reduces frustration
    c. children prefer negative reinforcement to no attention at all
    d. children watching aggressive models on television tend to be more passive after the program is over

20. Reinforcement studies have found that children learn more by being
    a. rewarded for good behavior than by being punished for bad behavior
    b. punished as a consequence of undesirable behavior
    c. ignored after desirable behavior
    d. none of the above; children's behavior is unpredictable

21. In her study of parenting styles and children's personalities, Baumrind concluded that children with permissive parents
    a. are the most mature
    b. tend to be highly exploratory and content
    c. lack self-control and are the least exploratory
    d. are the most withdrawn

22. Of the three kinds of parenting described by Baumrind, which one seems to nurture happier, healthier, more confident, respectful, secure children?
    a. authoritarian
    b. permissive
    c. authoritative
    d. none of the above

23. In the long run, specific parenting practices during a child's first 5 years may be less important than
    a. parents' socioeconomic status
    b. parents' level of education
    c. the number of friends a child has
    d. how the parents feel about their children and how they show those feelings

24. Which of the following statements about childhood play is most accurate?
    a. Lower-class children interact more with other children in play.
    b. Solitary play generally indicates poor social adjustment.
    c. Solitary play can be a sign of maturity and independence.
    d. Solitary play is common only among very young children.

25. According to recent research, children _____ tend to play more sociably than children _____ .
    a. attending a large university day care center; attending a private day care center
    b. from lower-class families; from middle-class families
    c. at an academically based day care center; at a day care center emphasizing social skills
    d. allowed to watch a great deal of television; whose parents participate in their children's activities

## Matching

Match each lettered item in the box below with the appropriate description in the numbered list following the box.

---

a. frustration
b. testosterone
c. penis envy
d. identification
e. imaginative play
f. permissive parenting
g. only children
h. authoritarian parents
i. cooperative play
j. television

---

1. creates highly gender-stereotyped attitudes _____

2. contributing factor in males' aggressive behavior _____

3. value self-expression and self-regulation _____

4. current subject of controversy in China _____

5. responsible for young girls' emotions toward their fathers _____

6. value control and total obedience _____

7. result of observing and imitating a model _____

8. trigger of aggression in young children _____

9. hindered by excessive television watching _____

10. observed in older, more developed children _____

## Completion

Suppply the term or terms needed to complete each of the following statements.

1. According to psychosexual theory, a girl in the phallic stage will experience the _____ complex, and a boy in the phallic stage will experience the _____ complex.

2. The aspect of the personality that represents the values communicated by parents and other agents of society was called the _____ by Freud.

3. Erikson's third crisis occurs during early childhood and is called _____ versus _____ .

4. At approximately age 2 a child becomes aware of being male or female; this is called gender _____ . Usually at about age 5 to 7 a child realizes that his or her sex will remain the same; this is called gender _____ .

5. According to Bem, a _____ is a mentally organized pattern of behavior that helps a child sort out perceived information.

6. The clearest gender difference between boys and girls is that males tend to be more _____ than girls.

7. Gender _____ are the behaviors, interests, attitudes, and skills that a culture considers appropriate for males and females and expects them to fulfill.

8. Bem coined the term _____ to describe the healthiest people, those who have a balance of characteristics from those thought appropriate for males and females.

9. Because differences among people of the same sex are _____ than the average variations between the sexes, _____ fails to explain large behavioral differences between the sexes.

10. The parent who is usually more accepting of "cross-gender" play (girls playing with trucks, boys playing with dolls) is the _____ .

11. A tendency for a child to show hostile actions intended to hurt someone or to establish dominance is called _____ ; concern for another person with no expectation of reward is called _____ .

12. _____ can heighten tendencies toward obesity and violence, and can convey distorted messages about drugs, alcohol, and gender roles.

13. The practice of altering children's behavior by rewarding approximations of desired behavior, or punishing undesirable behavior, is called _____ .

14. The less time elapses between behavior and punishment, the _____ the punishment will be.

15. Authoritative parents further their children's development by combining _____ with _____ .

16. If children's relationships with their _____ are marked by an easy trust and companionship, they may carry this pattern over to their dealings with playmates, classmates, and eventually friends and lovers in adulthood.

17. A study conducted with 4- to 7-year-olds confirmed the most important features of friendships at this time of life: _____ , _____ , _____ , and _____ .

18. Preschoolers who were _____ attached as infants tended to have more friends and were ranked by their teachers as more socially competent than other children.

19. Play in which children interact with others is called _____ play, whereas the forms of play which enhance children's cognitive development are called _____ play.

20. Children who watch a great deal of television tend not to play imaginatively, perhaps because they tend to absorb images _____ rather than generate their own images.

---

## ANSWERS FOR SELF-TESTS

---

### Multiple-Choice

1. b (page 211)
2. a (211)
3. c (211, 212)
4. d (213, 214)
5. a (214)
6. b (214)
7. b (214)
8. d (217)
9. c (217)
10. d (218)
11. a (219)
12. c (220)
13. a (221)
14. c (221)
15. a (222)
16. b (223, 224)
17. d (225, 226)
18. d (226)
19. c (227)
20. a (227)
21. c (228)
22. c (228, 229)
23. d (229)
24. c (235)
25. a (236)

### Matching

1. j (page 221)
2. b (223)
3. f (228)
4. g (231)
5. c (212)
6. h (228)
7. d (213)
8. a (223)
9. e (236)
10. i (234)

### Completion

1. Electra; Oedipus (pages 211, 212)
2. superego (212)
3. initiative versus guilt (212)
4. identity; conservation (*or* constancy) (214)
5. schema (215)
6. aggressive (217)
7. roles (217)
8. androgynous (218)
9. larger; biology (219)
10. mother (220)
11. aggression; altruism (222, 225)
12. television (225)
13. behavior modification (227)
14. more effective (227)
15. control; encouragement (228)
16. siblings (*or* brothers and sisters) (231)
17. common activities; affection; support; propinquity (232)
18. securely (232, 233)
19. social; cognitive (234)
20. passively (236)

# PHYSICAL AND INTELLECTUAL DEVELOPMENT IN MIDDLE CHILDHOOD

## INTRODUCTION

In Chapters 6 and 7 the development of children through kindergarten was discussed. Now, in **Chapter 8,** the discussion is shifted to the child of elementary school age. Where Chapter 6 focused on the physical and intellectual development of the preschooler, Chapter 8 examines the physical and intellectual development of the 6- to 12-year-old.

■ You will see, as you read Chapter 8, that the elementary school years are marked by further growth, strength, and agility and the mastery of skills that first appeared or were just learned during early childhood.

■ Probably the most significant aspect of development at this age is the fact that children spend a large proportion of their time in school. Intellectual development takes place in the context of formal schooling, entry into which coincides with significant changes in the way children think and organize knowledge.

■ Moreover, in middle childhood, moral and ethical thinking begins to develop in significant ways that are related to changes in the way children understand their world.

■ Chapter 8 concludes with a description of these cognitive changes and a discussion of how they are affected by the experience of school.

## CHAPTER OUTLINE

**PHYSICAL DEVELOPMENT**

**I. GROWTH DURING MIDDLE CHILDHOOD**

A. GROWTH RATES

B. NUTRITION AND GROWTH

**II. HEALTH, FITNESS, AND SAFETY**

A. CHILDREN'S HEALTH

1. Obesity

2. Minor Medical Conditions

3. Vision

4. Dental Health

5. General Fitness

6. Improving Health and Fitness

B. CHILDREN'S SAFETY

**III. MOTOR DEVELOPMENT IN MIDDLE CHILDHOOD**

**INTELLECTUAL DEVELOPMENT**

**IV. ASPECTS OF INTELLECTUAL DEVELOPMENT IN MIDDLE CHILDHOOD**

A. COGNITIVE DEVELOPMENT: PIAGET'S STAGE OF CONCRETE OPERATIONS

1. Operational Thinking

2. Conservation

a. What is conservation?

b. How is conservation developed?

B. MORAL DEVELOPMENT: THREE THEORIES

1. Piaget and Moral Stages

2. Selman and Role-Taking

3. Kohlberg and Moral Reasoning

a. Kohlberg's moral dilemmas

b. Kohlberg's levels of moral reasoning

c. Evaluating Kohlberg's theory

C. DEVELOPMENT OF MEMORY: INFORMATION PROCESSING

1. How Memory Works: Encoding, Storing, and Retrieving

2. Mnemonic Devices: Strategies for Remembering

a. Rehearsal

b. Organization

c. Elaboration

d. External aids

3. Metamemory: Understanding the Processes of Memory

D. DEVELOPMENT OF LANGUAGE: COMMUNICATION

1. Grammar: The Structure of Language

2. Metacommunication: Understanding the Processes of Communication

E. DEVELOPMENT OF INTELLIGENCE: PSYCHOMETRICS

1. IQ Tests

2. Norms, Reliability, and Validity

---

## KEY TERMS

attention deficit hyperactivity disorder (ADHD) (page 268)

concrete operations (248)

conservation (249)

conventional morality (252)

convergent thinking (270)

culture-fair (261)

culture-free (261)

decenter (249)

divergent thinking (270)

dyslexia (267)

elaboration (256)

external aids (256)

giftedness (269)

horizontal décalage (249)

learning disabilities (LDs) (267)

mainstreaming (268)

metacommunication (258)

metamemory (256)

mnemonic strategies (255)

morality of constraint (250)

morality of cooperation (250)

operational thinking (249)

organization (256)

Otis-Lennon School Ability Test (258)

postconventional morality (252)

preconventional morality (252)

rehearsal (255)

role-taking (250)

self-fulfilling prophecy (265)

Wechsler Intelligence Scale for Children (WISC-R) (258)

## LEARNING OBJECTIVES

After finishing Chapter 8, you should be able to:

1. Explain the importance of nutrition and fitness for continued healthy growth.

2. Describe the medical conditions common in middle childhood that might jeopardize growth and development.

3. Explain the typical progression of motor development in middle childhood.

4. Describe typical cognitive development in the elementary school years.

5. Recognize and explain the characteristics of *operational thinking* in general, and of *concrete operational thought* in particular.

6. Explain the development of *conservation,* a concept studied by Piaget.

7. Summarize the following people's theories of moral development.
   a. Piaget

   b. Selman

   c. Kohlberg

8. Compare and contrast the approaches to moral development of Piaget, Selman, and Kohlberg.

9. List and describe the four *mnemonic strategies*.
   a.

   b.

   c.

   d.

10. Explain what is meant by *metamemory*.

11. Describe the development of language in children of elementary school age, and their use of language.

12. Compare and contrast the purpose and use of the *WISC-R* and the *Otis-Lennon School Ability Test,* both of which are used to assess "intelligence."

13. Describe the ongoing controversy over IQ scores and cultural bias.

14. Explain why Japanese and Chinese children in a 1985 cross-cultural study outperformed American children in school achievement.

15. Describe some strategies for developing thinking and reasoning skills.

16. Explain how teachers' expectations can influence children's achievement.

17. List some of the ways parents can influence their children to succeed in school.

18. List and describe the four levels of mental retardation.
    a.

    b.

    c.

    d.

19. Describe what educational opportunities schools provide for children with physical disablilties or *learning disabilities.*

20. Describe what educational opportunities schools provide for children who are *gifted,* talented, or creative.

## SUPPLEMENTAL READING

This article is a reprint from *Newsweek*, Special Issue, Summer 1991.

## The Good, the Bad, and the Difference

### Barbara Kantrowitz

Like many children, Sara Newland loves animals. But unlike most youngsters, she has turned that love into activism. Five years ago, during a trip to the zoo, the New York City girl learned about the plight of endangered species, and decided to help. With the aid of her mother, Sara—then about 4 years old—baked cakes and cookies and sold them on the sidewalk near her apartment building. She felt triumphant when she raised $35, which she promptly sent in to the World Wildlife Fund.

A few weeks later, triumph turned into tears when the fund wrote Sara asking for more money. "She was devastated because she thought she had taken care of that problem," says Polly Newland, who then patiently told her daughter that there are lots of big problems that require continual help from lots of people. That explanation worked. Sara, now 9, has expanded her causes. Through her school, she helps out at an inner-city child-care center; she also regularly brings meals to homeless people in her neighborhood.

A sensitive parent can make all the difference in encouraging—or discouraging—a child's developing sense of morality and values. Psychologists say that not only are parents important as role models, they also have to be aware of a child's perception of the world at different ages and respond appropriately to children's concerns. "I think the capacity for goodness is there from the start," says Thomas Lickona, a professor of education at the State University of New York at Cortland and author of *Raising Good Children*. But, he says, parents must nurture those instincts just as they help their children become good readers or athletes or musicians.

That's not an easy task these days. In the past, schools and churches played a key role in fostering moral development. Now, with religious influence in decline and schools wavering over the way to teach values, parents are pretty much on their own. Other recent social trends have complicated the transmission of values. "We're raising a generation that is still groping for a good future direction," says psychologist William Damon, head of Brown University's education department. Many of today's parents were raised in the '60s, the age of permissiveness. Their children were born in the age of affluence, the '80s, when materialism was rampant. "It's an unholy combination," says Damon.

These problems may make parents feel they have no effect on how their children turn out. But many studies show that parents are still the single most important influence on their children. Lickona says that the adolescents most likely to follow their consciences rather than give in to peer pressure are those who grew up in "authoritative" homes, where rules are firm but clearly explained and justified—as opposed to "authoritarian" homes (where rules are laid down without explanation) or "permissive" homes.

The way a parent explains rules depends, of course, on the age of the child. Many adults assume that kids see right and wrong in grown-up terms. But what may be seen as "bad" behavior by an adult may not be bad in the child's eyes. For example, a young child may not know the difference between a fanciful tale and a lie, while older kids— past the age of 5—do know.

Many psychologists think that in children, the seeds of moral values are emotional, not intellectual. Such traits as empathy and guilt—observable in the very young—represent the beginning of what will later be a conscience. Even newborns respond to signs of distress in others. In a hospital nursery, for example, a bout of crying by one infant will trigger wailing all around. Research on children's attachment to their mothers show that babies who are most secure (and those whose mothers are most responsive to their needs) later turn out to be leaders in school: self-directed and eager to learn. They are also most likely to absorb parental values.

The first modern researcher to describe the stages of a child's moral development was Swiss psychologist Jean Piaget. In his groundbreaking 1932 book, *The Moral Judgment of the Child,* he described three overlapping phases of childhood, from 5 to 12. The first is the "morality of constraint" stage: children accept adult rules as absolutes. Then comes the "morality of cooperation," in which youngsters think of morality as equal treatment. Parents of siblings will recognize this as the "If he got a new Ninja Turtle, I want one, too," stage. In the third, kids can see complexity in moral situations. They can understand extenuating circumstances in which strict equality might not necessarily mean fairness. ("He got a new Ninja Turtle, but I got to go to the ball game, so it's OK.")

Although Piaget's conclusions have been expanded by subsequent researchers, his work forms the basis for most current theories of moral development. In a study begun in the 1950s, Lawrence Kohlberg, a Harvard professor, used "moral dilemmas" to define six phases. He began with 50 boys who were 10, 13 and 16. Over the next 20 years, he asked them their reactions to carefully constructed dilemmas. The most famous concerns a man named Heinz, whose wife was dying of cancer. The boys were told, in part, that a drug that might save her was a form of radiation discovered by the town pharmacist. But the pharmacist was charging 10 times the cost of manufacture for the drug and Heinz could not afford it—although he tried to borrow money from everyone he knew. Heinz begged the pharmacist to sell it more cheaply, but he refused. So Heinz, in desperation, broke into the store and stole the drug. Kohlberg asked his subjects: Did Heinz do the right thing? Why?

Kohlberg and others found that at the first stage, children base their answers simply on the likelihood of getting caught. As they get older, their reasons for doing the right thing become more complex. For example, Lickona says typical 5-year-olds want to stay out of trouble. Kids from 6 to 9 characteristically act out of self-interest; most 10- to 13-year olds crave social approval. Many 15- to 19-year-olds have moved on to thinking about maintaining the social system and being responsible.

Over the years, educators have used these theories to establish new curricula at schools around the country that emphasize moral development. The Lab School, a private preschool in Houston, was designed by Rheta DeVries, a student of Kohlberg's. The teacher is a "companion/guide," not an absolute authority figure. The object of the curriculum is to get kids to think about why they take certain actions and to think about consequences. For example, if two children are playing a game and one wants to change the rules, the teacher would ask the other child if that was all right. "Moral development occurs best when children live in an environment where fairness and justice is a way of life," says DeVries.

Not everyone agrees with the concept of moral development as a series of definable stages. Other researchers say that the stage theories downplay the role of emotion, empathy and faith. In *The Moral Life of Children,* Harvard child psychiatrist Robert Coles tells the story of a 6-year-old black girl named Ruby, who braved vicious racist crowds to integrate her New Orleans school—and then prayed for her tormentors each night before she went to bed. Clearly, Coles says, she did not easily fall into any of Kohlberg's or Piaget's stages. Another criticism of stage theorists comes from feminist psychologists, including Carol Gilligan, author of *In a Different Voice.* Gilligan says that the stages represent only *male* development with the emphasis on the concepts of justice and rights, not female development, which, she says, is more concerned with responsibility and caring.

But many psychologists say parents can use the stage theories to gain insight into their children's development. At each phase, parents should help their children make the right decisions about their behavior. In his book, Lickona describes a typical situation involving a 5-year-old who has hit a friend over the head with a toy while playing at the friend's house. Lickona suggests that the parents, instead of simply punishing their son, talk to him about why he hit his friend (the boy played with a toy instead of with him) and about what he could do next time instead of hitting. The parents, Lickona says, should also discuss how the friend might have felt about being hit. By the end of the discussion, the child should realize that there are consequences to his behavior. In Lickona's example, the child decides to call his friend and apologize—a positive ending.

For older children, Lickona suggests family "fairness meetings" to alleviate tension. If, for example, a brother and sister are constantly fighting, the parents could talk to both of them about what seem to be persistent sources of irritation. Then, youngsters can think of ways to bring about a truce—or at least a cease-fire.

Children who learn these lessons can become role models for other youngsters—and for adults as well. Sara Newland tells her friends not to be scared of homeless people (most of them rush by without a glance, she says). "Some people think, 'Why should I give to them?'" she says. "But I feel that you should give. If everyone gave food, they would all have decent meals." One recent evening, she and her mother fixed up three plates of beef stew to give out. They handed the first to the homeless man who's always on the corner. Then, Sara says, they noticed two "rough-looking guys" down the block. Sara's mother, a little scared, walked quickly past them. Then, she changed her mind and asked them if they'd like some dinner. "They said, 'Yes, God bless you,'" Sara recalls. "At that moment, they weren't the same people who were looking through a garbage can for beer bottles a little while before. It brought out a part of them that they didn't know they had."

## Questions about the Reading

1. As you were growing up, someone probably told you, "Let your conscience be your guide." How do you think your own "conscience" and values were formed?

2. In the United States today, what do you think has the greatest impact on formation of a child's values, and why: church, school, family, television, peers, government, the local newspaper, books, MTV, or advertising?

## SELF-TESTS

### Multiple-Choice

Circle the letter of the response which best completes or answers each of the following statements and questions.

1. Which of the following statements about growth is most accurate?
   a. Boys grow faster than girls from birth through adulthood.
   b. Girls grow faster than boys from birth through adulthood.
   c. Girls' growth rate outdistances boys' rate starting at about age 10; but boys overtake girls at about age 12 or 13.
   d. Growth rates around the world are similar for all races, national origins, and socioeconomic levels.

2. Normally, the years between ages 6 and 12 are
   a. among the healthiest in the life span
   b. no different from any other period with regard to health
   c. a continuous series of short-term colds, flu, and other illness
   d. the most dangerous because of the threat of major illnesses

3. The major health issue in the United States for children 6 to 11 years old has been found to be
   a. vision difficulties
   b. dental decay
   c. obesity
   d. broken bones

4. Lack of physical fitness among today's schoolchildren is mainly due to
   a. poor nutrition
   b. insufficient activity
   c. inherited weaknesses
   d. overeating

5. The leading cause of death and disability in middle childhood is
   a. contagious diseases and infections
   b. AIDS virus from blood transfusions
   c. child abuse
   d. accidents, particularly head injuries from bicycle accidents

6. Differences in physical skills and motor abilities between boys and girls aged 6 to 12 are largely due to
   a. inherent differences in anatomy
   b. hormonal differences that affect the development of muscle
   c. differences in eating patterns and nutrition
   d. differences in participation and expectations

7. Piaget's stage of cognitive development that is characteristic of most children in the middle years is referred to as
   a. sensorimotor
   b. preoperational
   c. concrete operations
   d. formal operations

8. Operational thought differs from earlier thought in that it involves
   a. using physical operations that correspond to thoughts
   b. using symbols to carry out operations, or mental activities, and the ability to understand another's view
   c. translating thought into action through physical operations
   d. operations (manipulating objects) as a basis for thought

9. Children in the middle years develop the different types of conservation (substance, weight, volume, etc.)
   a. at different times
   b. all within a short period of time relative to each other
   c. almost simultaneously
   d. by transferring what they have learned from one area to another

10. In developing conservation, children go through three stages:
    a. conservation through modeling, overgeneralization, mastery
    b. failure to conserve, transition, conserving and justifying
    c. concrete, symbolic, abstract conservation
    d. one-way, bidirectional, reversible conservation

11. Research shows that the development of conservation is influenced
    a. almost exclusively by maturation
    b. mainly by inherited characteristics
    c. primarily by cultural variables
    d. by both maturation and culture

12. Piaget and Kohlberg say that sound moral judgments are not likely until children have
    a. become capable of symbolic mental representations
    b. fully developed the ability to conserve
    c. matured beyond egocentric thinking
    d. mastered the fundamentals of symbolic logic

13. According to Piaget, the two stages of moral development are
    a. morality of constraint and morality of cooperation
    b. preconventional morality and conventional morality
    c. situational morality and universal morality
    d. morality of convenience and morality of commitment

14. Nicole is very concerned about a friend who has just broken her leg and cannot attend school or continue playing on the soccer team.  Nicole's role-taking is most closely associated with whose theory?
    a. Piaget's
    b. Freud's
    c. Selman's
    d. Kohlberg's

15. The technique of using moral dilemmas to study moral development is most associated with
    a. Piaget
    b. Freud
    c. Selman
    d. Kohlberg

16. From a research perspective, one shouldn't generalize about the results of Kohlberg's study of moral development because the subjects
    a. were males only
    b. were from western cultures only
    c. might say that they would act in a certain way when considering a hypothetical moral dilemma, but in actuality might act differently
    d. all of the above

17. Which of the following is *not* a mnemonic strategy?
    a. formalization
    b. rehearsal, repetition
    c. organization
    d. elaboration

18. A person's understanding of how his or her own memory processes operate is known as
    a. metamemory
    b. preoperational thinking
    c. operational memory
    d. operational thinking

19. During middle childhood, children are beginning to master the part of language called *syntax,* which is the
    a. definition of words
    b. spelling of words
    c. way words are organized in phrases and sentences
    d. none of the above

20. Knowledge of the processes of communication is known as
    a. metacomprehension
    b. metacommunication
    c. procedural knowledge
    d. syntax

21. Which of the following statements about IQ tests is the most accurate?
    a. Scores on IQ tests are not necessarily good predictors of grades in schools.
    b. IQ tests overlook some importance aspects of intelligence, such as creativity.
    c. The most widely used IQ tests are culturally biased.
    d. all of the above

22. In a cross-cultural study of American, Japanese, and Chinese children in first and fifth grade (1985), an international research team assessed cognitive abilities and found that
    a. Chinese and Japanese children spend more time per year in school and more time per day in school than American children
    b. Chinese and Japanese children spend more time on homework and get more help from their parents than American children
    c. Chinese and Japanese children performed better than American children on mathematics tests
    d. all of the above

23. The tendency of students to achieve according to what is expected of them is commonly called the
    a. expectancy effect
    b. Hawthorne effect
    c. self-fulfilling prophecy
    d. convergence of expectations and achievement

24. Which of the following statements about school achievement is true?
    a. Teachers' expectations have by far the greatest influence on children's school achievement.
    b. Parents and the home environment are the only significant influence on children's achievement.
    c. Children's friends have the greatest influence on achievement.
    d. Children's achievement is affected both by teachers' expectations and by parents' influence.

25. Public Law 94.142, landmark legislation passed by Congress in 1975, guarantees
    a. full mainstreaming for all retarded children
    b. a high school diploma for every disabled child
    c. appropriate public education for all children with disabilities—paving the way for mainstreaming and integration
    d. federal money for programs to provide year-round vocational training for any disabled learner

## Matching

Match each of the lettered items in the box with the appropriate description in the numbered list following the box.

---

a. Kohlberg
b. culture-free
c. mainstreaming
d. operational thinking
e. dyslexia
f. Piaget
g. Chomsky
h. norms
i. reliability
j. validity
k. culture-fair
l. divergent thinking
m. mnemonic strategy
n. attention deficit disorder
o. Selman

---

1. thinking with symbols _____
2. psychologist who described morality of cooperation _____
3. device to aid memory _____
4. having content common to various cultures _____
5. psychologist who posed moral dilemmas _____
6. five stages of role-taking _____
7. having no culture-linked content _____
8. integrating disabled students into regular classes _____
9. learning disability related to reading _____
10. thinking which comes up with fresh, unusual ideas _____
11. inappropriate activity, low tolerance for frustration, inability to attend to a task _____
12. if a test meets this criterion, it can correlate with other test results _____
13. studied language and syntax _____
14. standards established using a representative group of test takers _____
15. if test meets this criterion, a person who takes the test twice should score nearly the same both times _____

## Completion

Supply the term or terms needed to complete each of the following statements.

1. Sometime between 5 and 7 years of age, according to Piaget, children enter the stage of _____ , when they can think logically about the here and now but not yet about abstractions.

2. Children's inability to transfer what they learned about one type of conservation to another was called _____ by Piaget.

3. Piaget's first moral stage, _____ , is characterized by rigid, simplistic judgments.

4. The attainment of the stage of moral development that Piaget called *morality of cooperation* depends on a decrease in the child's _____ thinking.

5. In response to "Heinz's" dilemma as posed by Kohlberg, a child says, "It's all right to steal the drug, because his wife needs it and he wants her to live." This child is probably operating at the _____ stage of moral reasoning, according to Kohlberg's theory.

6. Kohlberg characterized children as _____, who work out their moral systems by independent discovery.

7. Mnemonic strategies include these four devices to aid memory: _____ , _____ , _____ , and _____.

8. Older children are more conscious of how memory works, and this knowledge, called _____ , develops in middle childhood.

9. Knowledge of the processes of communication is called _____ .

10. The most widely used *individual* IQ test for schoolchildren is the _____.

11. One of the major issues concerning IQ tests is _____ , the tendency to include test elements that are more familiar to people of certain cultures.

12. Asian Americans often do better in school than other American children. Studies indicate that the reasons for this are _____.

13. Miss Jones believes that her math class is of less than average ability (even though the children are really above average), and it is likely that her students will be affected by her belief. This phenomenon is called the _____.

14. The direct or indirect involvement of _____ improves children's grades and their scores on IQ and achievement tests, as well as their behavior and attitude toward school.

15. The four categories of mental retardation, based on severity, are _____ , _____ , _____ , and _____.

16. It is believed that the syndrome called _____—characterized by inattention, impulsivity, and low tolerance of frustration—is probably caused by a combination of genetic, neurological, biochemical, and environmental factors.

17. In 1975, Congress passed important legislation enacting the Education for All Handicapped Children Act, Public Law _____ , which ensures an appropriate public education for all disabled children.

18. It is estimated that approximately _____ percent of the population are gifted.

19. The use of IQ tests to identify gifted children goes back to _____ , the professor who brought the Binet test to the United States in the 1920s.

20. Three elements essential to the flowering of gifts and talents seem to be _____ , _____ , and _____.

## ANSWERS FOR SELF-TESTS

### Multiple-Choice

1. c (page 243)
2. a (244)
3. c (245)
4. b (246)
5. d (247)
6. d (248)
7. c (248)
8. b (249)
9. a (249)
10. b (249)

**11.** d (250)

**12.** c (250)

**13.** a (250)

**14.** c (250)

**15.** d (252)

**16.** d (254, 255)

**17.** a (255, 256)

**18.** a (256)

**19.** c (257)

**20.** b (258)

**21.** d (260)

**22.** d (262, 263)

**23.** c (265)

**24.** d (265, 266)

**25.** c (268)

## Matching

**1.** d (page 249)

**2.** f (250)

**3.** m (255)

**4.** k (261)

**5.** a (252)

**6.** o (250)

**7.** b (261)

**8.** c (268)

**9.** e (267)

**10.** l (270)

**11.** n (268)

**12.** j (260)

**13.** g (257)

**14.** h (260)

**15.** i (260)

## Completion

**1.** concrete operations (page 248)

**2.** horizontal décalage (249)

**3.** morality of constraint (250)

**4.** egocentric (250)

**5.** instrumental purpose and exchange (*or* second; stage 2) (253)

**6.** moral philosophers (254)

**7.** rehearsal; organization; elaboration; external aids (255, 256)

**8.** metamemory (256)

**9.** metacommunication (258)

**10.** WISC-R (258)

**11.** cultural bias (261)

**12.** cultural (263)

**13.** self-fulfilling prophecy (265)

**14.** parents (266)

**15.** mild; moderate; severe; profound (266)

**16.** hyperactivity (268)

**17.** PL 94.142 (268)

**18.** 3 to 5 (269)

**19.** Terman (270)

**20.** inborn ability; drive to excel; encouragement by adults (270)

# CHAPTER 9

# PERSONALITY AND SOCIAL DEVELOPMENT IN MIDDLE CHILDHOOD

## INTRODUCTION

Cognitive changes of middle childhood were described in Chapter 8. As **Chapter 9** describes, these are accompanied by personality and social changes. From the ages of 6 to 12, children's lives expand socially through greater interaction with peers, friends, neighbors, and families. Personal awareness of individual capabilities also expands as children enter school and other activities. Through these interactions, children can explore and develop their attitudes, values, and skills.

■ Two major accomplishments during this stage are development of the self-concept and a centering of control from outside the child to within the child. Even though the family remains a vital influence, children during this stage become more independent of their parents.

■ Because family structures have changed considerably over the past few generations (there are more divorces, more single parents, more working mothers, more children in day care, etc.), some children do not develop healthy self-esteem and may be more susceptible to stress, child abuse, depression, and emotional disorders.

■ Some psychologists are concerned about the "hurried" child of our society. Yet some "resilient" children are able to cope with stress. A variety of techniques are described to help children develop a healthy self-concept before entering the next stage of development, adolescence.

## CHAPTER OUTLINE

**I. THE SELF-CONCEPT**

A. COMPONENTS OF THE SELF-CONCEPT

1. Self-Recognition and Self-Definition

2. Self-Regulation

3. Self-Esteem

B. THEORETICAL PERSPECTIVES ON THE SELF-CONCEPT

1. Psychosexual Theory: Freud's Latency Period

2. Psychosocial Theory: Erikson's Crisis 4— Industry versus Inferiority

3. Social-Learning Theory

4. Cognitive-Developmental Theory

5. Information-Processing Approach

**II. ASPECTS OF PERSONALITY DEVELOPMENT IN MIDDLE CHILDHOOD**

A. EVERYDAY LIFE

1. How Do Children Spend Their Time?

2. With Whom Do Children Spend Their Time?

B. THE CHILD IN THE PEER GROUP

1. Functions and Influence of the Peer Group

2. Makeup of the Peer Group

3. Friendship

4. Popularity

   a. The popular child

   b. The unpopular child

      (1) Why are some children unpopular?

      (2) How can unpopular children be helped?

C. THE CHILD IN THE FAMILY

1. Parent-Child Relationships

   a. Issues between parents and children

   b. Discipline

   c. Control and coregulation

2. Parents' Work: How It Affects Their Children

   a. Mothers' work

      (1) The mother's psychological state

      (2) Interactions in working-mother families

      (3) Working mothers and children's values

      (4) Children's reactions to mothers' work

   b. Fathers' work

3. Children of Divorce

   a. Children's adjustment to divorce

      (1) "Tasks" of adjustment

      (2) Influences on children's adjustment to divorce

         (a) Parenting styles and parents' satisfaction
         (b) Remarriage of the mother
         (c) Relationship with the father
         (d) Accessibility of both parents

   b. Long-term effects of divorce on children

4.  The One-Parent Family

   a.  Current trends

   b.  Stresses on children

   c.  Effects on schooling

   d.  Long-term effects

5.  Stepfamilies

6.  Sibling Relationships

## III. CHILDHOOD EMOTIONAL DISTURBANCES

A.  TYPES OF EMOTIONAL PROBLEMS

1.  Acting-Out Behavior

2.  Anxiety Disorders

   a.  Separation anxiety disorder

   b.  School phobia

3.  Childhood Depression

B.  TREATMENT FOR EMOTIONAL PROBLEMS

1.  Therapies

2.  Effectiveness of Therapy

## IV. STRESS AND RESILIENCE

A.  SOURCES OF STRESS: LIFE EVENTS, FEARS, AND THE "HURRIED CHILD"

B.  COPING WITH STRESS: THE RESILIENT CHILD

---

## KEY TERMS

acting-out behavior (page 296)

affective disorder (297)

childhood depression (297)

coregulation (287)

discipline (286)

ideal self (277)

industry versus inferiority (279)

prejudice (283)

psychological maltreatment (300)

real self (277)

school phobia (297)

self-awareness (276)

self-care children (289)

self-concept (276)

self-definition (277)

self-esteem (278)

self-recognition (276)

self-schema (280)

separation anxiety disorder (296)

## LEARNING OBJECTIVES

After finishing Chapter 9, you should be able to:

1. Explain what is meant by a person's sense of self, or *self-concept,* which begins to develop during middle childhood.

2. Discuss the following aspects of the self-concept.
   a. Describe the development and importance of healthy *self-esteem* or self-image.

   b. Describe the parenting style which tends to foster a healthy self-concept.

3. Explain what Freud meant by the latency period in middle childhood.

4. Describe Erikson's fourth crisis, *industry versus inferiority,* and its successful resolution.

5. Explain what shapes a child's personality and social development during middle childhood according to each of the following.
   a. social-learning theory

   b. cognitive-developmental theory

c. information-processing approach

6. Explain some positive and negative effects of the peer group.
   a. positive effects

   b. negative effects

7. Differentiate between how a young child views a friend and how a child in the middle years views a friend.

8. Explain some personality characteristics of popular children and unpopular children.

10. Briefly describe the kinds of issues that arise between children in middle childhood and their parents concerning the following.
    a. *discipline*

    b. control and regulation

11. Briefly explain some research findings concerning mothers' working and its effects on the following.
    a. infants and toddlers

    b. school-age children

    c. adolescents

12. Briefly describe the research on how men's work (or unemployment) affects their families.

13. Describe some common reactions of children to parents' divorce.

14. List five suggestions for helping children adjust to divorce.
    a.

    b.

    c.

    d.

    e.

15. Explain some of the common stressors on children from one-parent families.

16. Describe the following nonphysical disturbances and list some possible treatments.
    a. *acting-out behavior*

    b. *separation anxiety disorder*

    c. *school phobia*

    d. *childhood depression*

17. Name and explain the treatment techniques for emotional disturbances.
    a. psychological therapies (three forms)

    b. drug therapy

18. Explain the term *psychological maltreatment* and its relationship to child abuse.

19. Explain what David Elkind and other psychologists mean by the term *hurried child*.

20. Describe some factors that help a child cope with and be more resilient to stress.

## SUPPLEMENTAL READING

This article is a reprint from *Newsweek*, Special Issue, Summer 1991.

### Helping Themselves

#### Charles Leerhsen

The subject was football—which was odd, because the problem was divorce. As a half dozen other fourth graders sat around him, thinking about the discord in their own homes, the boy spun endless accounts of gridiron glory. None of what he said was relevant, and very little seemed true. For two weeks David Rollins, a counselor at Shallowford Falls Elementary School in suburban Atlanta, just listened. Then, as the 10-year-old embarked on yet another tale of touchdowns and tackles, Rollins gently interrupted. "I wonder if we ever think about something so much that we really believe in it," he said. "I wonder if we talk about it so much because we don't want anyone to know how we are hurting." Rollins's remark was risky. The boy could have retreated deeper into his denial. But he fell instead into a thoughtful silence. When he spoke again it was to say how uncertain he felt about almost everything now that his parents had split up.

Score another small victory for school support groups. The same self-help revolution that swelled the ranks of Alcoholics Anonymous—and spawned a raft of similar organizations—is now reaching kids as young as 5. And schools are the usual setting because, as Donald J. Steadman, dean of the school of education at the University of North Carolina says, "Children have rich emotional lives—and child counselors have realized that these emotions are not confined to the home."

Movements don't get much more grass-roots than this. "This is people solving their own problems," says Dr. Magda Pollenz, a psychiatrist in Briarcliff Manor, N.Y. The groups started forming spontaneously about 10 years ago, as teachers noticed more kids having problems with divorce, drugs in the family and domestic violence. Formats vary widely. The Irvine Unified School District in California provides a counselor-run program which helps 5-to 18-year olds cope with "life changes." At St. Clement's Catholic School in Chicago, kids attend weekly meetings where they discuss similar topics with one another and with teacher-moderators. A two-year-old New York City program, Network in the Schools, allows kids to express joy in their daily accomplishments and form a modest plan to make their lives a little better.

Not only do most counselors embrace this idea, many see the groups as one sign of a major cultural shift—away from shame and guilt toward a greater self-awareness. "The beauty part of these sessions," says Dr. Margaret Dawson, president of the National Association of School Psychologists, is that "they are dedicated to the notion that you don't have to have family secrets." Parents, however, don't always exhibit the same openness. Sometimes when a teacher notices a child being aggressive or withdrawn and suggests a support group, she gets a flat no from a parent who may be ashamed of what's happening at home. "The reason some kids are having problems is that their mothers and fathers aren't 'fessing up to reality," says Carol Hacker, a psychologist in Colorado's Jefferson County school system.

For some children, the sessions are the most fun they have all day. Group leaders often suggest playing games that allow for self-expression. "What the little kids are really looking for is attention," says Kathy Eslinger, a teacher at St. Clement's. Dawson stresses that the sessions are not group therapy, which "is geared toward more serious problems." The support groups, she says, work best for kids who are already coping but who could benefit from a boost in self-esteem or a practical suggestion.

Even counselors agree that group guidance is often preferable to the one-on-one approach. "The best medicine," says Paul Cborowski, a professor of psychology at Long Island University, "is often the news that, no matter what your problem, you are not alone." Steven Chinlund, who runs Network in the Schools, goes further. "The act of affirming yourself in public has an effect that is almost magical," he says. The neatest trick of all may be that these groups help educators cope, too. "We live in an era when we have little money for guidance programs, but studies show an increase in the number of troubled kids," says Hacker. "You could call these support groups a lucky break." Or a dire necessity.

## Questions about the Reading

1. On the basis of what you have read in Chapter 9, what research would you cite to a parent to encourage inclusion of his or her child in a school-based support group?

2. How might you encourage a child at this stage of development to consider participating in a school-based support group?

3. Does this article support the authors' findings about the significance of peer relationships?

## SELF-TESTS

### Multiple-Choice

Circle the letter of the response which best completes or answers each of the following statements and questions.

1. Which of the following is *not* considered an important task of middle childhood?
   a. expanding understanding of the self and society
   b. developing trust in significant others
   c. developing acceptable behavioral standards
   d. managing one's own behavior

2. Coopersmith concluded that people base their self-image on which of the following criteria?
   a. popularity, intelligence, wealth
   b. peer approval, parental approval, teacher approval
   c. significance, competence, virtue, and power
   d. none of the above

3. The successful resolution of Erikson's fourth crisis, industry versus inferiority, is
   a. popularity
   b. love
   c. the virtue of purpose
   d. competence

4. Social-learning theorists believe that a child's self-concept during middle childhood is shaped by
   a. approval or disapproval of parents, teachers, peers
   b. the capacity for productive work
   c. growth in moral reasoning and ability
   d. all of the above

5. Which of the following statements about middle childhood is *false?*
   a. The two main things children choose to do are playing and watching television.
   b. Children who read every day are likely to watch less television.
   c. Children watch television more in middle childhood than during any other period of childhood.
   d. Children spend a great deal of their free time with parents.

6. In Furman's study in which children rated the important people in their lives, it was found that
   a. children look to their friends for affection, guidance, and enhancement of worth
   b. children rated their parents as the most important people in their lives
   c. boys relied more on their best friends than girls did
   d. fathers got higher companionship ratings than mothers

7. In the elementary school years, peer groups are usually
   a. all girls or all boys
   b. of the same or similar socioeconomic status
   c. formed naturally among children who live in the same neighborhood or go to school together
   d. all of the above

8. According to Selman, which of the following statements regarding childhood friendship is the most accurate?
   a. Girls value depth of relationships, while boys value number of relationships.
   b. Friendship plays only a minor role in a child's development.
   c. From ages 9 to 15, children value friends for material or physical attributes.
   d. Most school-age children respect friends' needs for both autonomy and dependency.

9. In middle childhood, a friend is
   a. someone a child feels comfortable with and can share secrets with
   b. someone who lives nearby and has lots of toys
   c. someone the child wants to be like
   d. none of the above

10. Which of these factors would probably *not* account for a child's unpopularity?
    a. unattractive appearance
    b. antisocial parents
    c. expecting to be well-liked
    d. a learning disorder

11. Which of the following statements is *least* accurate?
    a. Unpopular children are more likely to become delinquent.
    b. Children who expect to be liked actually are less liked by their peers.
    c. Rejected children need to learn how to make other children like them.
    d. Antisocial behavior in children often shows up first in the family.

12. Which of the following statements is true of parent-child relationships during middle childhood?
    a. The people in the child's home are the most important to him or her.
    b. Most parents are not concerned about the child's schoolwork.
    c. Most parents are not concerned about where their children are or with whom they play.
    d. Children and parents rarely disagree about household tasks.

13. In order for the transitional phase of coregulation to work, how should parents act toward children in middle childhood?
    a. Allow children to adopt their own standards and control their own behavior.
    b. Communicate clearly with children and provide support, guidance, and general supervisory control.
    c. Impose rigid rules and regulations on children and constantly scrutinize children's actions.
    d. Influence children to adopt values and standards like their own.

14. One finding from studies on mothers' working outside the home is that
    a. boys of lower socioeconomic status had lower IQs, and their academic achievement was worse, when their mothers worked full time during their preschool years
    b. working mothers' homes tend to be more structured, with clear-cut rules; and thier children are usually encouraged to be more independent
    c. there is much greater stress in working mothers' homes, and their children form insecure attachments
    d. as in infancy, girls are more vulnerable than boys if the mother is working full time

15. Johnny comes from a middle-class family, and his mother works outside the home; his friends' mothers are homemakers. Which of the following can we reasonably infer?
    a. As society adjusts to the growing number of working mothers, Johnny will be less affected by his mother's employment.
    b. Johnny's father will tend to be less nurturing and less involved than his friends' fathers.
    c. Johnny will acquire more stereotypes about gender roles than his peers.
    d. Johnny's home will tend to be less structured than his friends', with few rules and regulations.

16. Jerome's father recently lost his job and has become very irritable and depressed. How might we expect Jerome's behavior to change as a result?
    a. Jerome will set high aspirations for himself and try to avoid the failure his father has suffered.
    b. Jerome may become a behavioral problem in school and grow depressed as well.
    c. Jerome's behavior will remain unaffected by his father's crisis.
    d. Jerome will develop into a well-behaved child in order to mask his family's turmoil.

17. Which of the following scenarios is most common among remarried mothers?
    a. Daughters of remarried women often experience more problems coping than these women's sons.
    b. Remarried mothers tend to be less happy and less satisfied with their lives.
    c. The daughters of remarried women usually never adjust to coexistence with their stepfathers.
    d. Sons of remarried women often experience more problems coping than these women's daughters.

18. Recent studies on teenagers with divorced parents tend to show that
    a. three-quarters of the girls and boys remain severely troubled for at least 10 years after the crisis
    b. girls are far more likely to be lonely and unattached than boys
    c. many such children survive the painful experience, adjust well, and develop increased compassion for others
    d. the majority of children remain unaffected by their parents' divorce

19. Children living with a single parent
    a. are more likely to require disciplinary action than children with two parents
    b. do not usually have problems in school
    c. welcome a stepparent to take over the absent parent's role in the family
    d. usually stay in the same residence for a long time

20. Depressed children can be recognized by the fact that they
    a. are unable to have fun and unable to concentrate
    b. are frequently tired or extremely active
    c. talk little but cry a great deal
    d. all of the above

21. Which therapy involves all members of a family and points out their patterns of functioning?
    a. preventive
    b. family
    c. supportive
    d. play

22. Which therapy uses principles of learning theory to alter behavior?
    a. behavior modification
    b. preventive therapy
    c. play therapy
    d. supportive therapy

23. Action or inaction which damages children's behavior or their cognitive, emotional, or physical functioning is called
    a. institutional maltreatment
    b. psychological maltreatment
    c. resilience
    d. compensation

24. The child psychologist David Elkind, concerned about the pressures on children today, coined which of the following terms?
    a. resilient child
    b. depressed child
    c. abnormal child
    d. hurried child

25. Which of the following factors seems/seem to contribute to children's resilience to stress?
    a. good relationship with parents
    b. observation of positive models and experience solving problems
    c. compensating experiences and successful experiences in and outside the home
    d. all of the above

## Matching

Match each of the lettered items in the box with the appropriate description in the numbered list that follows the box.

a. self-awareness
b. ideal self
c. latency period
d. self-schema
e. siblings
f. developing friendships
g. reciprocal, two-way
h. rejected children
i. discipline
j. stepfamily

1. the self-concept is a set of knowledge structures which organize and guide these _____

2. relationship with these usually involves most conflict _____

3. a great milestone in human development _____

4. stage of friendship for 6- to 12-year-olds _____

5. "knowledge" or "instruction" _____

6. the realization that we are separate from others _____

7. Freud described this as a time of relative sexual calm _____

8. also called *blended* or *reconstituted* _____

9. the person we would like to be _____

10. children most likely to develop emotional and behavioral difficulties later in life _____

## Completion

Supply the term or terms needed to complete each of the following statements.

1. The gradual realization that we are beings separate from other people and from other things, with the ability to reflect on ourselves and our actions, is called _____ ; and each person's evaluation of himself or herself is called _____ .

2. By establishing _____ rules, we let children know what behavior is expected of them.

3. The _____ , according to _____ , is a time of relative calm between the turbulence of childhood and the storminess of adolescence.

4. Erikson's crisis of middle childhood is _____ versus _____ , and its successful resolution leads to _____ .

5. According to Piaget's _____ theory, changes during middle childhood permit growth in _____ and the ability to consider _____ as well as personal needs.

6. The two main things that children choose to do during middle childhood are _____ and _____ .

7. In middle childhood, a _____ is someone the child is comfortable with, someone with whom the child can share feelings and secrets, and someone with whom the child is able to give and receive respect.

8. Children who have trouble getting along with their peers are more likely to have _____ problems, to drop out of school, and to become _____ .

9. Today, almost _____ out of 10 married women with children under 18 and _____ out of 10 single mothers are in the work force.

10. Children who regularly care for themselves at home without adult supervision because one or both parents work outside the home are called _____ children.

11. The best custody arrangement for children of divorce seems to be with _____ .

12. The average income of families headed by women is _____ than that of families with two parents.

13. Siblings help each other develop a _____ , learn how to resolve _____ , learn to _____ for what they want, and learn how to deal with _____ in relationships.

14. Misbehavior that is an outward expression of emotional turmoil is referred to as _____ behavior.

15. The pain of physical abuse may heal quickly, but its _____ may never go away for some children.

## ANSWERS FOR SELF-TESTS

### Multiple-Choice

1. b (page 277)
2. c (278)
3. d (280)
4. a (280)
5. d (281)
6. b (281)
7. d (283)
8. a (283)
9. a (283)
10. c (284, 285)
11. b (285)
12. a (286)
13. b (287)
14. b (288)
15. a (289)
16. b (290)
17. a (291)
18. c (293)
19. a (294)
20. d (297)
21. b (298)
22. a (298)
23. b (300)
24. d (300)
25. d (301)

## Matching

1. d (page 280)
2. e (282)
3. f (283)
4. g (284)
5. i (286)
6. a (276)
7. c (279)
8. j (294)
9. b (277)
10. h (285)

## Completion

1. self-awareness; self-esteem (276, 278)
2. clear (*or* consistent) (279)
3. latency period; Freud (279)
4. industry; inferiority; competence (279, 280)
5. cognitive-developmental; moral reasoning; social (280)
6. play; watch television (281)
7. friend (283)
8. psychological; delinquent (285)
9. 7; 8 (287)
10. self-care (*or* latchkey) (289)
11. the parent of the same sex (293)
12. less than half (293)
13. self-concept; conflicts; negotiate; dependency (295)
14. acting-out (296)
15. psychological scars (300)

# PHYSICAL AND INTELLECTUAL DEVELOPMENT IN ADOLESCENCE

## INTRODUCTION

**Chapter 10** discusses physical and intellectual development in adolescence. Physically, adolescence is a time of moving from pubescence to puberty, toward sexual and physical maturation.

■ The chapter begins by examining the physiological changes of adolescence and their psychological impact.

■ Health and nutrition are discussed, as are the problems of drug abuse and sexually transmitted diseases.

■ Intellectual development is examined from the perspective of two different models—Piaget's and Kohlberg's—and adolescent egocentrism is discussed.

■ The influence of high school is examined, and home influences on achievement in high school are discussed.

■ Finally, career planning in late adolescence is considered, with a description of the stages of vocational planning and a discussion of the influences on vocational planning.

## CHAPTER OUTLINE

**I. ADOLESCENCE:
A DEVELOPMENTAL TRANSITION**

**PHYSICAL DEVELOPMENT**

**II. MATURATION IN ADOLESCENCE**

A. PHYSICAL CHANGES

    1. Puberty and the Secular Trend

    2. The Adolescent Growth Spurt

    3. Primary Sex Characteristics

    4. Secondary Sex Characteristics

    5. Menarche

B. PSYCHOLOGICAL IMPACT
OF PHYSICAL CHANGES

    1. Effects of Early and Late Maturation

       a. Early and late maturation in boys

       b. Early and late maturation in girls

    2. Reactions to Menarche and Menstruation

    3. Feelings about Physical Appearance

**III. HEALTH CONCERNS OF ADOLESCENCE**

A. NUTRITION AND EATING DISORDERS

    1. Nutritional Needs

    2. Obesity

    3. Anorexia Nervosa and Bulimia Nervosa

       a. Anorexia

       b. Bulimia

       c. Treatment for anorexia and bulimia

B. USE AND ABUSE OF DRUGS

    1. Current Trends

    2. Alcohol

    3. Marijuana

    4. Tobacco

C. SEXUALLY TRANSMITTED DISEASES (STDs)

    1. What Are STDs?

    2. STDs and Adolescents

**INTELLECTUAL DEVELOPMENT**

**IV. ASPECTS OF INTELLECTUAL
DEVELOPMENT IN ADOLESCENCE**

A. COGNITIVE DEVELOPMENT:
PIAGET'S STAGE OF FORMAL OPERATIONS

    1. Cognitive Maturity:
The Nature of Formal Operations

    2. Tracing Cognitive Development:
The Pendulum Problem

    3. What Brings Cognitive Maturity About?

    4. Assessing Piaget's Theory

B. ADOLESCENT EGOCENTRISM

    1. Finding Fault with Authority Figures

    2. Argumentativeness

    3. Self-Consciousness

    4. Self-Centeredness

    5. Indecisiveness

    6. Apparent Hypocrisy

C. MORAL DEVELOPMENT:
   KOHLBERG'S LEVELS OF MORALITY

   1. Level I: Preconventional Morality

   2. Level II: Conventional Morality

   3. Level III: Postconventional Morality

## V. HIGH SCHOOL

A. HIGH SCHOOL TODAY

B. HOME INFLUENCES ON
   ACHIEVEMENT IN HIGH SCHOOL

   1. Parents' Interest

   2. Parenting Styles

   3. Socioeconomic Status

C. DROPPING OUT OF HIGH SCHOOL

   1. Who Drops Out?

   2. Why Do They Drop Out?

   3. What Happens to Dropouts?

   4. How Can Dropping Out Be Prevented?

## VI. DEVELOPING A CAREER

A. STAGES IN VOCATIONAL PLANNING

B. INFLUENCES ON VOCATIONAL PLANNING

   1. Part-Time Work

   2. Parents

   3. Gender

---

## KEY TERMS

adolescence (page 308)

adolescent growth spurt (311)

anorexia nervosa (317)

bulimia nervosa (318)

formal operations (324)

imaginary audience (326)

menarche (313)

obesity (316)

personal fable (327)

primary sex characteristics (312)

puberty (308)

secondary sex characteristics (312)

secular trend (311)

sexually transmitted diseases (STDs) (320)

## LEARNING OBJECTIVES

After finishing Chapter 10, you should be able to:

1. Describe maturation in *adolescence.*

2. Explain the process of *puberty,* and identify the approximate time when it takes place.

3. Discuss the various physiological changes of *adolescence,* and how they differ in boys and girls.

4. List the *primary sex characteristics* and *secondary sex characteristics.*

5. Understand *menarche* and menstruation and their psychological effect.

6. Discuss the psychological impact of physical changes and the effects of early and late maturation.

7. Describe adolescents' concerns about physical appearance.

8. List the major health concerns during *adolescence.*

9. Explain the difference between various nutrition problems and eating disorders, and describe their effect on teenagers.

10. Discuss the drugs most commonly used by adolescents and the problems of abuse for this age group.

11. List the most common *sexually transmitted diseases* (STDs) and their effects, and describe how they are transmitted.

12. Identify which STDs are curable, which are not, and which are life-threatening.

13. Discuss Piaget's stage of *formal operations* in cognitive development.

14. Describe egocentrism in the adolescent, and give examples.

15. List and describe Kohlberg's three levels of morality.

    a.

    b.

    c.

16. Discuss the effects of high school on adolescents' development, and describe the influence of home and of socioeconomic status on achievement.

17. Discuss dropping out of high school.

18. Discuss career development, and the stages and influence of vocational planning.

---

## SUPPLEMENTAL READING

---

Grace Slick formerly sang with the rock group Jefferson Airplane, where she was called the "Acid Queen" in reference to the drug-oriented rock culture of which she was a part. Now, a recovering alcoholic, she lives with her husband in Mill Valley, California.

### Highs and Lows

#### Grace Slick

When I took acid in the '60s, I wanted to open up and explore life. In the '70s I took alcohol to close down and shut out the "noise." The former experience was a kind of reaching up. The latter was a downward spiral. Both experiences taught me worthwhile lessons—lessons that proved valuable when my daughter, China, was growing up and finding her way.

In 1965 I was a new singer, a new adult and a member of a generation trying to develop new ethics. We thought we were invincible. But as the '70s melted, and the world didn't go in the right direction fast enough, some of us crawled into a bottle or a needle looking for peace. Wrong move. Long-term peace—except maybe "rest in peace"—is not found in a chemical. Being half conscious always slaps back. In my case the blow was administered in a roundabout way. In 1977 I was a heavy drinker and a fast driver. A car,

"the California necessity," was my way to exercise personal freedom. So when the highway patrol said quit drinking or you lose your driver's license, I decided to get sober. That was 13 years ago. I am now 50.

Nobody knows for sure what makes someone get high. In some cases, they're genetically predisposed. Or they may be environmentally conditioned. Either way, the result is the same—you go nowhere fast, though I didn't realize that until later in life. As a kid, the times I saw my father open up were when he was drinking. He would sing, laugh and generally enjoy himself when he got loaded. Looked like a good deal to me. Of course, I didn't have to feel the pain the next morning. I didn't feel the depression, humiliation and loneliness that every alcoholic or addict experiences sooner or later.

Kids start using drugs earlier now. Many of them sober up, or die from an overdose, by the time they're 14 or 15. China drank for six months, but because I had been open with her about my past—and because she had gone to support-group meetings with me ever since she was 7 years old—she was able to recognize the symptoms of alcoholism in herself.

One night when she was 16, I picked China up from a party at a friend's house. She got in the car and said, "Mom, do you know what I've been drinking? Cooking sherry. And I threw up about 10 times and I was kissing this guy I don't even like and calling people on the phone and crying. I think I need to raise my hand at a meeting."

I was surprised—not that she had been drinking and certainly not that she had decided to confide in me. What surprised and pleased me was that she had been so quick to catch her own error. I felt a great sense of relief that she had skipped all those painful years of floundering before recognition of her problem. She's now 19 and has been sober for three years.

There's no telling how things would have turned out if China and I had had a different relationship. Most adults have a way of lording it over their kids, and that keeps the kids from telling their parents what's going on in their lives. But China and I have always hung out together. She is an honest friend as well as a daughter.

No subject is off-limits. She tells me things I never would have told my parents, and I tell her things my mother wouldn't have dreamed of telling me. We express our feelings—sometimes negative, sometimes positive, but always no holds barred. She feels free to call me on my bullshit, and often she is able to get me to see when I'm off the mark. When I'm in the middle of a lot of pontificating, she calls me "Mom Dass," after the spiritual leader Ram Dass. And to her credit, she is usually able to see the truth in a situation, even if it means she is wrong.

Hiding things from children—or worse, lying to them— inevitably leads to a phony set of manners. If I had played the uptight parent about drinking and drugs, nagging China

with an "I know what's best for you" attitude, neither of us would have been much help to each other. Instead I chose to tell her about my experience and let her do whatever she must with that knowledge. Hopefully, as she continues to grow, she will remain open to a wide variety of ideas, rather than restrict herself to the sanctimoniousness of one individual.

I know I've just thrown a lot of words at you, and I realize that every family has its own dynamic. But platitudes notwithstanding, part of the reason China and I feel like whole individuals today is because, simply, we get what we give. Consider your child a friend, not a possession, and things will lighten up considerably.

## Questions about the Reading

1. When your children ask you about activities you consider harmful or unhealthy, but which you may have participated in as a teenager, how will you respond to them?

2. What can parents do to improve the openness of communication with their adolescent children?

---

## SELF-TESTS

---

## Multiple-Choice

Circle the letter of the response which best completes or answers each of the following statements and questions.

1. The term *puberty* refers to
   a. the process of attaining sexual maturity
   b. onset of adolescence
   c. initial appearance of primary sex characteristics
   d. reaching age 13

2. The stage of physical development during which the reproductive organs mature and secondary sex characteristics appear is called
   a. adolescence
   b. puberty
   c. pubescence
   d. menarche

3. Which of these is *not* typically a characteristic of adolescence?
   a. spurt in physical growth
   b. tendency toward obesity
   c. appearance of pubic hair
   d. increasingly oily skin, often resulting in acne

4. Characteristics directly related to reproduction are called
   a. secondary sex characteristics
   b. primary sex characteristics
   c. secular trends
   d. pubescence indicators

5. Characteristics which are signs of sexual maturation, but which do not directly involve the sex organs, are called
   a. secondary sex characteristics
   b. primary sex characteristics
   c. secular trends
   d. pubescence indicators

6. The most common health problems of adolescence include
   a. cardiovascular (i.e., heart and lung) diseases
   b. cancer, especially leukemia, and blood diseases
   c. hormonal abnormalities and endocrine and pituitary problems
   d. eating disorders, drug abuse, and sexually transmitted diseases

7. Which of the following statements about adolescents and nutrition is the most accurate?
   a. Most adolescents need not worry about diet and nutrition.
   b. Since they eat so much, adolescents usually receive all necessary nutrients and vitamins and minerals.
   c. The diet of average Americans is deficient in iron, and many adolescents' diets are also deficient in calcium.
   d. Many adolescents' diets are deficient in the carbohydrates and fats needed to sustain their rapid physical growth.

8. Adolescents' increasing tendency to take risks is reflected in their high death rate from
   a. sexually transmitted diseases (STDs)
   b. use of drugs, alcohol, or both
   c. accidents, homicide, and suicide
   d. catastrophic illnesses

9. Anorexia nervosa is characterized by
   a. being 20 percent over one's ideal body weight
   b. episodes of eating binges followed by self-induced vomiting
   c. compulsive and excessive eating to the point of illness
   d. obsessive dieting resulting in self-starvation

10. Bulimia is characterized by
    a. being 20 percent over one's ideal body weight
    b. episodes of eating binges followed by self-induced vomiting
    c. compulsive and excessive eating to the point of illness
    d. obsessive dieting resulting in self-starvation

11. Today, the use of drugs among adolescents is
    a. more prevalent than it was in the 1960s
    b. about the same as it was in the 1960s
    c. less prevalent than it was in the 1960s
    d. dramatically higher during the past decade

12. The drugs most popular with adolescents are
    a. alcohol, marijuana, and tobacco
    b. marijuana and crack
    c. cocaine and barbiturates
    d. stimulants

13. Which of the following statements about adolescents' drinking is most accurate?
    a. Girls are more likely than boys to drink every day.
    b. Most teenagers start to drink because it seems grownup.
    c. College-bound teenagers drink more than those not planning to go to college.
    d. Most young people do not have their first drink until sometime after entering high school.

14. The leading cause of death among 15- to 24-year-olds is
    a. drug abuse and drug-related activities
    b. sexually transmitted disease
    c. alcohol-related vehicle accidents
    d. tobacco-related disease

15. Which of the following sexually transmitted diseases is *not* curable?
    a. genital herpes
    b. gonorrhea
    c. syphilis
    d. chlamydia

16. The most prevalent sexually transmitted disease is
    a. genital herpes
    b. AIDS
    c. syphilis
    d. chlamydia

17. The highest Piagetian stage of cognitive development, often achieved in adolescence, is
    a. sensorimotor
    b. preoperational
    c. concrete operations
    d. formal operations

18. According to Piaget, cognitive maturity is brought about by
    a. maturation of brain structures
    b. widening social environments and hence broader experiences
    c. interaction of brain maturity and broader experiences
    d. hormonal changes that characterize adolescence

19. Which of the following statements about egocentric thinking in adolescence is the most accurate?
    a. It takes the form of faultfinding, argumentativeness, and self-consciousness.
    b. It takes the form of being unable to view a problem from more than one (i.e., one's own) perspective.
    c. It is almost nonexistent in adolescents, who are much more socially oriented and therefore aware of other perspectives.
    d. Although not completely absent, egocentrism is rapidly decreasing as the adolescent matures to adulthood.

20. Most adolescents are at which stage of moral development, according to Kohlberg?
    a. morality of constraint
    b. conventional
    c. morality of cooperation
    d. postconventional

21. The central organizing experience of most teenagers' intellectual and social lives is their
    a. family, which provides them with adult role models
    b. peer group
    c. growing sense of personal identity
    d. high school

22. Teenagers who do well in school are those whose parents
    a. have allowed them complete freedom and independence
    b. are involved with their lives, both in and outside of school
    c. monitor their schoolwork but are uninvolved otherwise
    d. monitor their social activities but not their schoolwork

23. Which of the following statements most accurately describes the relationship between adolescents' grades and their parents' degree of involvement?
    a. Grades are directly related to parental involvement in children's lives.
    b. Grades are inversely related to parental involvement in children's lives.
    c. Grades are minimally related to parental involvement in children's lives.
    d. Grades are not related to parental involvement in children's lives.

24. Which of the following statements about high school dropouts is the most accurate?
    a. Surprisingly, most dropouts tend to be gifted.
    b. African Americans have the highest dropout rate among ethnic groups.
    c. Most dropouts eventually reenter some educational program.
    d. Dropping out is more prevalent among young people whose parents are poorly educated.

25. With respect to the relationship between gender and career choice, which of the following statements is the most accurate?
    a. Gender-typing in occupational choice is more prevalent today than ever before.
    b. Although many gender stereotypes have been broken down, gender still influences occupational choice.
    c. Gender still affects career choice, and this proves that there are innate intellectual differences between males and females.
    d. Gender stereotypes are as strong today as they ever were, but they do not seem to have any relationship to occupational choice.

## Matching

Match each of the lettered items in the box with the appropriate description in the numbered list that follows the box.

| |
|---|
| **a.** bulimia |
| **b.** menarche |
| **c.** secular trend |
| **d.** puberty |
| **e.** anorexia |
| **f.** personal fable |
| **g.** imaginary audience |
| **h.** adolescence |
| **i.** sexually transmitted disease |
| **j.** formal operations |
| **k.** abstract thought |
| **l.** obesity |
| **m.** secondary sex characteristics |
| **n.** growth spurt |
| **o.** primary sex characteristics |

1. most common eating disorder in the United States _____

2. fantasy observer _____

3. developmental transition between childhood and adulthood _____

4. adolescent's increase in height and weight _____

5. characteristics not related to sex organs _____

6. disorder characterized by eating binges followed by forced vomiting _____

7. disease transmitted by sexual contact _____

8. characteristic of cognitive maturity _____

9. characteristics related to reproduction _____

10. first menstruation _____

11. pattern seen over several generations _____

12. process of attaining sexual maturity _____

13. feeling that one's experience is unique _____

14. highest Piagetian stage _____

15. self-starvation _____

## Completion

Supply the term or terms needed to complete each of the following statements.

1. Puberty is defined as the process that leads to the attainment of _____ maturity.

2. The stage when reproductive functions mature, rapid growth occurs, the primary sex organs enlarge, and the secondary sex characteristics appear is known as _____ .

3. The primary sex characteristics are those that are directly related to _____ .

4. Secondary sex characteristics are physical signs of maturation that do not directly involve _____ .

5. A girl's first menstrual period is called _____ .

6. The most common eating disorder in the United States is _____ .

7. Piaget's highest level of intellectual development, formal operations, is characterized by the ability to think _____ .

8. Many adolescents behave self-consciously, as if they were being watched by a/an _____ , an observer who exists only in their own minds and who is as concerned with their thoughts and behaviors as they are themselves.

9. Most adolescents are at Kohlberg's _____ stage of moral development.

10. The conviction—especially strong in adolescence—that one is special and that one's own experience is unique is called the _____ .

11. Of girls who drop out of school, more than half say that they left because of _____ .

12. At around the time of puberty, most adolescents are at the second stage of career development, called the _____ period.

13. Work seems to _____ school performance.

14. The choice of a career is closely tied with a central personality issue of adolescence: the continuing effort to define _____ .

15. Research has revealed large differences between gifted boys and girls on the _____ portion of the Scholastic Aptitude Test.

---

## ANSWERS FOR SELF-TESTS

---

### Multiple-Choice

1. a (page 308)
2. b (310)
3. b (310–312)
4. b (312)
5. a (312)
6. d (316)
7. c (316)
8. c (316)
9. d (317)
10. b (318)
11. c (318)
12. a (319)
13. b (319)
14. c (320)
15. a (320–322)
16. d (321)
17. d (324)
18. c (325)
19. a (326)
20. b (327)
21. d (328)
22. b (329)
23. a (329)
24. d (331)
25. b (334)

### Matching

1. l (page 316)
2. g (326)

3. h (308)
4. n (311)
5. m (312)
6. a (318)
7. i (320)
8. k (324)
9. o (312)
10. b (313)
11. c (311)
12. d (308)
13. f (327)
14. j (324)
15. e (317)

### Completion

1. sexual (page 308)
2. puberty (310)
3. reproduction (312)
4. sex organs (312)
5. menarche (313)
6. obesity (316)
7. abstractly (324)
8. imaginary audience (326)
9. conventional (327)
10. personal fable (327)
11. pregnancy or marriage (331)
12. tentative (332)
13. undermine (333)
14. self (334)
15. mathematics (334)

# PERSONALITY AND SOCIAL DEVELOPMENT IN ADOLESCENCE

## INTRODUCTION

The search for identity is a major theme of adolescence, a time when a person's physical, cognitive, emotional, and social development will reach a peak. In **Chapter 11** we learn that adolescence is a period of both struggle and triumph. During this eventful period, the quest for identity is influenced by several factors; in particular, the adolescent's peer group and family play significant roles.

■ The chapter begins with a discussion of several important theories on the nature of adolescence. The major question of adolescence is, "Who am I?" and each theory suggests different methods that individuals may use in resolving the question.

■ The findings of recent research, which suggests that adolescents can be described as being in one of four identity states, are explained.

■ The changing relationships between adolescents and their families and peers are described.

■ Some current sexual practices and attitudes among adolescents are described, including a persistent problem associated with adolescence: pregnancy. Various preventive measures used by families and society are presented.

■ Another problem of adolsecence, juvenile delinqency, is also discussed.

■ The chapter concludes with a discussion of the many special personality strengths of adolescents. Three cohort studies providing a positive view of adolescence are described.

# CHAPTER OUTLINE

## I. UNDERSTANDING PERSONALITY DEVELOPMENT

### A. THEORETICAL PERSPECTIVES

1. G. Stanley Hall: "Storm and Stress"

2. Margaret Mead: The Cultural Factor

3. Sigmund Freud: The Genital Stage

4. Anna Freud: Ego Defenses of Adolescence

5. Erik Erikson: Crisis 5
—Identity versus Identity Confusion

### B. RESEARCH ON IDENTITY

1. Identity States

2. Gender Differences in Identity Formation

## II. ASPECTS OF PERSONALITY DEVELOPMENT IN ADOLESCENCE

### A. RELATIONSHIPS WITH PARENTS

1. How Adolescents and Their Parents Conflict

    a. The roots of conflict

    b. The nature of conflict

2. What Adolescents Need from Their Parents

3. How Adolescents Are Affected by Their Parents' Life Situation

    a. Parents' employment

    b. "Self-care" adolescents

### B. RELATIONSHIPS WITH PEERS

1. How Adolescents Spend Their Time —and with Whom

2. Friendships in Adolescence

3. Peer Pressure versus Parents' Influence

### C. ACHIEVING SEXUAL IDENTITY

1. Studying Adolescents' Sexuality

2. Sexual Attitudes and Behavior

    a. Masturbation

    b. Sexual orientation

        (1) What determines sexual orientation?

        (2) Homosexuality

    c. Attitudes, behavior, and the "sexual evolution"

## III. TWO PROBLEMS OF ADOLESCENCE

### A. TEENAGE PREGNANCY

1. Consequences of Teenage Pregnancy

2. Why Teenagers Get Pregnant

3. Who Is Likely to Get Pregnant?

4. Preventing Teenage Pregnancy

5. Helping Pregnant Teenagers and Teenage Parents

### B. JUVENILE DELINQUENCY

1. Statistics

2. Personal Characteristics of Delinquents

3. The Delinquent's Family

4. Dealing with Delinquency

## IV. A POSITIVE VIEW OF ADOLESCENCE: THREE COHORT STUDIES

## KEY TERMS

adolescent rebellion (page 346)

asceticism (342)

commitment (344)

crisis (344)

foreclosure (344)

genital stage (341)

heterosexual (355)

homosexual (355)

identity achievement (344)

identity diffusion (345)

identity versus identity confusion (343)

intellectualization (342)

libido (341)

masturbation (355)

moratorium (345)

reaction formation (342)

sexual orientation (355)

status offender (362)

storm and stress (341)

## LEARNING OBJECTIVES

After finishing Chapter 11, you should be able to:

1. Name the five theories discussed in the textbook that address the development of personality in adolescence, and briefly describe the major points of each.
   a.

   b.

   c.

   d.

   e.

2. In your own words, define the following defense mechanisms:
   a. *intellectualization*

   b. *asceticism*

3. Discuss some of the ways that adolescents resolve the conflict of *identity versus identity confusion*.

4. Describe the dangers of not being able to resolve the conflict of identity versus identity confusion.

5. James Marcia identified four specific identity states. Name each state and explain its main characteristics.

  a.

  b.

  c.

  d.

6. Describe some of the differences between males and females in the formation of identity.

7. Compare the importance of an adolescent's peer group with that of the family, and describe how each influences adolescents' attitudes and behaviors.

8. Explain some of the disadvantages for an adolescent in a single-parent household.

9. Discuss some of the current sexual practices and attitudes among adolescents.

10. Briefly explain how adolescents' attitudes regarding sex differ from their actual sexual practices.

11. Describe some of the causes of teenage pregnancy.

12. Describe some of the consequences of teenage pregnancy.

13. Discusse some of the disadvantages of being the child of a teenage parent.

14. Discuss the problem of juvenile delinquency.

15. List some of the special personality strengths of adolescents.

## SUPPLEMENTAL READING

This article originally appeared in a special issue of *Newsweek* magazine that was published late in the summer of 1990.

## The Dangers of Doing It

### Barbara Kantrowitz

Street wisdom drives 16-year-old Meta Jones crazy. Sexually transmitted diseases (STDs) are at record-high levels among teens, yet the kids Meta knows at Coolidge Senior High in Washington, D.C., have more faith in superstition than science. "They believe in the 'quick-withdrawal method,'" she says. "They think you can't catch anything if he pulls out quickly enough." A lot of boys don't worry, she says, because "they think it's the girls who catch [diseases] more easily. And everyone seems to think STDs are someone else's problem. They say, 'We're young. This isn't going to happen to us.'"

Meta knows they're wrong. Every week for the past year, she and 10 other Washington high school students have met in a conference room at the Center for Population Options, a nonprofit educational organization. As members of the center's volunteer Teen Council, they are preparing a pamphlet on STDs to be distributed to high-school students around the country.

The need for such information is acute. Experts on adolescent health say that ignorance of how STDs are spread is one of the main reasons 15- to 19-year-olds have a higher risk of getting many of these diseases than any other age group. But even though sex-education classes have become more prevalent in the last few years, many schools don't include information about STDs in their curriculum. And those that do often concentrate on diseases such as gonorrhea and syphilis—neglecting more common infections such as chlamydia and genital warts.

Since the 1960s, when more and more teens started having sex at younger and younger ages, the infection rates of several STDs have increased steadily, says Dr. Stuart Berman of the Centers for Disease Control (CDC). Only 3 percent of women born between 1938 and 1940 had had sex by the time they were 15. By 1988, more than a fourth of all 15-year-old girls were sexually experienced. Teens who have sex early are more likely to have multiple partners, which increases their risk of infection. Teens have also been the age group least likely to practice safe sex because they tend to have spontaneous rather than planned intercourse. And, like Meta Jones's friends, they believe they are immune to illness. AIDS seems to be one of the few things that has altered teens' behavior. Recent surveys show more young people using condoms.

Treating infected teens is as troublesome as trying to prevent illness. Because some of the most common STDs don't always have overt symptoms, young people may be unwitting carriers. And those who do receive medical attention may still end up infected. Doctors say adolescents frequently stop taking medication after the first few days—when the symptoms begin to disappear—and don't finish their prescriptions. Often, teens have more than one infection, which complicates treatment.

Some of the diseases threatening teens:

### AIDS

Although teens say they fear AIDS more than any other illness, fewer than 1 percent of all reported AIDS cases involve adolescents. That does not mean that teens are AIDS-free. Nearly a fifth of all people with AIDS are in their 20s and it can be as long as 10 years between infection and the onset of symptoms. That means that many of the young adults who have AIDS today probably got the disease as teenagers. Many researchers think today's teens may have similar rates of infection as they get older. Particularly at risk are inner-city kids. In a 1988 study of adolescent AIDS cases in New York, 58 percent were black and Hispanic males. Even more disturbing: the high levels of AIDS infection among babies born to teen mothers at urban hospitals around the country.

### CHLAMYDIA

Although it doesn't get as much attention as AIDS, chlamydia—probably the most common bacterial STD—is potentially a more serious threat to teenagers. Girls 15 to 19 years old appear to have the highest infection rates of any age group. Chlamydia often has no overt symptoms, but it can also cause abdominal pain, nausea and low fever in women, and a discharge from the penis or painful urination in men. These symptoms can easily be confused with other conditions, making chlamydia a difficult disease to detect. Left untreated, chlamydia can have disastrous consequences for men and women. In women the infection usually begins in the cervix and spreads to the fallopian tubes or ovaries. The result can be pelvic inflammatory disease, a major cause of sterility. Men can also become sterile.

### GENITAL WARTS

The human papillomavirus causes small growths that can be found on the vulva, vagina, cervix, anus, penis and urethra. Certain strains also occasionally show up in the throat. They're usually painless, but they may itch. Some studies have indicated that as many as a third of all sexually active teenagers have genital warts. A few growths are not necessarily dangerous, but if they keep growing they may eventually block body openings. Doctors are also concerned about an apparent association between genital warts and cervical cancer that researchers still don't fully understand. Like chlamydia, warts sometimes go undetected. There's no permanent cure: warts can be removed but at least 20 percent grow back.

### HERPES

Although herpes got a lot of attention a few years ago, researchers think it is not quite as common as genital warts among teenagers. There is evidence, however, that infection rates may be increasing. Although herpes has no cure, medication does ease the pain when sores are active. Undiagnosed herpes during pregnancy is a serious threat. The virus can cause miscarriage and stillbirth and can damage infants during childbirth. Obstetricians perform Caesarean sections if the virus is active.

### GONORRHEA

In the past 15 years the total number of gonorrhea cases in teenagers has declined considerably, largely because of a national gonorrhea-control program that was begun in the 1970s, says Dr. Willard Cates of the CDC. However, among black teenagers, rates of infection actually increased in the 1980s. By 1988 the numbers of young blacks reported with

the disease were 20 to 40 times greater than those of white teens, according to the CDC. Researchers blame the gap on inadequate health care.

### SYPHILIS

Teenagers have fewer cases of syphilis than other age groups, but they have not been immune to what Cates describes as a syphilis epidemic in the 1980s. In 1989, he says, syphilis-infection rates among the general population were at their highest level since post-World War II. The most dramatic increase among teenagers was among 15- to 19-year-old black girls. That trend threatens babies born to these young women, especially if the mothers have no prenatal care. There's also some evidence that open syphilis sores may increase the risk of contracting the AIDS virus. These complications, and so many others, have turned sex for teens into a medical minefield.

## Questions about the Reading

1. If you are—or can imagine yourself—the parent of a teenager today, what advice would you give him or her about sexual activity?

2. Would your advice to a son be different from your advice to a daughter? If so, how?

---

## SELF-TESTS

---

## Multiple-Choice

Circle the letter of the response which best completes or answers each of the following statements and questions.

1. Two of the most important preoccupations during adolescence are
   a. trust and autonomy
   b. industry and initiative
   c. integrity and generativity
   d. identity and intimacy

2. In their psychosexual theories, Hall and Freud agree that physiological changes of adolescence cause a person to have
   a. conflict
   b. apathy
   c. inner peace
   d. neuroses

3. According to Freud, the need to masturbate prepares a young person for eventual sexual release with a partner; after the person has been involved in a sexual relationship, the need to masturbate
   a. increases
   b. remains the same
   c. decreases
   d. causes impotence in males

4. Which of the following defense mechanisms translates sexual impulses into abstract thought, helping adolescents deal with body changes?
   a. asceticism
   b. sublimation
   c. intellectualization
   d. reaction formation

5. According to Erikson, which of the following is the active agent in identity formation?
   a. id
   b. ego
   c. libido
   d. superego

6. What is the fundamental "virtue" that arises from Erikson's identity crisis?
   a. fidelity
   b. empathy
   c. love
   d. faith

7. "True intimacy cannot take place until a stable identity is achieved." According to Erikson, this is true of
   a. both males and females
   b. females only
   c. males only
   d. people in late adulthood

8. People who possess rigid strength and a passive acceptance of other people's plans for their lives are said to be in which identity state?
   a. identity achievement
   b. foreclosure
   c. identity diffusion
   d. moratorium

9. A person in the status of identity diffusion has which attitude?
   a. strong commitment to his or her own beliefs
   b. strong commitment to others' beliefs
   c. strong commitments to the beliefs of his or her peer group
   d. no commitment at all

10. Of the following, which is the most powerful bonding agent during adolescence?
    a. race
    b. age
    c. gender
    d. social status

11. Which of the following statements is true of frienships in adolescence?
    a. Male friendships are rarely as close as female friendships.
    b. Female friendships are rarely as close as male friendships.
    c. Males and females have a relatively equal amount of friends.
    d. Males have fewer friends than females.

12. In one study, girls who had the closest friendships reported
    a. strained relationships with their mothers
    b. affectionate relationships with their mothers
    c. having authoritarian mothers
    d. having mothers who were single parents

13. During adolescence, which of the following would probably be most important in forming a friendship?
    a. similarity
    b. dissimilarity
    c. egocentricity
    d. identity status

14. According to the text, peers have more influence than parents on teenagers' decisions about
    a. moral dilemmas
    b. what job to take
    c. everyday social issues
    d. what education to pursue

15. Adolescents who have close friendships
    a. have low self-esteem
    b. consider themselves competent
    c. consider themselves incompetent
    d. do poorly in school

16. What adolescent need or needs does sexual activity satisfy?
    a. physical pleasure
    b. proof of maturity
    c. enhancement of intimacy
    d. all of the above

17. Which view of the specific causes of homosexuality has received the most support?
    a. Interaction of hormonal and environmental events is crucial in determining a person's sexual preference.
    b. Homosexuality is a specific mental disorder.
    c. Genetic factors create homosexual tendencies.
    d. A chance homosexual encounter during a critical period determines homosexuality.

18. In a recent Harris poll, what was the chief reason adolescents gave for being sexually active at an early age?
    a. expression of love
    b. social pressure
    c. curiosity
    d. lust

19. Teenage mothers are less likely than other teenager girls to
    a. finish high school
    b. have money troubles
    c. have repeat pregnancies
    d. receive public assistance

20. What is the primary reason given when adolescents are asked why they do not use an effective method of birth control?
    a. They didn't expect to have intercourse.
    b. They lack information.
    c. Contraception makes sex less enjoyable.
    d. They want to get pregnant.

21. Which of the following characterizes girls who are likely to use effective birth control?
    a. Their grades are low.
    b. They do not participate in sports.
    c. They are not likely to participate in other extracurricular activities.
    d. They have career aspirations.

22. In one study, how did the babies of mothers who received "parenthood training" differ from babies whose mothers received no training?
    a. They weighed more.
    b. They had more advanced motor skills.
    c. They were hyperactive.
    d. both a and b

23. Which of the following could result in being classified as a status offender?
    a. committing a robbery
    b. being sexually active at age 12
    c. committing a rape
    d. committing a murder

24. Which of these statements about adolescents and criminal activities is the most accurate?
    a. Teenagers commit proportionally fewer crimes against property.
    b. Girls are more likely than boys to get into trouble with the law.
    c. Teenagers are responsible for more than their share of certain crimes.
    d. Boys and girls are equally likely to commit crimes.

25. The strongest predictor of juvenile delinquency is
    a. adolescents' socioeconomic status
    b. adolescents' peer group
    c. parents' education
    d. amount of family supervision

## Matching

Match each of the lettered items in the box with the appropriate description in the numbered list that follows the box.

    a. storm and stress
    b. masturbation
    c. foreclosure
    d. asceticism
    e. libido
    f. intellectualization
    g. commitment
    h. status offender
    i. sexual orientation
    j. moratorium
    k. reaction formation
    l. identity versus identity confusion
    m. identity diffusion
    n. adolescent rebellion
    o. genital stage

1. translating sexual impulses into abstract thought _____
2. self-stimulation _____
3. Hall's view of adolescence _____
4. Erikson's conflict of adolescence _____
5. heterosexual or homosexual _____
6. Freud's stage of adolescence _____
7. no commitment _____
8. self-denial _____
9. truant, runaway, or sexually active minor _____
10. commitment without crisis _____
11. general alienation from adult society _____
12. expressing the opposite of what one feels _____
13. personal investment _____
14. in crisis _____
15. basic energy source for the sex drive _____

## Completion

Supply the term or terms needed to complete each of the following statements.

1. In Freud's terminology, mature adult sexuality is the _____ stage.

2. According to Freud, the _____ is the basic energy source that fuels the sex drive.

3. Hall believed that young people go through a period of _____ and _____ , during which time they adjust to their changing bodies.

4. When people express feelings opposite to their real feelings, they are using a defense mechanism called _____ .

5. _____ is a defense mechanism that allows people to translate sexual impulses into abstract thoughts.

6. As a defense against fear of losing control over their impulses, adolescents engage in a type of self-denial that is formally called _____ .

7. According to Erikson, the chief task of adolescence is to resolve the conflict of _____ versus _____ .

8. By _____ , James Marcia means a period of conscious decision making, and he defines _____ as a personal investment in an occupation or a system of beliefs.

9. According to Marcia, a person who has gone through a crisis and has made a sincere commitment to his or her beliefs would be categorized as in the state of _____ .

10. A person who has made a commitment without crisis is in Marcia's status of _____ .

11. Marcia's status of _____ describes people who are in a crisis without having made any serious commitments.

12. The _____ may encompass not only conflict within the family but a general alienation from adult society and hostility toward its values.

13. _____ is many young people's first sexual experience.

14. Being a homosexual or heterosexual is referred to as _____ .

15. The _____ is a young person who has been truant, has run away from home, has been sexually active, or has done something else that is ordinarily not considered criminal—except when done by a minor.

---

## ANSWERS FOR SELF-TESTS

---

### Multiple-Choice

1. d (page 340)
2. a (341)
3. c (342)
4. c (342)
5. b (343)
6. a (343)
7. c (343)
8. b (344)
9. d (345)
10. b (346)

11. a (352)
12. b (353)
13. a (353)
14. c (353)
15. b (353)
16. d (355)
17. a (356)
18. b (357)
19. a (358)
20. a (359)
21. d (361)

22. d (361)

23. b (362)

24. c (362)

25. d (362)

## Matching

1. f (page 342)

2. b (355)

3. a (341)

4. l (343)

5. i (355)

6. o (341)

7. m (345)

8. d (342)

9. h (362)

10. c (344)

11. n (346)

12. k (342)

13. g (344)

14. j (345)

15. e (341)

## Completion

1. genital (page 341)

2. libido (341)

3. storm; stress (341)

4. reaction formation (342)

5. intellectualization (342)

6. asceticism (342)

7. identity; identity confusion (343)

8. crisis; commitment (344)

9. identity achievement (344)

10. foreclosure (344)

11. moratorium (345)

12. adolescent rebellion (346)

13. masturbation (355)

14. sexual orientation (355)

15. status offender (362)

# CHAPTER 12

# PHYSICAL AND INTELLECTUAL DEVELOPMENT IN YOUNG ADULTHOOD

## INTRODUCTION

**Chapter 12** examines the physical and intellectual development which occurs in young adulthood, from about 20 to 40 years of age.

■ The chapter begins with a discussion of the general physical condition of young adults, focusing on health issues especially pertinent in young adulthood.

■ Aspects of intellectual development are be reviewed, including psychometrics, or measuring the increase or decrease of intelligence during adulthood.

■ Theoretical approaches commonly used to describe stages of cognitive development are described, and the development of morality during young adulthood is discussed.

■ The college experience as a part of the life of many young adults is considered, and the chapter concludes with an exploration of career development and satisfaction with work.

# CHAPTER OUTLINE

## PHYSICAL DEVELOPMENT

### I. SENSORY AND PSYCHOMOTOR FUNCTIONING

### II. HEALTH IN YOUNG ADULTHOOD
A. HEALTH STATUS

B. INFLUENCES ON HEALTH AND FITNESS

  1. Diet

    a. Diet and weight

    b. Diet and cholesterol

    c. Diet and cancer

  2. Exercise

  3. Smoking

  4. Alcohol

  5. Stress

    a. Can stressful life events lead to illness?

    b. Why does stress affect some people more than others?

      (1) "Control" and stress

      (2) Personality and stress: Behavior patterns and heart disease

  6. Indirect Influences on Health

    a. Socioeconomic factors

    b. Education

    c. Gender

      (1) Biological differences

      (2) Behavioral and attitudinal differences

    d. Marital status

## INTELLECTUAL DEVELOPMENT

### III. ADULT THOUGHT: THEORETICAL APPROACHES
A. K. WARNER SCHAIE: STAGES OF COGNITIVE DEVELOPMENT

B. ROBERT STERNBERG: THREE ASPECTS OF INTELLIGENCE

C. BEYOND JEAN PIAGET: POSTFORMAL THOUGHT

### IV. ADULT MORAL DEVELOPMENT
A. HOW DOES EXPERIENCE AFFECT MORAL JUDGMENTS?

B. ARE THERE GENDER DIFFERENCES IN MORAL DEVELOPMENT?

### V. COLLEGE
A. WHO GOES TO COLLEGE?

B. INTELLECTUAL GROWTH IN COLLEGE

C. GENDER DIFFERENCES IN ACHIEVEMENT IN COLLEGE

D. LEAVING COLLEGE

### VI. STARTING A CAREER
A. WORK AND AGE

  1. How Young Adults Feel about Their Jobs

  2. How Young Adults Perform on the Job

B. WORK AND GENDER

## KEY TERMS

achieving stage (page 381)

acquisitive stage (381)

componential element (383)

contextual element (383)

executive stage (382)

experiential element (383)

postformal thought (384)

premenstrual syndrome (PMS) (380)

reintegrative stage (382)

responsible stage (382)

stress (377)

tacit knowledge (383)

"Type A" behavior pattern (378)

"Type B" behavior pattern (378)

## LEARNING OBJECTIVES

After finishing Chapter 12, you should be able to:

1. Describe the sensory and psychomotor functioning of a typical young adult.

2. Discuss health during young adulthood, including the factors that influence health and fitness.

3. Describe the specific things an individual can do to improve his or her health.

4. Describe the relationship between *stress* and health.

5. Explain how good health is related to such indirect factors as socioeconomic status, education, gender, and marital status.

6. Discuss some of the factors that account for differences between men and women in health and in death rates.

7. Describe the intellectual development and functioning of the young adult.

**8.** Describe Schaie's five stages of cognitive development.

   **a.**

   **b.**

   **c.**

   **d.**

   **e.**

**9.** Describe the three aspects of intelligence formulated by Sternberg.

**10.** Describe the characteristics of mature, or *postformal,* thought.

**11.** Describe Kohlberg's theory of moral development as it applies to young adults.

**12.** Discuss the issue of possible gender differences in moral development.

**13.** Explain who goes, and who does not go, to college.

**14.** Describe how the college experience affects intellectual growth.

**15.** Discuss how the college experience differs for men and women.

**16.** Describe how a person's age, or stage of life, affects the way he or she thinks about work.

**17.** Discuss the relationship between work and gender.

**18.** Discuss dual-earner families and how they cope with *stress* and conflicting demands.

---

## SUPPLEMENTAL READING

---

Carla Rohlfing is the associate health editor for *Family Circle* magazine.

## Are You a Victim of Silent Stress?

### Carla Rohlfing

Most of us are, say the experts. Here's how it sneaks into your life—and puts your health at risk.

When was the last time you felt *really* relaxed? Can't remember? You're not alone. According to some health experts, many Americans are suffering from post-traumatic stress disorder, a syndrome usually associated with war veterans (hallmarked by fatigue, irritability, lack of concentration and other symptoms). While most of us haven't been through a war in the literal sense, we are constantly being worn down by the little battles of everyday life—balancing family and work, dealing with deadlines, fighting traffic, stretching the budget, plus job insecurity, junk mail, jangling telephones, lack of sleep, fear of crime—you name it.

According to the newest research, a heavy load of "silent" stressors—from waiting to see the doctor to having no time for yourself—may be as harmful to your physical and emotional health as the bigger, more obvious ones, such as losing your job or moving to another city. Studies now indicate that what's most stressful about a "big event" is not the event itself but, rather, the small changes it forces you to make in your day-to-day habits.

Take a recently divorced woman, for example. Friends and family may have lent support throughout the divorce itself, but she may actually be more stressed by all the household responsibilities she must now shoulder alone—from paying bills to mowing the lawn. Those added duties are her silent stressors.

A steady diet of such hassles can suppress your immune system and cause you to become physically ill more often. Worse, being under chronic mild stress may impair your memory and even cause your brain to age prematurely. And evidence is growing that chronic stress increases your risk of life-threatening ailments.

Despite the dangers, the fact is we all need some stress in our lives to fuel creativity and provide us with the energy needed to complete demanding tasks. Stress doesn't have to be debilitating; the first step to making it work for you is understanding how it builds.

The term *stress* comes from engineering, according to Andrew Goliszek, Ph.D., author of *Breaking the Stress Habit*. He defines it as an external force that produces a strain on a structure. In humans, the external force is called a *stressor*, and it can be almost anything: arriving late for work, getting

married, having a baby sitter cancel at the last minute—whatever pushes your buttons. Your reaction is stress.

When you're under stress, your body undergoes several biochemical changes that over time can have a profound effect on your health, according to University of Kentucky neuroscientist Philip Landfield, Ph.D. "First, the adrenal glands pump out the hormones *cortisol* and *adrenaline*," he explains. Together, these hormones hike your heart rate, blood pressure and blood flow, pushing extra oxygen into your muscles. (This prepares your body for physical action: to fight or flee.) Blood glucose (sugar) is also diverted from your internal organs to your brain to increase your alertness. Most bodily functions not vital to fighting or fleeing—such as digestion—are temporarily suppressed. Finally, the body releases *endorphin,* a natural tranquilizer that brings hormone levels back down to normal.

All of these functions were useful eons ago, when coping with stress meant outrunning a lion, but the stress response is far from ideal in most modern settings. Whether you're being called on the carpet at work or you're dealing with silent stressors—a slow checkout line, for example—there's no physical fight to prepare for, but the hormones surge just the same.

If this happens on a now-and-then basis, research indicates that your body is resilient enough to bounce back with no long-term harm. But chronic stress can alter the way your body functions, keeping adrenaline and cortisol elevated. "One consequence can be higher blood cholesterol," says Dr. Landfield. "When stress diverts glucose to the brain, your internal organs begin to break down stores of fat for energy." As that fat circulates in your system, cholesterol levels rise. Chronic stress has also been linked to heart disease, hypertension, ulcers, depression, upper respiratory infections, psoriasis and other serious ailments.

### BODY AND BRAIN BREAKDOWNS

How stress may lead to illness isn't fully understood. In some cases, however, illness appears to result from the damage stress does to the immune system. In two separate studies, researchers at the University of Pittsburgh School of Medicine followed two groups of healthy adults ages 18 to 45—one for four weeks and the other for six months. The subjects kept daily records of the irritating situations they faced each day and their overall health and symptoms. At regular intervals the researchers also tested the subjects' level of *natural killer* cells (the body's first line of defense against common colds and certain other infections).

"We found that people who experienced the greatest number of hassles per day also had the least active natural killer cells." says immunologist Theresa Whiteside, Ph.D. Not surprisingly, this same group also caught colds and had flu more often. Worse off, according to Dr. Whiteside, were "those under 30, probably because they didn't have the maturity to deal with irritating events."

Other new research suggests that living with chronic mild stress may produce permanent memory loss. In animal research, Dr. Landfield studied three groups of rats—young, middle-aged and elderly. Within each group, half were exposed to regular bouts of mild stress for six months—for rats, that meant running through tunnels and receiving mild electric shocks on an unpredictable basis. "These animals were tense and anxious even when they weren't running the course, making them a good model for chronic human anxiety," says Dr. Landfield. In people, this experience would be similar to, say, toiling away as an air traffic controller or feeling stuck in an unhappy marriage.

"We found that stress hormones in the animals were elevated throughout and after the test period," says Dr. Landfield. "We know from previous research that these hormones are toxic to brain cells." Specifically, he found that chronic stress had prematurely aged the brains of young and middle-aged rats by interfering with the electrophysiological transmission of information between brain cells. "In human terms, this may be why you always lose your keys when you're under a lot of stress," Dr. Landfield explains. Your memory simply isn't processing correctly. Fortunately, this type of damage is reversible if stress is eased.

Most alarming, however, was the condition of the elderly rats; they experienced brain-cell death in the *hippocampus*, which is critical for learning and memory. "The loss of cells was almost double the amount you normally see associated with aging," says Dr. Landfield. "And once the brain cells are gone, they cannot be regenerated."

## GOOD VERSUS BAD: IS ALL STRESS THE SAME?

One tantalizing question that remains to be answered is whether all stress can be harmful to your health. In other words, is the go-go type who loves to juggle many different tasks as susceptible as someone who faces the same pressures but doesn't enjoy them? "We don't know yet," says Dr. Landfield. "In large part, stress is how you perceive it. Most people associate stress with feeling anxious," he points out. "But in someone who is not upset by multiple demands, we may find that the levels of stress hormones aren't as high as in the person who feels overwhelmed. If there is no message of alarm transmitted, the stress response may not be as severe."

Not all experts agree. According to Ronald Kessler, Ph.D., program director at the Institute for Social Research at the University of Michigan, "Even if you feel fine under stress, adrenaline is still elevated," and still can do harm. Dr. Kessler is currently supervising the National Survey of Health and Stress, in which 25,000 Americans will be interviewed. The researchers hope to answer questions about how different types of stress affect emotional and physical health. If all goes as planned, Dr. Kessler will have some answers by early next year. In the meantime, without any solid data on

good versus bad stress, most experts advise keeping stress to a minimum.

## ZEROING IN ON SILENT STRESSORS

While many of the so-called major stressors are relatively easy to spot—you know it if you've had a fight with your husband, for instance—the trouble with little hassles is that they're often so subtle you may not know you're at risk. For example, you may not realize that your noisy, bumper-to-bumper commute is the real reason you hit the ceiling at a gum-cracking co-worker or whining toddler; you simply can't take one more irritation. Such clashes—when your reaction is out of proportion to the incident at hand—are silent stress points. They reflect something else going on in your life that you can't cope with.

Susceptibility to silent stress may be on the rise. According to Dennis D. Embry, Ph.D., executive director of Project Me, Inc., a Tucson, Arizona, organization dedicated to improving family relationships, "Research suggests that people in general are feeling more stressed nowadays." One reason: overexposure to bad news, particularly through television. "Watching 'media-mediated' violence—such as the much-played videotape of Los Angeles police beating a suspect—distorts your ability to perceive everyday events in a positive light," he says. Regular exposure to such images can eventually cause you to see innocuous events—someone walking down your street, for instance—in a threatening light.

How you react to feeling stressed can also compound existing tensions. If your response to seemingly insurmountable demands is to worry, smoke, eat or drink too much, for instance, your stress will only intensify. "When you're chronically stressed, you're also more likely to fly off the handle at family, friends and co-workers," says Dr. Embry—worsening the very relationships you need for emotional support. In addition, the persistent erosion of the family—a traditional stress buffer—is also a factor in compounding stress. Left unchecked, stress can eventually lead to depression. "That's because chronic stress can make you feel helpless, that you have no control over your life." he says.

According to Dr. Embry, your stress reaction is largely "programmed" by family influences. It "appears to be a combination of heredity and learned behavior," adds Dr. Kessler. For example, chronic stress may put you at greater risk for heart disease or ulcers if those diseases run in your family. But you also learn by example: If your mother always responded to stress by overeating, you may fall into the same trap.

Your response is also conditioned by stressors you've faced previously, Dr. Embry says. If you have little control over your workload and a demanding supervisor, just hearing the boss call your name may send your adrenaline soaring. Similarly, anticipating a stressful evening of housework and cooking dinner while also trying to give attention to your husband and children can rev your stress response before you even walk in the door.

Not all stress reactions are bad, however. Identifying your silent stressors can motivate you to scale back commitments, reorganize priorities and do whatever it takes to reduce pressure. "Most people are very resilient in the face of stress," says Dr. Kessler, once they've identified the cause. Getting to the root of your stress helps you regain a sense of control—and feeling in charge of your life is the key to coping with all kinds of pressures.

## Questions about the Reading

1. What "silent stressors" exist in your daily life now?

2. What can you do to reduce the adverse impact of these stressors?

3. What changes can you anticipate in your life during the next year or so? How will these changes affect your stress levels? What can you do to minimize that anticipated stress?

---

## SELF-TESTS

---

## Multiple-Choice

Circle the letter of the response which best completes or answers each of the following statements and questions.

1. With regard to health and safety, young adults in the United States as an age group are
   a. most accident-prone
   b. most injury-prone
   c. least healthy
   d. healthiest

2. Which of the following makes/make a significant difference in both rates and causes of death?
   a. gender
   b. race
   c. ethnicity
   d. all of the above

3. An organism's physiological and psychological reaction to demands made on it is called
   a. response latency
   b. stress
   c. psychomuscular reaction
   d. entropy

4. Which of the following statements about stress is the most accurate?
   a. Stress always impairs health.
   b. Stress is not inevitable in life.
   c. Some stress is essential, and some is actually energizing.
   d. Stress is an abnormal reaction to everyday problems.

5. Which of the following describes people with the "Type A" behavior pattern?
   a. impatient, competitive, aggressive, hostile
   b. concerned, inquisitive, intelligent, articulate
   c. moody, belligerent, argumentative, sarcastic
   d. relaxed, easygoing, unhurried

6. Which of the following describes people with the "Type B" behavior pattern?
   a. impatient, competitive, aggressive, hostile
   b. concerned, inquisitive, intelligent, articulate
   c. moody, belligerent, argumentative, sarcastic
   d. relaxed, easygoing, unhurried

7. Premenstrual syndrome (PMS) is a disorder characterized by
   a. emotional instability and physical weakness
   b. mental confusion and physical lethargy
   c. physical discomfort and emotional tension
   d. emotional instability without any physical symptoms

8. Which of the following statements about marriage and health is the most accurate?
   a. Marriage seems to be healthful for both women and men.
   b. Marriage seems to be healthful for men but not women.
   c. Marriage seems to be healthful for women but not men.
   d. There is no relationship between marriage and health.

9. In which of K. Warner Schaie's stages are information and skills learned for their own sake, without regard to context?
   a. reintegrative
   b. executive
   c. acquisitive
   d. responsible

10. In which of K. Warner Schaie's stages are people more selective about the tasks on which they choose to expend energy and more concerned about the purpose of what they do?
    a. reintegrative
    b. executive
    c. acquisitive
    d. responsible

11. In which of K. Warner Schaie's stages do people need to integrate complex information on a number of levels?
    a. reintegrative
    b. executive
    c. acquisitive
    d. responsible

12. In which of K. Warner Schaie's stages are people concerned with long-range goals and practical problems?
    a. reintegrative
    b. executive
    c. acquisitive
    d. responsible

13. Which of Sternberg's aspects of intelligence refers to how people approach novel and familiar tasks?
    a. achieving
    b. experiential
    c. contextual
    d. componential

14. Which of Sternberg's aspects of intelligence refers to how efficiently people process and analyze information?
    a. achieving
    b. experiential
    c. contextual
    d. componential

15. A component of practical intelligence that involves such things as knowing how to win a promotion or cut through red tape is called
    a. tacit knowledge
    b. academic knowledge
    c. intuitive knowledge
    d. concrete knowledge

16. Which of Sternberg's aspects of intelligence refers to how people deal with their environment?
    a. achieving
    b. experiential
    c. contextual
    d. componential

17. Practical intelligence involves the application of "inside" information, or "savvy"; the technical term for this kind of knowledge is
    a. componential
    b. theoretical
    c. research
    d. tacit

18. The kind of intelligence that relies on subjectivity and intuition is called
    a. formal thought
    b. postformal thought
    c. concrete operational thought
    d. sensorimotor thought

19. Moral judgments in adulthood are often based on
    a. theory
    b. experience
    c. research
    d. intuition

20. Which of the following statements about the relationship between stages of cognitive development and stages of moral development is the most accurate?
    a. The moral stage sets the upper limit for the cognitive stage.
    b. The moral stage sets the lower limit for the cognitive stage.
    c. The cognitive stage sets the upper limit for the moral stage.
    d. The cognitive stage sets the lower limit for the moral stage.

21. According to Kohlberg, one type of experience that advances moral development is
    a. being responsible for one's own welfare
    b. being responsible for the welfare of other people
    c. associating with people whose values are similar to one's own
    d. living independently

22. Carol Gilligan, arguing that Kohlberg's theory does not address the way women think about moral issues, holds that with respect to reasoning about moral issues
    a. men think more in terms of fairness while women consider responsibility to specific people
    b. women think more in terms of fairness while men consider responsibility to specific people
    c. men think more in concrete, specific terms while women think in more general, abstract terms
    d. men seem to advance through the stages of moral development at a slightly slower rate than women of equal cognitive ability

23. Studies of women in college showed that
    a. girls—who outshone boys in elementary and high school—often slipped behind the boys academically in college
    b. girls—who outshone boys in elementary and high school—continued to outshine them academically in college
    c. although women no longer performed better than men in college, their self-esteem and career aspirations were higher
    d. there were no noticeable differences between women and men by the time they had completed the first year of college

24. Studies show that younger workers (those under age 40) are
    a. more satisfied with their jobs than any other age group
    b. more committed to their employers than they will be later
    c. less likely than older workers to change jobs
    d. less satisfied with their jobs than they will be later

25. Younger workers, compared with older workers, are more concerned about
    a. friendliness of supervisors
    b. friendliness of coworkers
    c. how interesting their work is
    d. receiving help with their work

## Matching

Match each of the lettered item in the box with the appropriate description in the numbered list that follows the box.

---

    a. tacit knowledge
    b. contextual element
    c. acquisitive stage
    d. Type A
    e. experiential element
    f. postformal thought
    g. achieving stage
    h. reintegrative stage
    i. componential element
    j. responsible stage
    k. self versus others
    l. executive stage
    m. Type B
    n. stress
    o. premenstrual syndrome

---

1. stage of learning without regard for context _____

2. stage of learning for social responsibility _____

3. women's central moral dilemma _____

4. mature thinking _____

5. stage of learning for real-life problems _____

6. intelligence measured by traditional IQ tests _____

7. "inside" information _____

8. condition affecting 20 to 40 percent of all women _____

9. stage of learning in late adulthood _____

10. intelligence in dealing with the environment _____

11. organism's reaction to demands made on it _____

12. impatient and competitive _____

13. stage of learning to achieve competence _____

14. insightful part of intelligence _____

15. relaxed and easygoing _____

## Completion

Supply the term or terms needed to complete each of the following statements.

1. The typical young adult is a healthy physical specimen; _____ , _____ , and _____ are at their peak.

2. The senses are at their sharpest during _____ .

3. Given the healthy state of most young adults, it is not surprising that _____ is/are the leading cause of death at this age.

4. Although today the percentage of young adults who smoke tobacco is the lowest recorded, the number of _____ who smoke has risen dramatically.

5. _____ abuse is a major cause of death from automobile accidents.

6. Even if they eat fatty foods, smoke, and do not exercise, _____ people rarely have heart attacks before age 70.

7. Recent research has found little evidence for a relationship between _____ and heart disease.

8. Psychometric tests of intelligence concentrate on the aspect that Sternberg called _____ intelligence.

9. _____ relies on subjectivity and intuition, as well as on the pure logic that is characteristic of formal operational thought.

10. A woman's central moral dilemma, according to Gilligan, is the conflict between _____ .

11. Studies show that student's thinking changes in definable stages while they are in college. The last stage is characterized by freely chosen _____ .

12. A majority of all college students are _____ .

13. Although most college dropouts have lower average aptitude scores than people who stay in school, they are usually doing _____ work.

14. About _____ percent of all people who enter college never receive a degree.

15. Younger workers tend to have more _____ absences from work than older workers.

---

## ANSWERS FOR SELF-TESTS

### Multiple-Choice

1. d (page 371)
2. d (371)
3. b (377)
4. c (377)
5. a (378)
6. d (378)
7. c (380)
8. a (381)
9. c (381)
10. a (382)
11. b (382)
12. d (382)

13. b (383)
14. d (383)
15. a (383)
16. c (383)
17. d (383)
18. b (384)
19. b (384)
20. c (385)
21. b (385)
22. a (387)
23. a (388)
24. d (390)
25. c (390)

## Matching

1. c (page 381)
2. l (382)
3. k (386)
4. f (384)
5. j (382)
6. i (383)
7. a (383)
8. o (380)
9. h (382)
10. b (383)
11. n (377)
12. d (378)
13. g (381)
14. e (383)
15. m (378)

## Completion

1. strength; energy; endurance (page 370)
2. young adulthood (371)
3. accidents (371)
4. women (376)
5. alcohol (377)
6. Type B (378)
7. Type A (379)
8. componential (383)
9. postformal thought (384)
10. herself and others (386)
11. commitments (387)
12. women (388)
13. satisfactory (388)
14. 50 (388)
15. avoidable (390)

# PERSONALITY AND SOCIAL DEVELOPMENT IN YOUNG ADULTHOOD

## INTRODUCTION

Following the period of adolescence, during which all aspects of development proceed at an almost alarming rate, most young adults have reached the point where physical growth has stabilized. However, development of the adult personality continues throughout life. Young adults are at the stage where they are just learning to maximize their physical and intellectual capabilities and realize that social and emotional development is a lifelong process. **Chapter 13** looks specifically at how the major events of young adulthood influence an individual's personality and social development.

■ Two models of personality development in young adulthood are discussed: the normative-crisis model and the timing-of-events model. The normative-crisis model describes human development in terms of a predictable sequence of chronological changes. The timing-of-events

model suggests that adult development proceeds according to individual experiences in relation to the time in a person's life when they occur.

■ The chapter then focuses on the desire of young adults to form intimate sexual relationships. This need to develop intimate relationships is discussed from the perspective of the influence it will have on future social and emotional development.

■ The advantages and disadvantages of various lifestyles—marriage, divorce, cohabitation, and single life—are discussed.

■ The text discusses parenthood as a developmental experience for both parent and child. The alternative of remaining childless is also discussed.

■ The chapter concludes with a discussion of the characteristics of friendships in young adulthood.

## CHAPTER OUTLINE

b. Adoption

c. New methods of becoming a parent

   (1) Artificial insemination

   (2) In vitro fertilization

   (3) Donor eggs

   (4) Surrogate motherhood

   (5) Technology and conception: Ethical issues

4. The Transition to Parenthood

5. Parenthood as a Developmental Experience

H. REMAINING CHILDLESS

I. FRIENDSHIP

1. Characteristics of Adult Friendship

2. Benefits of Friendship

---

## KEY TERMS

adaptive mechanisms (page 399)

artificial insemination (418)

career consolidation (399)

cohabitation (414)

donor eggs (418)

dream (401)

in vitro fertilization (418)

infertility (417)

intimacy versus isolation (398)

life structure (401)

mentor (401)

nonnormative life events (404)

normative life events (404)

normative-crisis model (398)

surrogate motherhood (418)

timing-of-events model (404)

triangular theory of love (408)

## LEARNING OBJECTIVES

After finishing Chapter 13, you should be able to:

1. Describe personality development in young adulthood according to the *normative-crisis model* and the *timing-of-events model.*
   a. normative-crisis model

   b. timing-of-events model

2. Describe the crisis of young adulthood according to Erikson.

3. Describe Vaillant's formulation of the mechanisms by which people adapt to life circumstances.

4. Describe the developmental changes that occur during each phase of young adulthood, according to Levinson.

5. List some of the ways that personality development in young adulthood is different for males and females.

6. Describe in what way or ways the normative-crisis model is misleading.

7. Explain the differences between *normative life events* and *nonnormative life events,* and give an example of each.
   a. normative

   b. nonnormative

8. Discuss how young adults' attitudes toward life events can be influenced by society.

9. Describe the *triangular theory of love.*

10. List some of the advantages of married life.

11. Discuss the relationship between marriage and each of the following.
    a. happiness

    b. health

12. List some of the factors related to success in marriage.

13. Discuss the problem of violence in marriage.

14. Discuss the phenomenon of divorce, including its causes and consequences.

15. Discuss single life and *cohabitation* as alternatives to marriage.

16. Describe sexuality and sexual activity during young adulthood.

17. Describe the reasons for becoming a parent.

18. Discuss the trend toward delayed parenthood, and identify its advantages and disadvantages.

19. List and describe some of the alternative methods for becoming a parent.

20. Describe the process of becoming a parent in developmental terms.

21. Discuss various aspects of the choice to remain childless.

22. Describe the importance of friendship during young adulthood.

---

## SUPPLEMENTAL READING

---

This article originally appeared in the December 1990 issue of *Mademoiselle* magazine.

### They've Got to Have It

**Jill Neimark**

Get married: This was the one mission my grandmother had when she was 16. She met a 24-year-old man at a dance and they eloped when she was 17. For the next 50 years she funneled her life into her husband and children. My grandfather became a dentist; she became his receptionist. She laid out his clothes every night for him, cooked his meals and spent his money on mink coats and Cadillacs. The phone in their house was constantly ringing, for my grandmother's friendships were as varied and intense as love affairs. I'll always remember her ensconced in the plush cocoon of their enormous bed, with its white lace coverlet and deep rows of down pillows.

But there was a drawback to her glorious marriage: My grandfather (like most men of that time) always made the big decisions, and when he decided on early retirement in Florida, there was no question about them moving. My grandmother lost a way of life she had worked 30 years to build. Down in Miami, he spent his days fishing, and she spent her days feeling lonely. There was great love between my grandparents, but the day she married, I realized, my grandmother relinquished her freedom.

That's no longer a woman's legacy, and most of us are glad. "Young women today don't expect to marry the American dream, they expect to become it themselves," notes Ruth Sidel, Ph.D., a sociologist at Hunter College in New York City and author of *On her Own* (Viking Penguin).

Lately, there's been a lot of talk about exactly what dream it is that young women today want to become. Trend-watchers say that twentysomething women (and men) are clearly distinct, in values and goals, from those who have come before them. In fact, both *Fortune* and *Time* magazines have given this generation a name—"the baby-busters"—to distinguish them from the baby-boomers and all others who preceded them. These young men and women, media pundits say, want to work and get married, but they want to do it on their own terms; they're determined to have a life they're totally in control of. Unlike the baby-boomers, for instance, they'll supposedly say no to slaving 80 hours a week for a corporation—no matter what the salary or perks—since, they figure, doing so would interfere with their enjoyment of life.

That character analysis is true to some extent. If the '80s was the era of the material girl (work hard and spend hard), the '90s has a new theme for young women: Lead a sane life. They want to work hard, sure, but they plan also to have plenty of time for a personal life. They do want to get married—but just not right out of college, thanks.

In order to have everything, they know they have to plan a balanced life. Because they choose not to devote every second of their twenties to their career, they may not be able to buy a BMW by age 28. So what, they say. A Honda will do.

All the same, they are driven, and their journey to personal fulfillment is far from stress-free. Knowing that you have to say "no" to some options may be easy to swallow in the abstract, but each particular instance that requires a choice—turning down a promotion, say, because it involves moving to another state and you don't want to leave the home and the social circle you've established—can be stressful. "Am I right to say no to this job?" you end up asking yourself at least once.

And though women today may not let their job become everything to them, meaningful work still matters tremendously to us. The thought of merely clocking in at an office and doing something trivial eight hours a day just to pass the time and earn a few dollars is inconceivable.

It's no surprise that for some of us, the twenties turn out to be the "trauma years," according to Judith Sills, Ph.D., a clinical psychologist in private practice in Philadelphia, and the author of *A Fine Romance: The Passage of Courtship from Meeting to Marriage* (Ballantine Books). "Establishing full lives as powerful people with loving families and meaningful work is an awesome task. You inevitably ask yourself early on: Am I going to lay the tracks my parents want for me, am I going to lay my own, will I do it by myself for now or with somebody soon, who should the somebody be, and what in God's name should I really do anyway?"

We're all probably a little more daunted at times than we'd like to admit. When I was 24, I was hired as an acquisitions editor at a major publishing house, the youngest in my department. I was nervous but I tried to appear nonchalant and confident. After two weeks, another 24-year-old editor was hired. I'd heard she lived in Greenwich Village, in a doorman building I had always coveted. Why can't I afford to live in that building yet, I wondered. Her first day, I checked out her left hand—she didn't have an engagement ring, either. So she wasn't "ahead" of me in the marriage department, I sighed with relief.

At 24, no matter how sure of yourself you are, life sometimes seems like the final race of the Kentucky Derby—everything is at stake and it might all be over in a flash. I couldn't help but compare myself to others my own age, not so much because I wanted to beat them at anything, but because I wanted to be reassured that I wasn't falling behind in my own life plan. According to Dr. Sidel, "Young women today feel they have to make each move count."

Even when we're not working, many of us feel pressured to be active, to enjoy and experience life. If you're not going to be at the office until eleven at night (and who wants to be more than once a year?), then you've got to prove you're having fun. And it has to be brilliant, gorgeous, dance-all-night-and-eat-breakfast-at-dawn fun.

Whether partying or exercising hard at the gym, throwing dinner parties to show off our latest boyfriends, hunting thrift shops for designer bargains or blowing a week's pay in the hushed salons of fine department stores on manicures and haircuts, or traveling to the south of France or Tibet, we're determined to experience all of life. To many of us the legacy of the women's movement, the words "you can do anything," has come to mean, "you must do everything—if not all at once." We have been born into a generation of women who believe they can—and therefore must—make their mark on the world.

Why exactly are young women so ambitious about life? At first it seems easy to pinpoint the source of women's desire: We've just come out of the Reagan '80s and the age of affluence; we're dazzled and driven by the success stories of young Wall Streeters, anchorwomen, entrepreneurs; yet we live in a time of upheaval, scandal and fragmentation, when nothing seems to last—so we subconsciously conclude we'd better do it all before the world falls apart. Feminism has won us freedom, but also brought responsibility. The message has been drummed into our subconsciouses: We must earn money and take care of families.

Most young women today bring the same arc of ambition to love that they do to a career. The average age of first marriage has jumped from 19 to 24 in the last 40 years—and because we're focusing on careers first and delaying marriage, we feel more pressured than ever to make the correct choice of a mate when we do settle down.

For a lot of young women, dating eventually takes on an edge of high seriousness: Romance has to be big with the possibility of marriage. We can't just experiment for years; that would be like working at only temp jobs forever. Old-fashioned weddings are back in style, and every issue of *Bride's* magazine is as thick as a volume of the encyclopedia. We see marriage as another measure, perhaps, of having fully arrived at adulthood.

Even though being single feels great most of the time, many of us have felt the pressure to marry by 30, to have it be one of the things we accomplish in our twenties. "The slogan of the seventies was 'You're okay, I'm okay,'" quips Dr. Sidel. "The slogan of today is 'We're okay, I'm okay.'"

One summer my live-in boyfriend and I flew to my hometown for my best friend's wedding. I'd known her since I was 12. At the wedding ceremony her family gave the kind of sentimental speech that makes you cry, and even though I'd been fighting with my boyfriend for months, I suddenly and desperately wanted to marry him. When the groom whispered, "He's nice," I was a goner. A few champagne glasses later, I dragged my boyfriend outside. "Are you going to marry me before I turn thirty?"

Women today are confident they can do it all. But every once in a while, we do have moments of doubt. We ask ourselves if we're really going to be able to have all we want, when we want.

I often ask myself, am I going to be like a flawless trapeze artist—and master all life's moves now? My grandmother knew what (and who) she wanted at 17. Her choices were so much easier, and sometimes, I envy her that; I like to pretend then that I'm sleeping in her palatial, snowy-white bed. She knew a security I've never known. Still, I wouldn't trade my freedom for it. I don't think any of us would.

## Questions about the Reading

1. How do the trends described in this article fit with the normative-crisis model? With the timing-of-events model?

2. What problems are young adults, and women in particular, likely to encounter if they strive to "have it all"?

---

## SELF-TESTS

---

## Multiple-Choice

Circle the letter of the response which best completes or answers each of the following statements and questions.

1. Erikson's crisis of early adulthood is intimacy versus
   a. stagnation
   b. isolation
   c. self-absorption
   d. despair

2. According to the normative-crisis model, human development can be described as
   a. following a definite sequence
   b. depending on gender
   c. unpredictable
   d. both b and c

3. According to Erikson, what is the ultimate goal for young adults involved in heterosexual relationships?
   a. total intimacy
   b. independence from their parents
   c. satisfactory development for their own children
   d. marriage

4. Which of the following is a major criticism of Erikson's sixth crisis?
   a. He limits healthy development to loving, heterosexual relationships that produce children.
   b. He places too much emphasis on the male pattern of development.
   c. He asserts that the search for identity continues through adulthood.
   d. both a and b

5. According to Vaillant, what determines a person's level of mental health?
   a. number of traumatic events in a person's life
   b. number of satisfactory relationships in a person's life
   c. development of the "virtue" of love
   d. person's adaptation mechanisms for dealing with life circumstances

6. Which of the following best describes a person who, according to Vaillant, uses immature mechanisms to adjust to life situations?
   a. enjoys helping others
   b. develops aches and pains with no physical basis
   c. distorts reality
   d. develops irrational fears

7. Vaillant concluded that the best-adjusted men use which type of ego defense mechanisms?
   a. immature
   b. psychotic
   c. mature
   d. realistic

8. A life structure is the underlying design of a person's life, including
   a. people, places, and things a person considers important
   b. subconscious aspirations for autonomy and intimacy
   c. two ego defense mechanisms—projection and sublimation
   d. adaptation mechanisms for dealing with life circumstances

9. According to Levinson, a man seeks independence from his parents during
   a. the novice phase of early adulthood
   b. the preadulthood period
   c. culminating phase of young adulthood
   d. adolescence

10. According to Levinson, the divorce rate for men peaks during
    a. the novice phase of early adulthood
    b. the preadulthood period.
    c. the culminating phase of young adulthood
    d. adolescence

11. Studies indicate that men's "dreams" are mostly concerned with achievement, while women's are more concerned with
    a. relationships
    b. possessions
    c. separation from their families
    d. achievement and relationships

12. Which one of the following theorists is a supporter of the timing-of-events model?
    a. Erikson
    b. Levinson
    c. Vaillant
    d. Neugarten

13. Proponents of the timing-of-events model suggest that unexpected life events may result in
    a. relief
    b. stress
    c. confusion
    d. pleasure

14. According to research, women who found the age-30 transition most stressful were those who were unsatisfied with their
    a. personal relationships
    b. occupational achievement
    c. both a and b
    d. physical appearance

15. Which model suggests that people develop in response to the specific events in their lives and the specific times when these events occur?
    a. normative-crisis model
    b. nonnormative-crisis model
    c. life structure model
    d. timing-of-events model

16. Which of the following is *not* a factor affecting a person's ability to respond to life events?
    a. physical health
    b. social support
    c. life history
    d. All of the above *are* factors.

17. Research suggests that today, in comparison with the past, never-married people (especially men) are _____ , and married people (especially women) are _____ .
    a. happier; also happier
    b. less happy; also less happy
    c. less happy; happier
    d. happier; less happy

18. According to one survey, which of the following groups experiences the most health problems?
    a. divorced people
    b. widowed people
    c. single people
    d. married couples

19. According to one study, which of the following strategies for dealing with conflict seemed to be good for a marriage?
    a. arguing and showing anger
    b. withdrawing by walking away
    c. not talking about a problem
    d. none of the above

20. Men who abuse women tend to
    a. have higher-than-normal self-esteem
    b. be sexually inadequate
    c. be socially engaged and involved
    d. have no sense of jealousy or envy

21. The divorce rate in the United States is
    a. one of the lowest in the world
    b. one of the highest in the world
    c. rising more rapidly than ever before
    d. lowest among young adults

22. Which is the most accurate statement about the effects of adoption on children, as reported by researchers?
    a. Adopted children saw their adoptive parents as less nurturing than a control group of nonadopted children saw their biological parents.
    b. Adopted children got into trouble more than nonadopted children.
    c. Adopted children were generally more confident and felt in better control of their lives than nonadopted children.
    d. both a and b

23. Compared with parents, people who choose to remain childless
    a. have nontypical family backgrounds
    b. report less marital satisfaction
    c. spend less time in enjoyable activities as a couple
    d. have less traditional attitudes toward women

24. Which of the following groups has the greatest number of friendships?
    a. elderly people
    b. newlyweds
    c. adolescents
    d. middle-aged people

25. Which of the following statements about friendship in young adulthood is the most accurate?
    a. Most people's best friends are of the opposite sex.
    b. Romantic bonds have little in common with friendships.
    c. "Best friendships" are often seen as more stable than ties to a spouse or lover.
    d. Isolation from friends and family is related to better health.

## Matching

Match each of the lettered items in the box with the appropriate description in the list that follows the box.

---

a. normative-crisis model
b. intimacy versus isolation
c. adaptive mechanisms
d. life structure
e. mentor
f. timing-of-events model
g. nonnormative life events
h. normative life events
i. triangular theory of love
j. cohabitation
k. infertility
l. artificial insemination
m. in vitro fertilization
n. surrogate motherhood
o. dream

---

1. injection of sperm into women's cervix _____

2. unexpected life events _____

3. expected life events _____

4. woman "carries" a baby for another _____

5. takes place outside the mother's body _____

6. defines human development in a definite sequence of age-related changes _____

7. aspects include intimacy, passion, and commitment _____

8. inability to conceive _____

9. a vision of one's future _____

10. Erikson's sixth crisis _____

11. ways people adapt, according to Vaillant _____

12. underlying pattern of a person's life _____

13. views human development in terms of responses to life events _____

14. couple live together without being married _____

15. someone who offers guidance and inspiration, passes on wisdom, etc. _____

## Completion

Supply the term or terms needed to complete each of the following statements.

1. Erik Erikson's theory is an example of the _____ , which describes human development in terms of a definite sequence of age-related social and emotional changes.

2. The sixth of Erikson's eight crises—and what he considers to be the major issue of young adulthood—is _____ .

3. Vaillant identified four types of _____ , or characteristic ways in which people adapt to life situations.

4. The stage of _____ is characterized by preoccupation with strengthening one's career.

5. The underlying pattern or design of a person's life at a given time is his or her _____ .

6. Men often enter adulthood with a _____ of the future, couched in terms of a career.

7. A _____ offers guidance and inspiration and passes on wisdom, moral support, and practical help in both career and personal matters.

8. The _____ model views development as a result of the times in people's lives when important events take place.

9. Expected life events are called _____ life events, and unexpected life events are known as _____ life events.

10. An increasingly common living arrangement is _____ , in which an unrelated man and woman live together.

11. Ten to fifteen percent of American couples experience _____ , the inability to conceive after trying for 12 to 18 months.

12. Some couples are able to produce children through means of _____ , that is, injection of a man's sperm directly into the woman's cervix.

13. _____ , fertilization that takes place outside the body, is becoming increasingly common for women whose fallopian tubes are blocked or damaged.

14. Women who cannot produce normal ova may be able to bear children through the use of _____ , ova donated from fertile women—the female counterpart of AID.

15. _____ motherhood occurs when a woman who is not married to a man bears his baby and agrees to give the child to the biological father and his wife.

---

## ANSWERS FOR SELF-TESTS

---

### Multiple-Choice

1. b (page 398)

2. a (398)

3. c (398)

4. d (399)

5. d (399)

6. b (399)

7. c (399)

8. a (401)

9. a (401)

10. c (401)

11. d (403)

12. d (404)

13. b (404)

14. c (404)

15. d (404)

16. d (405)

17. d (410)

18. a (410)

**19.** a (410)

**20.** b (410–411)

**21.** b (411)

**22.** c (418)

**23.** d (422)

**24.** b (423)

**25.** c (423)

## Matching

**1.** l (page 418)

**2.** g (404)

**3.** h (404)

**4.** n (418)

**5.** m (418)

**6.** a (398)

**7.** i (408)

**8.** k (417)

**9.** o (401)

**10.** b (398)

**11.** c (399)

**12.** d (401)

**13.** f (404)

**14.** j (414)

**15.** e (401)

## Completion

**1.** normative-crisis model (page 398)

**2.** intimacy versus isolation (398)

**3.** adaptive mechanisms (399)

**4.** career consolidation (399)

**5.** life structure (401)

**6.** dream (401)

**7.** mentor (401)

**8.** timing-of-events (404)

**9.** normative; nonnormative (404)

**10.** cohabitation (414)

**11.** infertility (417)

**12.** artificial insemination (418)

**13.** in vitro fertilization (418)

**14.** donor eggs (418)

**15.** surrogate (418)

# PHYSICAL AND INTELLECTUAL DEVELOPMENT IN MIDDLE ADULTHOOD

## INTRODUCTION

**Chapter 14** looks at physical and intellectual development in middle adulthood, between the ages of 40 and 65.

■ The physical changes which occur during this period are discussed, including changes in reproductive and sexual capacity and changes in appearance.

■ The general health status of middle-aged people is described, and various health concerns and problems of this age group are discussed.

■ In the area of intellectual development, the chapter examines intelligence and cognition in adults and discusses various aspects of the adult learner.

■ Vocational patterns and occupational factors such as stress and career changes are considered.

## CHAPTER OUTLINE

**PHYSICAL DEVELOPMENT**

### I. PHYSICAL CHANGES OF MIDDLE AGE

A. SENSORY AND PSYCHOMOTOR
   FUNCTIONING

   1. Vision, Hearing, Taste, and Smell

   2. Strength, Coordination, and Reaction Time

   3. Physiological Changes

B. SEXUALITY

   1. Sexual Activity

   2. Reproductive and Sexual Capacity

     a. Menopause

       (1) Physical effects of menopause

       (2) Managing menopause

     b. The male climacteric

C. APPEARANCE:
   THE DOUBLE STANDARD OF AGING

### II. HEALTH IN MIDDLE AGE

A. HEALTH STATUS

B. HEALTH PROBLEMS

   1. Diseases and Disorders

   2. Death Rates and Causes of Death

**INTELLECTUAL DEVELOPMENT**

### III. ASPECTS OF INTELLECTUAL DEVELOPMENT IN MIDDLE ADULTHOOD

A. INTELLIGENCE AND COGNITION

   1. Psychometrics:
      Does Intelligence Change in Adulthood?

   2. Mature Thinkers:
      Does Cognition Change in Adulthood?

     a. Integrative thinking

     b. Practical problem solving

B. THE ADULT LEARNER

### IV. WORK IN MIDDLE ADULTHOOD

A. OCCUPATIONAL PATTERNS

   1. Pattern 1: Stable Careers

   2. Pattern 2: Changing Careers

B. OCCUPATIONAL STRESS

C. UNEMPLOYMENT

D. WORK AND INTELLECTUAL GROWTH

## KEY TERMS

burnout (page 441)

climacteric (431)

crystallized intelligence (436)

estrogen (431)

fluid intelligence (436)

hypertension (434)

male climacteric (431)

menopause (431)

osteoporosis (431)

presbycusis (429)

presbyopia (429)

substantive complexity (442)

## LEARNING OBJECTIVES

After finishing Chapter 14, you should be able to:

1. Identify the period known as *middle age* and the markers that denote it.

2. List some common physical abilities which decline in middle adulthood and explain what compensations can be made for them.

3. Describe *menopause* and its effects, both physical and psychological.

4. Describe the *male climacteric* and its effects, both physical and psychological.

5. Describe the "double standard of aging" in the United States.

6. List the major health problems of middle age.

7. Describe the impact of race on health.

8. Discuss the results and appropriateness of standardized intelligence testing on middle-aged adults.

9. Describe the processes of integrative thinking and problem solving in middle age.

10. Identify the characteristics and attitudes of adults who attend school.

11. Describe two different occupational patterns of middle-aged people.
    a.  pattern 1



    b.  pattern 2

12. Describe how occupational stress can affect physical and emotional well-being.

13. Describe the characteristics of highly creative people.

14. Discuss how the work people do affects their intellectual growth.

---

## SUPPLEMENTAL READING

---

Nancy Kelton writes humorous essays and tries to date humorous men. She is on the faculty of New York University.

## Dating at Forty

### Nancy Kelton

My long time friend Sharon gave my telephone number to a man she claimed would be perfect for me. He never called. The other day she mentioned that he would not be available after all.

"What did you say about me?" I demanded.

"Nothing," she said. "He died."

"Where's he buried?" I asked. I figured it this way: The last several men I've dated have had addictions, ambivalence, or wives they have not quite divorced. Could "dead" make a man any more unavailable?

"A cemetary out on Long Island," Sharon said.

"You're right," I told her. "It's too far away."

I am not always so irreverent. But sick humor comes naturally when I talk about men and dating.

Dating in high school. It's about sweating out Saturday nights and worrying about the prom. I am 40 years old. I have a child, a career, a mortgage, bunions, stainless flatware for twelve, and a beautician who thinks I should touch up my gray. There is something ridiculous—positively ridiculous—about the fact that I still go out and watch some man I hardly know pick a white wine or his teeth.

Dating elicits everything from ecstasy to nausea, depending on the man, the restaurant, and whether the man offers to pick up the check. It also elicits hard-to-answer questions from my prepubescent daughter: "How come every man you go out with is bald?"

Her questions make me long for the days before marriage, when all I faced was the typical parental grilling: What does he do? What does he drive? What are his prospects? He's Jewish, isn't he?

My dates aren't all bald, yet they definitely come with some type of middle-age baggage. Love handles, children, lower-back ailments, periodontal problems, and a need to recapture lost youth have long since replaced the fraternity pins and traces of adolescent acne.

"Ron isn't bald," I tell my daughter somewhat defensively.

"But you don't see Ron anymore," she reminds me.

I see Ron when he is not busy getting over something. First it was his ex-wife. Then it was his last love. Lately it's been the flu.

"Could these be excuses for avoiding a relationship?" I asked him.

"That's what my therapist keeps pointing out," Ron said. "It's great getting in touch."

Terrific! Like many men, Ron didn't know what he was feeling until he hit 45. Then he got divorced, joined a men's group, and went into therapy to expand his self-awareness. Now he's aware that he's detached.

"Peter's not really bald," I tell my daughter about another man I've started dating.

"Ma," she says, "you've seen Peter five times. I've seen him twice. How come I noticed the bald spot?"

"I wasn't looking," I say.

With Peter, I'm trying to look inside his head instead of on top, because the sparks aren't exactly flying. Yet I like his compassion, warmth, and thirteen-year-old daughter, who helps fulfill my family fantasies when we do things as a foursome. I keep hoping they might compensate for the missing passion.

Dating at 40 is about "sort ofs," kissing lots of frogs, and shopping for the dress that fits. One man's unavailable. Another's unappealing. And the one I'm sure I'd definitely click with is dead.

With some dates, I know immediately whether we'll have a future or even much of a present. One man began talking about his ex-wife before we sat down to dinner. By the time our entrees came, I knew so much about her exercise routine, allergies, and the fiber content in her diet that I felt she was sitting between us and could have easily passed me the salt. I would have had a much better evening if he had left her at home or gotten her a date so we could have doubled.

Then there was a sixties man who, in 1988, believed that the meaning of life was in manual labor. He baked 93 loaves of bread a week for a living, yet he never got his hands dirty in a committed relationship. Only in dough.

There was a prosperous businessman who found his purpose through wheeling and dealing and investing and scheming. Over our cold antipasto appetizer, he gazed into my eyes and said, "I worry I may have lost my soul, if you get my drift."

Unfortunately I got his drift. I told him that he'd have to look elsewhere for his missing soul; it was certainly not inside me.

Most of my dates have fallen somewhere between the bread baker and the deal maker. There've been several lawyers who've now blended together in my mind into one 39-regular navy pin-striped suit. There've been psychotherapists who have told me what I was really feeling, then, after 50 minutes, have let me know—with a glance, with little beepers on their watches, or by standing—that our time was definitely up.

There was an extremely intelligent professor, with a Ph.D. in English literature from Harvard, who at the end of our second date was still discussing Jude the Obscure. And there was a very tan, very rich Park Avenue ophthalmologist with a serious drinking problem. About him, my mother still asks, "Can you make him stop?"

"How come you dump every man you go out with?" my daughter wants to know.

"I don't dump all of them," I say. I certainly didn't dump Robert, the man I dated for two and a half years shortly after my divorce. Whether I wasn't ready or he wasn't "it," I'm not sure, but when it seemed as though we had no future together, he moved on and got married.

"When it's right, you'll know it," my friend Susan always says.

I hope so. But isn't "right" about timing and patience and who is sitting to our left when we're ready to fall in love? I hope I'm not at the bus station when my ship comes in.

Dating fulfills a short-term need to have male companionship for movies, plays, dinners, and brunches, but that's not what it's about at all. It's more akin to job hunting, putting Mr. Potato Head together, and playing that game at the amusement park where you throw darts at the balloons; if you keep at it long enough, eventually you pop one.

My dating strategy has said more about me than about an array of unsuitable men. I've been looking with just one eye and getting back what I give. It all boils down to that line attributed to Groucho Marx: "I don't want to belong to any club that will accept me as a member."

I'm getting ready to play differently now. I'd much prefer to join.

In one of the first episodes of the TV show *Kate and Allie*, Allie nervously dresses for a first date. Kate tells her friend, "Dating isn't about having dinner. Dating's about finding somebody so you never have to date again."

Of course. That's why I keep at it. Keep looking inward, and keep going out. I would like to think I'll pop one balloon before my arm gets too tired.

## Questions about the Reading

1. How do the physical changes associated with middle age, which are were humorously described by the author of this article, affect interpersonal relationships during this period?

2. How do men and women react differently to the physical changes associated with middle age?

## SELF-TESTS

## Multiple-Choice

Circle the letter of the response which best completes or answers each of the following statements and questions.

1. Which of the following statements about middle age is true?
   a. Strength declines but coordination improves.
   b. Coordination declines but strength improves.
   c. Both strength and coordination decline.
   d. Both strength and coordination improve.

2. Which of the following statements about sensory functioning in middle age is correct?
   a. As the lens of the eye softens, many people become nearsighted.
   b. Hearing loss occurs, especially for high-frequency sounds.
   c. Taste sensation is more acute, and so the appetite increases.
   d. Sensitivity to smell declines noticeably.

3. Which of the following is *not* a common physical change associated with middle age?
   a. weakening of the diaphragm
   b. accelerated kidney functioning
   c. diminished ability to pump blood
   d. diminished gastrointestinal enzyme secretion

4. Which of the following statements about reproductive capacity in middle age is the most accurate?
   a. Women's ability to bear children comes to an end.
   b. Men's ability to father children comes to an end.
   c. Although women are still fertile, their interest in sex declines.
   d. Although men are now infertile, their interest in sex increases.

5. The cessation of ovulation and menstruation is known as
   a. menarche
   b. menorrhea
   c. menopause
   d. menorrhagia

6. The 2- to 5-year period during which the changes resulting in menopause occur is called the
   a. premenopausal period
   b. hormone-depletion stage
   c. menarche
   d. climacteric

7. Preceding menopause, the body reduces its production of
   a. estrogen
   b. progesterone
   c. testosterone
   d. adrenaline

8. Thinning of the bones, which increases the risk of fractures, is called
   a. osteomyelitis
   b. osteoporosis
   c. decalcification
   d. calcium deficiency syndrome

9. In one study of middle-aged women, the subjects reported, in comparison with their earlier years,
   a. a decrease in sexual interest
   b. a better sex life
   c. a decline in sexual activity
   d. no change in sexual interest or activity

10. *Male climacteric* refers to the
    a. cessation of sperm production
    b. inability to father children
    c. period of change in the male's reproductive system
    d. male's adjustment to reproductive changes in his female peers

11. The male climacteric brings
    a. decline in fertility
    b. increase of impotence
    c. lower libido
    d. all of the above

12. The "double standard of aging"
    a. does not affect men, since aging makes a man look distinguished
    b. is more likely to affect a husband's sexual response to his wife than vice versa
    c. does not affect women, since crow's feet and gray hair are seen as a sign of strength
    d. either a or b

13. Health problems in midlife are especially severe among
    a. African Americans
    b. Native Americans
    c. Hispanic Americans
    d. American women

14. Hypertension is
    a. high blood pressure
    b. excessive response to stress
    c. excessive worrying
    d. tightening of muscles, especially in the face and neck

15. Death in middle age is most likely to occur as a result of
    a. accidents
    b. violent crime
    c. natural causes
    d. suicide

16. Which of the following statements about mortality in middle age is accurate?
    a. Despite medical advances, there has been no decline in midlife mortality.
    b. As a result of medical advances and changing lifestyles, midlife mortality is the same as mortality in young adulthood.
    c. Midlife mortality decreased immediately after World War II, but there has been no change since 1950.
    d. There has been a significant decrease in midlife mortality during the past four decades.

17. According to theories of adult intelligence, mature thinking
    a. relies almost exclusively on logic
    b. is almost completely objective
    c. employs only formal operational reasoning
    d. relies on a certain amount of intuition

18. Research has shown that middle-age people perform better than younger people on tasks involving
    a. recall of factual information
    b. solving problems of a practical nature
    c. mental games
    d. using logic to solve abstract mental problems

19. Adults' thinking tends to be
    a. logical
    b. methodical
    c. integrative
    d. none of the above

20. The reasons given by most adult students for returning to school were related to
    a. their jobs
    b. personal fulfillment
    c. boredom in other areas of life
    d. the need to make new acquaintances

21. Compared with younger students, mature learners tend to be
    a. more motivated
    b. less anxious
    c. more self-confident
    d. less interested

22. During middle adulthood, the typical worker is likely to be
    a. at the peak of a career chosen in younger adulthood
    b. on the threshold of a new vocation
    c. frustrated by occupational stagnation
    d. either a or b

23. Emotional exhaustion and a feeling that one can no longer accomplish anything on the job are commonly known as
    a. midlife occupational stagnation
    b. burnout
    c. vocational menopause
    d. midlife crisis

24. In midlife, a major cause of daily stress on the job is
    a. difficulty in performing menial tasks
    b. dissatisfaction with work conditions
    c. conflicts with supervisors, subordinates, and coworkers
    d. either a or b

25. Gruber's studies of highly creative people concluded that they tend to be
    a. conservative, finding stability in the familiar
    b. fast workers, who quickly move on to new tasks
    c. goal-directed, with a strong sense of purpose
    d. loners, preferring to work in isolation

## Matching

Match each of the lettered items in the box with the appropriate description in the numbered list that follows the box.

---

a. hypertension
b. osteoporosis
c. presbyopia
d. climacteric
e. crystallized intelligence
f. burnout
g. menopause
h. estrogen
i. presbycusis
j. reaction time
k. cancer
l. practical problems
m. unemployment
n. complexity
o. calcium insufficiency

---

1. hearing loss associated with aging _____

2. leading cause of death in middle age _____

3. aspect of job affecting mental flexibility _____

4. biggest work-related stressor _____

5. farsightedness associated with aging _____

6. hormone produced in decreasing amounts _____

7. intellectual strong point in middle age _____

8. high blood pressure _____

9. job stress causing emotional exhaustion _____

10. cause of bone thinning _____

11. ability to remember and use learned information _____

12. thinning of the bones _____

13. cessation of ovulation and menstruation _____

14. 2- to 5-year period preceding menopause _____

15. slows by 20 percent from age 20 to age 60 _____

## Completion

Supply the term or terms needed to complete each of the following statements.

1. Farsightedness associated with aging is called _____ .

2. The gradual hearing loss that often occurs during middle age, especially for high-frequency sounds, is called _____ .

3. People who lead sedentary lives lose _____ and _____ and therefore become even less able to exert themselves physically.

4. During the climacteric, a woman's body reduces production of the hormone _____ .

5. Osteoporosis (bone thinning) can be prevented by increasing the daily intake of _____ .

6. The male climacteric usually begins about _____ years later than the female climacteric.

7. Blood pressure screening, a low-salt diet, and medication have prevented many deaths from _____ and _____ .

8. High blood pressure, or _____ , is strongly related to risk of heart attacks or strokes.

9. As in young adulthood, death rates in middle age are _____ for men than for women and _____ for white Americans than for black Americans.

10. According to Schaie's model of adult development, adults in middle age use their intelligence to focus on _____ problems.

11. Mature learners tend to be more _____ than younger learners.

12. Most community, business, and governmental leaders tend to be in their _____ years.

13. The single occupational factor having the most impact on psychological functioning was found to be the _____ of the work itself.

14. Research on highly creative adults found that they work _____ and _____ to master the knowledge and skills needed to solve a problem.

15. An accurate summary of midlife is that it is a time of _____ .

## ANSWERS FOR SELF-TESTS

### Multiple-Choice

1. c (page 429)
2. b (429)
3. b (430)
4. a (430–431)
5. c (431)
6. d (431)
7. a (431)
8. b (431)
9. b (431)
10. c (431–432)
11. d (431, 433)
12. d (433)
13. c (434)
14. a (434)
15. c (434)
16. d (434)
17. d (438)
18. b (438)
19. c (438)
20. a (439)
21. a (439)
22. d (440)
23. b (441)
24. c (441)
25. c (443)

### Matching

1. i (page 429)
2. k (434)
3. n (442)
4. m (442)
5. c (429)
6. h (431)
7. l (438)
8. a (434)
9. f (441)
10. o (432)
11. e (436)
12. b (432)
13. g (431)
14. d (431)
15. j (430)

### Completion

1. presbyopia (page 429)
2. presbycusis (429)
3. muscle tone; energy (430)
4. estrogen (431)
5. calcium (432)
6. 10 (431, 433)
7. heart disease; stroke (434)
8. hypertension (434)
9. higher; lower (434)
10. real-life (436)
11. motivated (439)
12. middle (440)
13. substantive complexity (442)
14. painstakingly; slowly (443)
15. reevaluation (444)

# PERSONALITY AND SOCIAL DEVELOPMENT IN MIDDLE ADULTHOOD

## INTRODUCTION

Midlife is a time of searching for meaning in life with respect to achievement of earlier goals and ambitions (particularly in careers and intimate relationships)—often with a recognition that if changes are to be made, one will need to act quickly.

■ **Chapter 15** begins with a discussion of the stressful period during the early to middle forties which supposedly accounts for the changes in personality and lifestyle that are common during middle adulthood. This period is referred to as the *midlife crisis.*

■ The chapter then examines middle adulthood (ages 40 to 65) from two theoretical perspectives: the normative-events approach (which holds that change will occur unless some-thing interferes with development) and the timing-of-events model (which holds that personality will remain stable unless a specific event occurs to produce change).

■ The text describes various important events in relation-ships such as changes in marriage (marriages often end in divorce at this time); in sexual relationships; and in relation-ships with siblings, friends, one's own maturing children, and parents. The problem of abuse of the elderly is also presented.

■ The chapter concludes with a discussion of the changes brought about as a result of the death of a parent and how that often produces changes in adults' attitudes toward time and death.

# CHAPTER OUTLINE

## I. MIDLIFE: THE NORMATIVE-CRISIS APPROACH

A. THEORIES AND RESEARCH

1. Carl Jung: Balancing the Personality

2. Erik Erikson: Crisis 7—
   Generativity versus Stagnation

3. Robert Peck:
   Four Adjustments of Middle Age

4. George Vaillant: Introspection and Transition

5. Daniel Levinson: Changing Life Structures

6. Women's Development
   in Middle Adulthood: Two Studies

   a. Women and the midlife transition

   b. Mastery, pleasure,
      and women's adjustment

B. EVALUATING THE
   NORMATIVE-CRISIS MODEL

1. Can the Findings of
   Normative-Crisis Research
   Be Generalized to Other Populations?

2. How Typical Is the Midlife Crisis?

3. Is Adult Development Age-Linked?

4. How Healthy Is the Male Model?

## II. PERSONAL RELATIONSHIPS AND TIMING OF EVENTS IN MIDLIFE

A. MARRIAGE AND DIVORCE

1. Marital Satisfaction in Midlife

2. What Makes Middle-Aged Couples
   Divorce or Stay Together?

B. RELATIONSHIPS WITH SIBLINGS

C. FRIENDSHIPS

D. RELATIONSHIPS WITH
   MATURING CHILDREN

1. Adolescent Children: Issues for Parents

2. When Children Leave: The "Empty Nest"

3. When Children Stay or Return:
   The Not-So-Empty Nest

4. Lifelong Parenting

E. RELATIONSHIPS WITH AGING PARENTS

1. Contact with Parents

2. Mutual Help

3. Caring for Parents

4. Reacting to a Parent's Death

   a. Personal changes

   b. Changes in other relationships

   c. Changes in attitudes
      toward time and death

## KEY TERMS

emotional flexibility versus emotional impoverishment (page 451)

"empty nest" (461)

generativity versus stagnation (451)

interiority (452)

mental flexibility versus mental rigidity (451)

midlife crisis (448)

socializing versus sexualizing in human relationships (451)

valuing wisdom versus valuing physical powers (451)

## LEARNING OBJECTIVES

After finishing Chapter 15, you should be able to:

1. Describe the characteristics of what is known as the *midlife crisis.*

2. Compare and contrast the major aspects of development in middle adulthood according to various theories that are based on the *normative-crisis model.*

3. Describe Jung's notion of balancing the personality in midlife.

4. Explain Erikson's seventh crisis—*generativity versus stagnation*—and identify the "virtue" of this period.

5. Describe the four psychological developments that Peck views as critical to successful adjustment to middle age.
   a.

   b.

   c.

   d.

6. Describe the findings of Vaillant's longitudinal Grant Study of Harvard University men.

7. Describe the changes in life structures that characterize midlife, according to Levinson.

8. Describe how women's adjustment in the middle adult years is influenced by mastery and pleasure.

9. Identify the major criticisms of the research on middle age, particularly of the normative-crisis model.

10. Describe how development in middle age seems to be influenced by people's respones to various aspects of marriage and personal relationships.

11. Describe some of the findings on sibling relationships in middle age.

12. Describe some of the findings on friendships in middle age.

13. Explain some of the findings about relationships between maturing children and their middle-aged parents.

14. Explain what is meant by the following terms.
    a. *empty nest*

    b. "not-so-empty nest"

15. List some of the findings about lifelong parenting.

16. Describe how relationships with older parents often change during middle age and how those changes affect the development of the middle-aged adult.

17. Discuss how the death of a parent can precipitate personal changes as well as changes in relationships with others.

## SUPPLEMENTAL READING

Rollene W. Saal is a literary agent who has written on such diverse topics as Edith Wharton and a changing Prague.

## On My Own

**Rollene W. Saal**

There are all kinds of ways to be single. There's the never-having-been-married single, there's the divorced single and the single person whose spouse has died. There is singleness by choice and not by choice. Each brings its own set of feelings, but I can speak only for mine. As a divorced person for the past 15 years, I have been single just about as long as I was married.

I liked being married. I liked the coupleness, the familiarity, the same warm cozying up to my cold toes night after winter night. There were other things I did not like about that specific duet, but this doesn't change the fact that I always liked the style of it, the "being married" part.

And then I got to be single again, only this time with three children. I even liked that, mostly because it was a relief to be on my own, to have my own bad moods and gray days and not someone else's rain cloud in the house. After a while I got to like being single for itself, not only for what it wasn't. I could see quite early on that being single has a definite lifestyle all its own. It isn't the same life as being married but done by ones instead of by twos. It isn't Noah's Ark in single file. It exists with its own joys and sorrows, not better or worse than those we dealt with in married life.

"How you *feel* about being single is important," says Dr. Sandra Steinman, a New York City psychotherapist, herself a divorced woman with two college-age children. "Whether one likes being single or not is often influenced by such factors as one's self-esteem. If you feel good about yourself, you can feel good about living a single life."

For a successful single life, it helps to have well-developed human skills such as being curious about meeting new people and being willing to try new activities. Married couples have a built-in companion; together they can always stay home, pay bills, call the kids and talk to the grandchildren.

"Singleness," says Dr. Steinman, "is another life experience. It's ever changing, and when we find those things that interest us as individuals—not as part of a pair—then we begin to develop ourselves. Otherwise we are just sitting it out, waiting for a man or woman to come to the rescue."

It is obviously more difficult for those who have had long marriages to adjust to a single life. Recently I met a man in his late 60s whose wife had died after 38 years of marriage. "You go from being married to being single in a minute. And your whole life changes," he said with a sigh. "My circle of friends has dwindled; the married couples don't know what to do with me as a single man." When I asked him if there was anything positive about being single, he thought for a moment and said, "Oh, yes. I've learned to cook frozen foods in a microwave oven."

Not everyone takes such a dismal view. At 61, David Shea, a silver-haired industrial-relations consultant, has been married, divorced, and for the past few years has enjoyed—really enjoyed—a single life. "I think that when people say they don't like being single, it may not mean that they want to be married. It just means that they don't want to be alone. That's quite a different thing."

For David Shea, being alone is neither frightening nor lonely. He enjoys browsing in a bookshop or hardware store. "When you do those things as part of a couple, it's different. For me, flexibility is a big plus of being single. I love to let things just unfold."

Not that he doesn't enjoy dating. "Some women are literary or intellectual, and I like to go with them to seen a play or a concert. Others may be charming company for dinner or a movie. I try to gear the activity to the person I'm asking to accompany me."

Unfortunately, it's not always easy for women to call the shots on who gets to go where with whom. Men still do most of the inviting, though I've heard about one woman who takes destiny into her own single hands. When she meets a man whose company she finds promising, she will invite him out to dinner, calling ahead to the restaurant to give them her credit-card number so that nothing so rude as a bill ever appears at the table.

I ran this story by several male friends, and the reactions ranged from "I wish someone would ask me out!" to "What does she do if he says no?"

What she does, of course, is face the risk of rejection, a part of the single state that many married people have long forgotten. Every single person, man or woman, faces daily the risks of living alone, of putting oneself out there without the buffer of one's mate. Fortunately for me, I tend to side with those who say whatever doesn't kill you makes you stronger.

I recently asked a woman whose husband died two years ago about the pros and cons of living alone. She remarked how lucky she was to have a job to keep her occupied and a loving grown daughter. I congratulated her on how well she had adapted to her new single life. "Yes, I'm doing well," she said. "But let me ask you, how do you share a wonderful moment?" That moment when you finally land the job you've dreamed of . . . or when a double rainbow suddenly appears.

I've reflected on this question, and I think the answer for me is that I do, in fact, often share it with a loved one. That may not be the husband she had in mind, but being single, I have learned to reach out to my children and family in an intimate way and, like many single people, can share life's riches with a network of cherished friends. Sometimes, only sometimes, I take that special moment and simply enjoy it by myself. And that isn't a bad thing to have learned.

## Questions about the Reading

1. How does a person's ability to adapt to being single depend on the reasons for being single (i.e., widowhood, divorce, never having married)?

2. Suppose that you are 45 years old. In what ways would your married friends and acquaintances treat you differently if you were single rather than married?

## SELF-TESTS

## Multiple-Choice

Circle the letter of the response which best completes or answers each of the following statements and questions.

1. It has been suggested that the midlife crisis, a stressful period which may occur in the early to middle forties, is brought on by
   a. living with teenagers
   b. dissatisfaction with one's career
   c. dissatisfaction with one's marriage
   d. awareness that one is mortal and that there may not be time to achieve one's ambitions

2. Much of the theory and research on adult development done in the past few decades has come from which of the following models?
   a. normative-crisis
   b. timing-of-events
   c. midlife-crisis
   d. transition

3. Jung's theory of personality development emphasized
   a. early development of self-esteem
   b. search for identity in midlife
   c. elimination of egocentrism in midlife
   d. quest for meaning in life

4. According to Jung, in the midlife transition
   a. men balance their personalities, but women tend to stagnate
   b. both men and women are free to balance their personalities
   c. women balance their personalities, but men tend to stagnate
   d. both men and women become locked into their existing personalities

5. Jung's notion of a "union of opposites" refers to the tendency of men and women in midlife to
   a. express those aspects of themselves that had been suppressed earlier
   b. become physically attracted to more members of the opposite sex
   c. find new partners who are very different from their original partners
   d. find new partners whose personalities are the opposite of their own

6. The virtue resulting from successful resolution of Erikson's seventh crisis—generativity versus stagnation—is
   a. love
   b. trust
   c. self-control
   d. care

7. Which aspect of Erikson's generativity theory is being questioned by psychologists today?
   a. People usually seek a mentor.
   b. People are concerned about their mortality.
   c. People who have not experienced parenthood do not easily achieve generativity.
   d. People value wisdom over physical power.

8. Which of the following was defined by Peck as the ability to make the best choices in life and appears to depend largely on sheer life experience and the opportunities of encountering a wide range of relationships and situations?
   a. emotional flexibility
   b. wisdom
   c. mental flexibility
   d. stagnation

9. Vaillant found that the male Harvard graduates he studied had a tendency toward
   a. depression
   b. introspection
   c. crisis
   d. happiness

10. An important task for men in midlife, according to Levinson's studies, is to deal with
    a. opposite tendencies
    b. career disappointments
    c. financial demands
    d. mental stagnation

11. Two personality traits which seem to remain relatively stable over a lifetime are
    a. affection and persistence
    b. loyalty and impulsivity
    c. extroversion and neuroticism
    d. kindness and greed

12. One common trend in midlife is that
    a. most traits become even stronger
    b. most adults seem to lose control of their lives
    c. most adults lose self-esteem
    d. men and women take on traits associated with the opposite sex

13. A critical event at midlife for women whose lives have been extremely family-centered is
    a. going back to school
    b. getting a new job
    c. taking care of infirm parents
    d. children's leaving home for college, careers, or marriage

14. Barnett, Baruch, and Rivers studied almost 300 women between the ages of 35 and 55 and found that two elements which appear to influence a woman's mental health are
    a. mastery of and pleasure from life
    b. nurturance and freedom
    c. freedom and pleasure
    d. individuality and sexuality

15. A major criticism of many models of adult development is that
    a. they are not based on longitudinal studies
    b. they are not based on current trends
    c. their subjects have been mostly white, middle-class men
    d. their samples were too diverse

16. A recent finding about marital satisfaction suggests that
    a. the happiest time is during the child-rearing years
    b. the least happy time is old age
    c. the years immediately after children leave home may bring as much contentment as the early years of the marriage
    d. the happiest time is when people are heavily involved in their careers

17. A major criticism of research on marital satisfaction is that
    a. samples have been too large
    b. samples have been cross-sectional rather than longitudinal
    c. samples were not random
    d. some couples have been studied longitudinally rather than on a cross-sectional basis

18. The reason/reasons most frequently given for lasting marriages is/are
    a. positive attitude toward the spouse as a friend and a person
    b. commitment to marriage
    c. agreement on aims and goals in life
    d. all of the above

19. In a survey by Lauer and Lauer, happily married couples said that
    a. they were generally satisfied with their sex life
    b. sex was not a primary reason for their happiness
    c. for some, their sex life had improved
    d. all of the above

20. Which of the following statements about friendships in middle age is *false?*
    a. Middle-aged people seem to have less time or energy for friendship than people in other stages of life.
    b. Friendships do persist through life and are a strong source of emotional support.
    c. Age is a more important factor than similarity of life events in making friends.
    d. Similarity of life events is a more important factor than age in making friends.

21. Which of the following statements about relationships with maturing children is true?
    a. Adolescence can be hard on everyone in the family.
    b. Children often overidentify with parents' ambitions.
    c. Children must realize that their parents have total control over them.
    d. According to research, the most frequent area of disagreement among middle-aged couples concerns adult children living at home.

22. The "empty nest" crisis is particularly difficult for
    a. fathers
    b. parents whose children do not become independent
    c. women who have not prepared for their children's leaving
    d. all of the above

23. If children do not leave home when the parents expect them to, there may be psychological conflict for which of the following reasons?
    a. Adult children living with parents may fall into dependent habits while parents continue as caregivers.
    b. Young adults are likely to feel isolated from peers and not develop intimacy.
    c. Parents may be deprived of freedom to renew intimacy and to resolve marital issues.
    d. all of the above

24. Which of the following statements about caring for elderly parents is *false?*
    a. Most older people feel that it would be easy to live with their children.
    b. The strain of caring for elderly parents most often shows up in physical and emotional exhaustion.
    c. Somehow, most people do not expect to have to take care of their parents and rarely plan ahead for it.
    d. Relationships between middle-aged adults and their parents are usually characterized by a strong bond of affection.

25. After the death of a parent, middle-aged adults often
    a. seek new relationships with elderly people
    b. abandon thier relationships with other elderly people
    c. review and evaluate their own lives and goals
    d. regress to an earlier developmental stage

## Matching

Match each of the lettered items in the box with the appropriate description in the numbered list that follows the box.

---

a. empty nest
b. interiority
c. mental flexibility
d. mental rigidity
e. emotional flexibility
f. emotional impoverishment
g. socializing
h. sexualizing
i. midlife transition
j. care
k. generativity versus stagnation
l. midlife crisis
m. mastery
n. quest for meaning in life
o. pleasure

---

1. best predicted by positive experience with husband and children _____

2. when the last child leaves home _____

3. valuing people as individuals and companions _____

4. control a woman feels she has over her life _____

5. Erikson's seventh stage _____

6. inability to shift emotional investment from one person to another _____

7. valuing people primarily as sex objects _____

8. introspection in middle age _____

9. stressful period during the early to middle forties _____

10. changes in personality and lifestyle during middle adulthood _____

11. virtue of Erikson's seventh stage _____

12. using experiences as guides to solving new problems _____

13. ability to shift emotional investment _____

14. emphasized by Jung _____

15. closed to new ideas _____

## Completion

Supply the term or terms needed to complete the each of the following statements.

1. A potentially stressful period during the early to middle forties, precipitated by an evaluation of one's life, is called the _____ .

2. According to the _____ approach to human development—popularized by Vaillant, Levinson, and Erikson—the human personality goes through a universal sequence of critical changes at certain ages.

3. Erikson's seventh crisis in development, which occurs at midlife, is _____ versus _____ .

4. _____ is the concern of mature adults for establishing and guiding the next generation (or for productivity or creativity), because people feel a need to participate in the continuation of life.

5. According to Erikson, if the seventh crisis is not resolved successfully, people will become _____ .

6. Peck's four critical psychological developments related to successful adjustment in middle age are valuing wisdom versus _____ , socializing versus _____ , emotional flexibility versus _____ , and mental flexibility versus _____ .

7. Neugarten's term for people's concern with introspection (their "inner" life) is _____ .

8. George Vaillant's Grant Study, a longitudinal study that followed male subjects into middle age, found that the best-adjusted men were the most _____ .

9. One study found that two main factors influenced middle-aged women's mental health: _____ and _____ .

10. The most influential normative-crisis theories of adult development have been based primarily on _____ subjects.

11. The _____ model suggests that personality development is influenced less by age than by what events people experience and when these events occur.

12. The time of transition for a couple when their last child leaves home, popularly called the _____ , may be a time of personal or marital crisis.

13. Usually during middle age, many people look at their parents objectively and see them as _____ and _____ .

14. Studies indicate that the person who is most likely to care for elderly parents is _____ .

15. Elderly parents tend to be somewhat selective, focusing their attention and aid on the child who _____ .

## ANSWERS FOR SELF-TESTS

## Multiple-Choice

1. d (page 448)
2. a (449)
3. d (449)
4. b (449)
5. a (449)
6. d (451)
7. c (451)
8. b (451)
9. b (452)
10. a (452)
11. c (453)
12. d (453)
13. d (454)
14. a (454)
15. c (455)
16. c (457)
17. b (458)

18. d (459)

19. d (459)

20. c (460)

21. a (461)

22. d (461)

23. d (462)

24. a (464)

25. d (465)

## Matching

1. o (page 454)

2. a (461)

3. g (451)

4. m (454)

5. k (451)

6. f (451)

7. h (451)

8. b (452)

9. l (448)

10. i (448)

11. j (451)

12. c (450)

13. e (451)

14. n (449)

15. d (450)

## Completion

1. midlife crisis (page 448)

2. normative crisis (449)

3. generativity; stagnation (451)

4. generativity (451)

5. stagnant (451)

6. physical powers; sexualizing; emotional impoverishment; mental rigidity (451)

7. interiority (452)

8. generative (452)

9. mastery; pleasure (454)

10. privileged white male (455)

11. timing-of-events (457)

12. empty nest (459, 461)

13. elderly (*or* aged) and becoming dependent on them (463)

14. a daughter (464)

15. needs them most (464)

# 16

# PHYSICAL AND INTELLECTUAL DEVELOPMENT IN LATE ADULTHOOD

## INTRODUCTION

**Chapter 16** examines physical and intellectual development in late adulthood, the last age-defined group discussed in the text. Many events and changes still lie ahead for the 65-year-old.

■ The chapter begins with an exploration of longevity and the aging process, physical changes, and health problems and concerns.

■ Changes in intelligence and intellectual functioning in late adulthood are discussed, as are changes in the functioning of memory.

■ The relationship between intellectual activity and intellectual functioning is discussed in the context of lifelong learning.

■ The chapter closes with an examination of the influence of work and the transition to retirement.

## CHAPTER OUTLINE

**I. OLD AGE TODAY**

A. WHAT IS OUR ATTITUDE TOWARD OLD AGE?

B. WHO ARE THE ELDERLY?

1. "Young Old" and "Old Old"

2. The Graying of the Population

3. The Oldest Old

C. HOW CAN WE MAKE THE MOST OF THE LATER YEARS?

## PHYSICAL DEVELOPMENT

**II. LONGEVITY AND THE AGING PROCESS**

A. LIFE EXPECTANCY

1. Trends in Life Expectancy

2. Death Rates and Causes of Death

3. Race, Gender, and Life Expectancy

   a. Racial differences

   b. Gender differences

B. WHY PEOPLE AGE: TWO THEORIES

1. Programmed Aging

2. Aging as Wear and Tear

**III. PHYSICAL CHANGES OF OLD AGE**

A. SENSORY AND PSYCHOMOTOR FUNCTIONING

1. Vision

2. Hearing

3. Taste and Smell

4. Sensitivity to Cold and Heat

5. Strength, Coordination, and Reaction Time

B. OTHER PHYSICAL CHANGES

C. RESERVE CAPACITY

**IV. HEALTH IN OLD AGE**

A. INFLUENCES ON HEALTH AND FITNESS

B. HEALTH CARE AND HEALTH PROBLEMS

1. Medical Conditions

2. Dental Health

3. Mental and Behavioral Disorders

   a. Reversible mental health problems

      (1) Depression

      (2) Overmedication

   b. Irreversible mental problems

      (1) Alzheimer's disease

         (a) Causes of Alzheimer's disease

         (b) Symptoms and diagnosis

         (c) Treatment

      (2) Other irreversible conditions

## KEY TERMS

ageism (page 472)

Alzheimer's disease (484)

dementia (483)

dual-process model (491)

gerontologists (472)

long-term memory (492)

mechanics of intelligence (491)

plasticity (489)

pragmatics of intelligence (491)

primary aging (478)

programmed-aging theory (478)

reserve capacity (481)

secondary aging (478)

selective optimization with compensation (491)

senescence (476)

sensory memory (492)

short-term memory (492)

terminal drop (488)

wear-and-tear theory (478)

## LEARNING OBJECTIVES

After finishing Chapter 16, you should be able to:

1. Describe common attitudes toward old age and the elderly.

2. Identify various categories of elderly people.

3. Explain several specific steps that one can take to help older people make the most of their lives.

4. Define *senescence*, and explain why changes in life expectancy in this century have focused attention on it.

5. Describe trends in life expectancy, death rates, and major causes of death among older people.

6. Describe the physical aspects of aging.

7. Discuss two theories of why people age.
   a. *programmed aging*

   b. *aging as wear and tear*

8. Distinguish between *primary aging* and *secondary aging*.

9. Discuss the physical changes of late adulthood in areas such as sensory and psychomotor abilities, responses, skin, and bones.

**10.** Define *reserve capacity,* and explain its relevance to aging.

**11.** Describe the general health of older people and the factors that influence health and fitness among the elderly.

**12.** Identify the health care issues and health problems that are of special concern to the elderly.

**13.** Discuss the causes, symptoms, and treatment of *Alzheimer's disease.*

**14.** Discuss theories of intelligence in older people, and describe some techniques for measuring changes in intellectual functioning.

**15.** List some physical and psychological factors that can influence older adults' performance on intelligence tests, and describe how older people continue to learn.

**16.** Discuss the *dual-process model* of intellectual functioning, which helps explain how some aspects of intelligence seem to increase with age.

**17.** Describe differences between young people and old people in the following areas, and summarize the various theories that seek to explain these differences.
 a. *sensory memory*

 b. *short-term memory*

 c. *long-term memory*

**18.** Discuss the importance of continued mental activity, and explain how learning and memory are interrelated.

**19.** Describe the effect of work and retirement on the older person.

## SUPPLEMENTAL READING

Leslie Lindeman writes and lectures on aging, health, and peace. He is a runner and lives in Chicago.

## Beating Time

### Leslie Lindeman

The horn sounds and Don Greetham uncoils like a spring as he sails out over the water. He hits with a splash, legs kicking, arms pulling, head turning rhythmically as he gulps in each breath.

In less than 17 seconds he reaches the far end of the 25-yard pool, executes a perfect flip-turn and heads back. The arms of half-a-dozen more competitors windmill wildly all around Greetham as the seven swimmers churn the water a frothy white.

Greetham holds the lead a quarter of the way through this 200-yard race. The swimmers go into their flip-turns like a row of trained dolphins. Down they go again and back they come on the second lap with Greetham barely in front. They hit, they turn, down they go, heading back for the three-quarter mark. At the turn, the swimmer two lanes to Greetham's right has pulled dead even.

Down they go one last time; they hit, they turn, and here they come for the final 25 yards to the finish, arms flying, legs churning and not a quart of water separating Greetham and his closest competitor.

The swimmers on the deck warming up for the next heat stop to look. The spectators in the bleachers come to their feet. The timers lean over the pool's edge as the swimmers in lanes three and five pull for the wall. Boom! They hit one-two so quickly you can hardly tell them apart. They emerge gasping in their slick caps and goggles.

Greetham hangs on the edge of the pool, chest heaving, mind not yet back into this world. He has no idea he won, or that it was the closest race of his life. He finished in 2:49.47—his competitor in 2:49.48.

Not a bad day's play for a 68-year-old, and it's only 11 a.m. By midafternoon he will swim nearly half a mile, win three gold medals and a silver, and become a little younger.

Younger? Compared with his performances in recent years, Don Greetham's times are going down. Like everyone else he is chronologically aging, but in terms of physical accomplishment there is no difference between the Don Greetham of today and who he was four or five years ago. Thanks to the training—an hour of swimming four or five nights each week, a mile to a mile-and-a-half per workout—he has stopped time, even made it go the other way.

Walk around this pool once or twice and you will meet a dozen Don Greethams.

Arnie Formo, a 63-year-old retired businessman from Wilson, North Carolina, glides through the 500-yard free-style, wins by less than a second and hops out grinning. Greetham's wife, Bernice (they met at a swim meet in Charlotte, North Carolina, in 1984 and now live in Raleigh), was an all-American in the 1940s but didn't swim a competitive stroke for 40 years. Now she's back into it and regularly keeps pace with women in their 30s and 40s.

There are more than a hundred older athletes around this pool today. Stripped down to their swimsuits they are a picture of 55- to 84-year-old fitness—all are clear-eyed, vibrant, full of life.

They are here for the finals of the North Carolina Senior Games, one of 55 national qualifying sites for the third biennial U.S. National Senior Sports Classic to be held in Syracuse, New York, from June 28 to July 3. In all, 1,528 athletes are in Raleigh this September weekend running track events, playing tennis, racing bicycles, shooting baskets, race walking—competing in 40 events.

Each one qualified to be here by placing first, second or third in one of 39 local competitions throughout the state. Multiply these numbers across the nation and you begin to get a sense of the growing phenomenon of senior athletics. Indeed, by this past March more than 200,000 athletes age 55 and over had competed in senior games, with 15,000 of them qualifying for the big event in Syracuse and about 5,000 expected to show up, according to Barbara McQuitty, director of marketing for the governing body, the U.S. National Senior Sports Organization (USNSSO).

All of this started in the late 1960s when grassroots organizations across the country began sponsoring senior games. By 1985, 40 communities were involved. The flavor of the games varied by region but there was one common denominator: five-year age groups (Men's/Women's 55–59; 60–64; etc.) that enabled older athletes to compete with their peers.

Then the organizers of the St. Louis games hit upon the idea of hosting a national contest and the first U.S. National Senior Olympics took place there in 1987. Last year, the organization reached an agreement with the United States Olympic Committee to drop the word "Olympic" from its name, and the games became the U.S. National Senior Sports Classic. Today USNSO has an annual budget of $1.5 million, which is provided by 12 corporate sponsors.

To take a reading on the growth of the senior athletic movement, we traveled to three of the national qualifying sites: Raleigh, St. Louis, and Palm Springs, California.

Support for older athletes runs strong in St. Louis, where they've been holding senior events for 11 years. At 9 a.m. on a cool spring day the parking lot of the Jewish Community Centers Association in suburban Creve Coeur is already filled with hundreds of cars.

Inside, the main building athletes finish late registration and pick up the numbers they will wear during competition. In one corner a video explains the history of the senior games; in another, yellow-shirted volunteers pass out paper cups of mineral water. In the gymnasium three-on-three basketball has already begun. Downstairs in the pool some of the 100-plus competitors in the swimming events have started their warmups. An hour from now the tennis tournament will begin on the courts outside. Next door, a quarter-mile cycling track has been set up in the parking lot surrounding a bowling alley. One of the day's first events—a five-mile race for cyclists ages 55–59—has just ended.

Two competitors lean on their bicycles breathing heavily. Jasper Savage, a 55-year-old machine-shop teacher at a local junior college, has a dark ring of perspiration around the neck of his cycling jersey. His $1,200 14-speed Italian racer is built from the same alloy used to make military jets. A tiny computer on the handlebars tells Savage his speed, distance traveled, and rpm—everything except what kind of strategy his buddy Tom Reichard is using. To help in that regard, he wears a tiny rear-view mirror attached to his glasses.

Reichard is 59 and newly retired from his career as a research physicist. He has always had "the fitness urge" and sports (he also speed skates) are a big part of his retirement.

He and Savage ride with a St. Louis cycling club and love nothing better than to go on cycling tours in the summer. They also go head to head in several races each year.

Reichard has dominated local senior competition. But in this race, Savage vowed not to get out in front where Reichard could draft (stay close behind and let Savage act as a wind break), then pass him at the last moment. On this morning it was Savage coming from behind in the last 20 meters to win a breathtaking race by about a wheel.

"I know Tom Reichard," Savage says, "and that's the only reason I beat him. I know he has a tremendous sprint so I couldn't let him stay right behind me."

"Jasper's been gunning for me for some years," says Reichard with a wink. "I'm sure we'll be racing again."

In 1940, Carla Convery was Italy's 800-meter-run champion, all set to compete in the Helsinki Olympics. World War II stole that opportunity—but since she discovered senior athletics some years ago she has been making up for it. Convery travels to competitions across the country year-round, competing in as many events as time allows. Among her favorites: discus, javelin, shot put, basketball, softball, billiards, table tennis, swimming and, of course, track. She probably has won more medals than any other senior games participant.

"I do it because I love the people," she says, "and because I love sports." Two years ago, Convery dropped out of a 5-kilometer race because she felt faint. The next day her doctor found her heart rhythm so dangerously irregular he ordered her flown by helicopter to a hospital where she had a pacemaker implanted. (She tells the story quickly, leaning forward, eyes intense and hands gesturing. She could easily pass for ten years younger than her 70 years.) She returned to athletics a month later and subsequently shattered her pacemaker while throwing the javelin. She now competes with a state-of-the-art model that adjusts itself to her level of exertion.

## SENIOR ATHLETES' SAFETY CHECK

While waiting to reenter a basketball game at the St. Louis Senior Games last summer, a 55-year-old player collapsed on the gymnasium floor. On-site paramedics quickly began lifesaving measures and an ambulance arrived within minutes, but he never regained consciousness. He was a daily six-mile jogger and weight-lifter.

The episode sent a momentary chill across the games and raised two familiar questions: Why do seemingly fit people sometimes suffer heart attacks during exercise? And is intense physical exertion safe for senior athletes?

We spoke first with 72-year-old George Sheehan, M.D., the noted cardiologist, philosopher and author known as "the patron saint of running."

"Nobody dies during exercise unless they have underlying heart disease," says Sheehan. "What I've discovered among the legion of runners who have consulted me—many of them older athletes—is that heart attacks are rare but heart disease is not infrequent."

Runners with persistently high cholesterol and/or a family history of heart disease are likely to develop the disease, he says, regardless of their exercise regimens. Athletes who are finely attuned to their bodies should know when something is wrong. But they must heed the early warning signs, says Sheehan.

He cites the case of a 73-year-old fellow member of the New York Road Runners Club who suffered a heart attack shortly after a five-mile race. "It turns out that for the previous few months he had been having pain when he ran," Sheehan recalls. "In up to 90 percent of heart attack cases, patients have told someone—a physician, friend or spouse—that they were experiencing symptoms."

Mary E. Case, M.D., the St. Louis County medical examiner, agrees that exercise does not lead to sudden death among those who do not have heart disease. Indeed, she officially listed the basketball player's probable cause of death as "arteriosclerotic heart disease," a narrowing of the arteries that supply the heart with blood and in this case most likely caused a fatal arrhythmia.

Based on her experiences, would she suggest that older people curtail their fitness activities?

"I would never advocate that," says Case, who works out regularly at a health club. "On balance, your health risks are much lower if you exercise."

Probably the most vociferous advocate of exercise for people of any age is Ken Cooper, M.D., the Dallas, Texas, cardiologist who founded the Aerobics Center—a combination health club, research center and preventive medicine clinic.

His favorite statistic: More than 10,000 men and women with an average age of about 43 have run nine million miles, cycled one million miles and swum 122,000 miles at his health club over the past 17 years with only one fatality. Cooper's secret is that men age 40 and over and women age 50 and over must have a stress test before being allowed to join, then have a repeat evaluation every three years.

Unlike Sheehan, Cooper believes that "as many as 40 percent of heart attack victims have no symptoms prior to sudden death."

Stress tests are not necessary for everyone, says Cooper, but since athletes are at greater risk of suffering heart attack if they have heart disease and don't know it, it only makes sense for them to be more aware.

All three physicians agree that athletics is not a panacea. If you are a senior athlete, heed the following:

—Be aware of your family history. Heart disease has strong genetic ties.

—Have a physical examination before beginning a fitness program. High-intensity athletes would do well to have periodic stress tests.

—Listen to your body for early warning signs of heart disease such as chest pain, dizziness or numbness, especially during workouts.

—Keep your cholesterol level low and develop a low-fat diet.

## Questions about the Reading

1. What do the examples provided in this article indicate with respect to the wear-and-tear theory of aging?

2. In what ways are older athletes different from their younger counterparts? From their nonathletic peers?

## SELF-TESTS

### Multiple-Choice

Circle the letter of the response which best completes or answers each of the following statements and questions.

1. *Ageism* refers to
   a. reverence and respect for elderly people
   b. prejudice or discrimination based on age
   c. belief that elderly people are especially wise
   d. scientific study of the aging processes

2. A person who studies the aged and the aging processes is called a/an
   a. ageist
   b. ageologist
   c. gerontologist
   d. portiologist

3. Which of the following statements about the elderly is true?
   a. People 85 years old and older are the fastest-growing age group in the United States.
   b. The elderly are generally poorly coordinated, feel tired most of the time, and are prone to infections.
   c. The elderly tend to become isolated from their families as they become self-pitying and cranky.
   d. The elderly have little or no interest in or desire for sexual relationships.

4. The period of the life span marked by declines in bodily functioning is known as
   a. burnout
   b. climacteric
   c. menopause
   d. senescence

5. Which of the following statements about old age is the most accurate?
   a. Because old age is the period during which deaths most frequently occur, the elderly are the smallest age group.
   b. The lengthening life span in modern times has swelled the population of the aging.
   c. The size of the elderly population has begun to decline and will continue to do so for several decades.
   d. The size of the elderly population has been stable for decades and is expected to remain so.

6. By far, the biggest killer of people over age 65 is
   a. cancer
   b. accidents
   c. heart disease
   d. respiratory illnesses

7. The life expectancy (in years) of newborns in the United States in 1987 was
   a. about 75
   b. about 80
   c. 68
   d. more than 80

8. Which of the following medical advances is/are responsible for the increase in life expectancy?
   a. dramatic decline in mortality rates of infants and children
   b. development of new drugs and treatments for fatal illnesses
   c. better living and working conditions
   d. both a and b

9. Which theory of biological aging holds that human bodies age in accordance with a normal developmental pattern built into each organism?
   a. primary aging
   b. secondary aging
   c. wear and tear
   d. programmed aging

10. Which theory holds that aging is a result of continuous use and of accumulated "insults" to the body?
    a. primary aging
    b. secondary aging
    c. wear and tear
    d. programmed aging

11. The gradual process of bodily deterioration that begins early in life and continues inexorably through the years is known as
    a. primary aging
    b. secondary aging
    c. wear and tear
    d. programmed aging

12. Aging that is due to disease, abuse, and disuse —factors often under our own control—is known as
    a. primary aging
    b. secondary aging
    c. wear and tear
    d. programmed aging

13. Which of the following statements about older people's senses is the most accurate?
    a. Farsightedness that begins in middle age will continue to worsen during old age, eventually resulting in functional blindness.
    b. Elderly people, whose other senses have deteriorated, rely more on their sense of smell, which actually improves with age.
    c. Because they generally have more body fat than younger people, the elderly are less sensitive to extremes of temperature.
    d. Hearing loss is very common in old age, affecting about 3 of 10 people over 65 and half of those over 75.

14. What causes the general "slowing down" of older people?
    a. environmental deprivation
    b. depression
    c. neurological changes
    d. all of the above

15. Which of these is *not* a physical change associated with old age?
    a. Varicose veins are more common.
    b. Women's hair becomes fuller.
    c. Skin becomes paler and splotchy.
    d. Skin loses elasticity.

16. Which of these statements about fitness for older people is *false?*
    a. It helps maintain speed and stamina.
    b. It can lead to arthritis because it overworks the joints.
    c. It improves mental alertness.
    d. It relieves anxiety and depression.

17. Symptoms of depression in older people include
    a. extreme sadness
    b. lack of interest or enjoyment in life
    c. tendency to do childish things
    d. both a and b

18. Which of the following statements about intellectual functioning in old age is the most accurate?
    a. Most psychologists agree that general intellectual decline in old age is largely a myth.
    b. Most psychologist recognize that deterioration of intellectual functioning is a normal part of aging.
    c. Since abilities related to solving novel problems are at the heart of intelligence, and since there is an increase in such abilities in old age, declining intelligence is not a general problem for the elderly.
    d. There is some disagreement among psychologists about the progress of intellectual functioning in old age.

19. The sudden decrease in intellectual performance shortly before death is known as
    a. terminal drop
    b. senile dementia
    c. anticipatory shutdown
    d. death anticipation syndrome

20. Variability in a person's intellectual performance is known as
    a. elasticity
    b. plasticity
    c. cognitive flexibility
    d. situational variability

21. "Content-free architecture of information processing and problem solving" refers to what aspect of intelligence?
    a. synergistics
    b. mechanics
    c. pragmatics
    d. dynamics

22. Practical thinking, application of accumulated knowledge and skills, specialized expertise, professional productivity, and wisdom are known as the _____ of intelligence.
    a. synergistics
    b. mechanics
    c. pragmatics
    d. dynamics

23. Aging has a significant effect on what kind of memory?
    a. sensory
    b. working
    c. short-term
    d. long-term

24. When a person looks up a telephone number, closes the directory, and then dials, the number is stored in a kind of memory which is relatively unaffected by age, namely
    a. sensory
    b. working
    c. short-term
    d. long-term

25. With regard to memory in old age, which of the following statements is accurate?
    a. Long-term memory for recent events deteriorates with old age.
    b. Memory for events far in the past declines with old age.
    c. Visual sensory memory deteriorates with advancing age.
    d. Short-term memory is most affected by old age.

## Matching

Match each of the lettered items in the box with the appropriate description in the numbered list that follows the box.

---

a. plasticity
b. senescence
c. ageism
d. geriatrics
e. terminal drop
f. secondary aging
g. dementia
h. Alzheimer's disease
i. primary aging
j. long-term memory for recent events
k. short-term memory
l. heart disease
m. wear-and-tear theory
n. programmed-aging theory
o. mechanics

---

1. area of intellect which declines with age _____

2. branch of medicine dealing with age _____

3. memory unaffected by increasing age _____

4. variability in cognitive performance _____

5. theory that a rate for aging is built into each person _____

6. memory most affected by advancing age _____

7. degenerative brain disorder of the aged _____

8. prejudice based on age _____

9. leading killer of the elderly _____

10. aging due to disease, abuse, and disuse _____

11. apparent intellectual deterioration _____

12. decrease in intellectual performance shortly before death _____

13. period of life marked by declines in body functioning related to aging _____

14. gradual process of bodily decline _____

15. theory that aging is due to continuous use of the body _____

## Completion

Supply the term or terms needed to complete each of the following statements.

1. _____ , the traditional marker of old age, is no longer a reliable guide.

2. On the average, life expectancy is _____ for white Americans than for black Americans, and _____ for men than for women.

3. The farsightedness that affects most people in middle age _____ at about age 60.

4. Older people can do most of the things that younger people do, but they do these things more _____ .

5. About 6 percent of older people are victims of _____ , a degenerative brain disorder that affects intelligence, awareness, and the ability to control bodily functions.

6. Schaie and Baltes maintain that some intellectual abilities, mostly _____ abilities, either hold their own or increase in later life.

7. The poor showings of older people in cross-sectional studies of intelligence may be due to _____ , a sudden decrease in intellectual functioning shortly before death.

8. _____ of intelligence is the area in which there is often an age-related decline.

9. _____ of intelligence includes such areas as practical thinking and the application of accumulated knowledge and skills.

10. Pragmatic intelligence can help older people maintain their intellectual functioning through _____ .

11. Images in _____ memory fade very quickly unless they are transferred to short-term memory.

12. One study of memory showed that older people had trouble in _____ items, but they did just as well as younger people in _____ items.

13. Researchers have recently become interested in how _____ factors account for individual differences in recall.

14. Older people can learn new skills, but they learn better when the instruction takes into account the _____ , _____ , and _____ changes they may be going through.

15. Two key elements in satisfaction with retirement are _____ and using _____ well.

---

## ANSWERS FOR SELF-TESTS

### Multiple-Choice

1. b (page 472)

2. c (472)

3. a (474–475)

4. d (476)

5. b (477)

6. c (477)

7. a (477)

8. d (477)

9. d (478)

10. c (478)

11. a (478)

12. b (478)

13. d (479–480)

14. d (480)

15. b (481)

16. b (482)

17. d (484)

18. d (486)

19. a (488)

20.  b (489)

21.  b (491)

22.  c (491)

23.  d (492)

24.  c (492)

25.  a (492)

## Matching

1.  o (page 491)

2.  d (475)

3.  k (492)

4.  a (489)

5.  n (478)

6.  j (492)

7.  h (484)

8.  c (472)

9.  l (477)

10.  f (478)

11.  g (484)

12.  e (488)

13.  b (476)

14.  i (478)

15.  m (478)

## Completion

1.  retirement (page 474)

2.  greater; less (477)

3.  stabilizes (479)

4.  slowly (480)

5.  Alzheimer's disease (484)

6.  crystallized (486)

7.  terminal drop (488)

8.  mechanics (491)

9.  pragmatics (491)

10.  selective optimization with compensation (491)

11.  sensory (492)

12.  recalling; recognizing (492)

13.  contextual (492–493)

14.  physiological; psychological; intellectual (493)

15.  planning beforehand; leisure time (495)

# CHAPTER 17

# PERSONALITY AND SOCIAL DEVELOPMENT IN LATE ADULTHOOD

## INTRODUCTION

How people adapt to aging depends on their personalities and on how they have adapted throughout life. They can experience the last stage of life positively and may even experience it as a time of growth and fulfillment.

■ **Chapter 17** begins with an examination of two theories of psychological development in late adulthood: Erikson's eighth crisis, integrity versus despair; and Peck's three crises of late adulthood.

■ The text describes several approaches to successful aging, including activity theory and disengagement theory.

■ Personality and patterns of aging are discussed; and four major personality types, with associated patterns of aging, are described.

■ The chapter describes several social issues related to aging, such as the importance of activity, changes in income, options for living arrangements (including nursing homes), aging in minority cultures, and vulnerability to crime.

■ A discussion of personal relationships in late life is provided, including such topics as marriage and marital happiness, divorce, surviving a spouse's death, remarriage, sexual relationships, relationships with siblings, and friendships.

■ The chapter concludes with an exploration of relationships with adult children, with a discussion of childlessness and grandparenthood.

## CHAPTER OUTLINE

### I. THEORY AND RESEARCH ON PERSONALITY DEVELOPMENT

A. ERIK ERIKSON: CRISIS 8
—INTEGRITY VERSUS DESPAIR

B. ROBERT PECK: THREE ADJUSTMENTS OF LATE ADULTHOOD

C. GEORGE VAILLANT: FACTORS IN EMOTIONAL HEALTH

D. RESEARCH ON CHANGES IN PERSONALITY

### II. AGING

A. APPROACHES TO "SUCCESSFUL AGING"

1. Activity Theory

2. Disengagement Theory

3. Personal Definitions of Aging Successfully

B. PERSONALITY AND PATTERNS OF AGING

C. SOCIAL ISSUES RELATED TO AGING

1. Income

2. Living Arrangements

  a. Living independently

  b. Living in institutions

    (1) Who lives in nursing homes?

    (2) What makes a good nursing home?

    (3) Problems in nursing homes

3. Abuse of the Elderly

### III. PERSONAL RELATIONSHIPS IN LATE LIFE

A. MARRIAGE

1. Marital Happiness

2. Strengths and Strains in Late-Life Marriage

B. DIVORCE

C. SURVIVING A SPOUSE

1. Adjusting to the Death of a Spouse

2. Living as a Widow or Widower

D. REMARRIAGE

E. SINGLE LIFE: THE "NEVER MARRIEDS"

F. SEXUAL RELATIONSHIPS

G. RELATIONSHIPS WITH SIBLINGS

H. FRIENDSHIPS

I. RELATIONSHIPS WITH ADULT CHILDREN

1. How Parents Help Children

2. How Children Help Parents

J. CHILDLESSNESS

K. GRANDPARENTHOOD AND GREAT-GRANDPARENTHOOD

## KEY TERMS

activity theory (page 503)

disengagement theory (504)

elder abuse (512)

integrity versus despair (501)

## LEARNING OBJECTIVES

After finishing Chapter 17, you should be able to:

1. Explain Erikson's eighth crisis—*integrity versus despair*—and the virtue that results from its successful resolution.

2. Describe the three psychological adjustments of late adulthood according to Peck.
   a. broader self-definition versus preoccupation with work roles

   b. transcendence of the body versus preoccupation with the body

   c. transcendence of the ego versus preoccupation with the ego

3. List some of the research findings on changes in personality in late adulthood.

4. Describe and compare the two theories of successful aging.
   a. *activity theory*

   b. *disengagement theory*

5. Describe the four major personality types found in elderly people, according to one study.
   a. integrated

   b. armor-defended

   c. passive-dependent

   d. unintegrated

6. Explain some findings about the following social issues related to aging.
   a. income



   b. living arrangements



   c. living independently



   d. living in institutions



   e. abuse of the elderly



7. Discuss aging among African Americans, Hispanic Americans, and other minority groups in the United States.



8. Describe some research findings about the following.
   a. marital happiness in long-term marriages



   b. late-life marriage



   c. divorce

   d. adjusting to the death of a spouse



   e. living as a widow or widower



   f. remarriage



   g. single life



   h. sexual relationships



9. Explain the significance and quality of relationships between elderly people and each of the following.
   a. siblings



   b. friends



   c. adult children



   d. grandchildren

## SUPPLEMENTAL READING

This article originally appeared in the July 14, 1991 issue of *Parade* magazine.

## Here, They See Age as an Asset

## Michael Ryan

Recently I traveled to Asheville, N.C., and met some of the community's leading citizens. Carolyn Rosenthal found time for me in between meetings of the reading groups she runs in the area. Earl Hitchcock squeezed me in during a busy day of administering a volunteer program. I tracked down Bob Etter in his physical chemistry lab and went to an inner-city school to find Mel Hetland and Evelyn Smith. Bob and Peggy Tinkler had a little more free time; they had just finished work on a grueling political campaign and were settling back into their more normal routines as college students. This was not a collection of native Ashevilleans— nor did they have much else in common. By training, they were a dancer, a businessman, a corporate research director, two educators, an insurance man and a travel agent. Some had lived in the upper Midwest and the Northeast; one had spent his career in places like Saigon and Buenos Aires. All had, at the age of 65 or so, wound down their primary careers. The rest of the world would call them retired. Asheville calls them leaders.

Approximately 13 percent of this country's citizens— around 32 million people—are 65 or older. Although no exact statistics are kept, experts believe that most of these individuals are in good health. Life expectancies for Americans vary by sex, race and other demographic factors, but many older people today can expect to live into their 80s. And in 30 years, as many members of the Baby Boom generation are reaching retirement age, the number of older Americans will start to rise by 50 percent.

Statistics like these led the University of North Carolina at Asheville to set up its North Carolina Center for Creative Retirement. "Until recently, most of the nation's concern for senior citizens was concentrated on the frail, the fragile and the impoverished," said Ronald J. Manheimer, the center's director. "Those people are very important. But other seniors were ignored."

With its reasonable cost of living, temperate climate and breathtaking view of the Blue Ridge Mountains, Asheville has grown increasingly popular as a place for older people: 16,000 of the city's 62,000 residents are retirees. About 1500 of those participate each year in the programs of the Center for Creative Retirement. In the center's non-credit College for Seniors, retirees can further their education. In its Senior Academy for Intergenerational Learning, they can pass on their knowledge to young people. Through Leadership Asheville Seniors, they work in the schools, hospitals and prisons of the community.

In Asheville, "retired" people are running discussion groups for adults in rural communities; helping hospitals, libraries and orchestras to organize their finances and marketing; and counseling college students on career choices. "These are people of talent—resourceful, bright and capable," said Ron Manheimer. "They had been an untapped resource."

The older people who take part in the center's programs live in their own homes and commute to their jobs and classes on and off-campus. Some might spend as little as two hours a week taking a course in poetry or physics or arms control at the College for Seniors. Others spend all or part of almost every weekday working on center-sponsored projects. "You don't see many people withering away or floundering around for something to do around here," Bob Tinkler, 67, told me. Earl Hitchcock, 72, certainly wasn't floundering around when I met with him. "I've got my hands full," he said cheerfully, gesturing at a thick pile of paperwork. A few years ago, Hitchcock was a businessman in New Jersey. Today, he coordinates the work of 80 volunteers in the public schools of the Asheville area. "When I retired, I didn't have anything specific in mind that I wanted to do," Hitchcock said. "I knew I wanted to play tennis—and I've done that. But my wife and I had always been active in the community—United Way, Cub Scouts, a family-counseling service—and we wanted to remain active."

Hitchcock attended the seven-week Leadership Asheville Seniors training course, in which political, educational and philanthropic leaders taught the participants about the community's needs. "They talked about drug addiction, dropouts, the usual litany of city problems. It occurred to us that every one of these problems was education-related."

Hitchcock and other members of his class worked together with area principals to bring older people into the public schools, matching them with students who needed tutors, remedial help or just an adult to talk to. One elderly volunteer tutored a young girl who had been through four foster homes in one school year. She knitted the girl a sweater, helped her with reading and gave a shoulder to cry on. Another volunteer helped a grade-school student who had been failing math, and the child scored an 85 on a math exam. "Some people said that seniors wouldn't be interested in schools, because they don't have kids in school anymore," Hitchcock said. "But absolutely nobody we talked to felt that way."

For Mel Hetland, 70, the center offers a very special way to serve his community while keeping his hand in the profession he loves. Hetland is one of a small group of volunteers from the center who work at Randolph Elementary School, in a downtrodden section of Asheville. Once a week, he teaches reading to first- and third-graders and devises science demonstrations for fifth-graders. "The big reward is that I'm helping some teachers develop techniques for relating to students—techniques that I had a lot of experience with during my own career as a curriculum supervisor and professor of education," he said.

In a laboratory at the University of North Carolina at Asheville, Prof. John Stevens and his students have been doing research on the Mössbauer effect—a nuclear technique that scientists use to study the structure of matter. Stevens has spent much of his career in this work and has introduced hundreds of eager undergraduates to research. Since last summer, he has been grouping his young students with people from the center. "It's been one of the most fruitful semesters I've had in 20 years of research," he said.

Bob Etter, 58, and Terri Spangler, 21, have begun a remarkable partnership. Bob, who has a Ph.D. in chemistry, retired two years ago as research vice president of Johnson's Wax; Terri is a UNC-Asheville junior. "I was expecting to be of service when I retired," Bob said. "I do a lot of volunteer things. But this is the only one I've found in which I can use my scientific background." Working as a team, Bob and Terri run painstaking analyses on specialized equipment, which they learn about as they work together.

The undergraduates in the program admit that they were apprehensive at first about having retired scientists looking over their shoulders. Now, though, Terri pays the program the ultimate compliment: "It's the kind of thing I'd like to do when I retire," she says.

You don't need to be a scientist or a business leader to benefit from the center. "Some of the smartest people in our classes only got as far as high school," said one College for Seniors participant. Carolyn Rosenthal, 67, a former librarian from New York City and Washington, D.C., has started a reading discussion group for adults in rural communities around Asheville. "At first," she recalled, "I had to convince them that they could be members of a reading group. Now, a lot of these people are candidates for courses at the College for Seniors."

Today, the scope of the North Carolina Center for Creative Retirement makes it one of a kind, but Ron Manheimer believes that other creative retirement centers could spring up around the country. With a budget of about $350,000—which comes in part from the university, foundation grants and the fees of its students—the center has relatively low costs. "The programs are replicable, if you have dedicated people," said Manheimer. Already, consultants from retirement communities and government have come to study the center. The White House named it one of President Bush's 1000 Points of Light.

Manheimer concedes that the Center for Creative Retirement is not for everyone; some people lead rich, happy retired lives just puttering in the garden, playing golf and visiting with the grandchildren. But retired people everywhere can learn an important lesson from its philosophy. As Earl Hitchcock put it: "If you can't think of anything to do when you retire, you don't have much imagination."

## Questions about the Reading

1. Explain the success of the program described in this article in terms of activity theory and wear-and-tear theory.

2. Discuss the likely resolution of Erikson's eighth stage of psychosocial development for the people involved in the program described in this article.

## SELF-TESTS

## Multiple-Choice

Circle the letter of the response which best completes or answers each of the following statements and questions.

1. The virtue resulting from successful resolution of Erikson's last crisis of personality development is
   a. will
   b. wisdom
   c. generativity
   d. care

2. According to Erikson, during the last developmental stage, people who do not gain a sense of order and meaning from their lives will experience
   a. bereavement
   b. overwhelming despair
   c. paranoia
   d. schizophrenia

3. According to Robert Peck, people need to redefine their worth as human beings, beyond their work roles, through a process he calls
   a. acceptance
   b. integrity versus despair
   c. broader self-definition
   d. transcendence

4. Peck suggests that in his second crisis (dealing with the physical decline which accompanies aging), a person should
   a. find compensatory satisfactions
   b. develop a focus on relationships
   c. concentrate on improving muscular coordination and strength
   d. both a and b

5. According to Peck, the most difficult task older people face is
   a. adapting to the prospect of death
   b. cultivating mental and social powers
   c. living alone
   d. living in institutions

6. It is possible for people to feel positive about their own death through
   a. children they have raised
   b. the way they have lived and their personal relationships
   c. contributions they have made to their culture
   d. all of the above

7. Many older people, instead of achieving self-transcendence, become preoccupied with
   a. intimate relationships
   b. ambition
   c. meeting their own needs
   d. accomplishments

8. The activity theory of aging suggests that
   a. the earlier people retire, the happier they are
   b. roles are a major source of satisfaction in life
   c. the happiest people are those involved in structured activities
   d. the less active people are, the more successfully they age

9. Disengagement theory suggests that
   a. people want to cut down on activities and commitments
   b. the older a person gets, the more active he or she becomes
   c. our culture encourages people to stay involved in work and work-related associations
   d. none of the above

10. One classic study of older people identified four major personality types. The largest group of people, who were functioning well with high levels of satisfaction, had a pattern of life the researchers called
    a. integrated
    b. armor-defended
    c. passive-dependent
    d. unintegrated

11. One of the major findings about older adults' income is that
    a. those who live alone are often more financially secure
    b. for most people, pensions and IRAs are the single largest source of income
    c. many older people are facing poverty for the first time
    d. old age is the time when people have the highest income

12. The majority of elderly people
    a. live in institutions
    b. live with spouses, children, or other relatives
    c. are widowed men
    d. are eager to give up their independence and prefer to live with their children

13. Living arrangements available for the elderly include
    a. group homes and retirement communities
    b. cooperatives, shared housing, and "granny" flats
    c. independent living and nursing homes
    d. all of the above

14. The primary source of emotional support for the elderly is
    a. friends and coworkers
    b. family
    c. both a and b
    d. neither a nor b

15. Abuse of the elderly is most likely to be committed by
    a. a spouse
    b. grandchildren
    c. children
    d. none of the above

16. It has been reported that there is greater marital satisfaction in late adulthood because
    a. people are at a stage when they can enjoy life in general
    b. the decision to divorce usually comes in the earlier years of a marriage
    c. there are fewer strains on a marriage at this time
    d. both a and b

17. Widowhood is widespread in late adulthood; it has been found that
    a. half the men in the United States over 65 are widowed
    b. half the women in the United States over 56 are widowed
    c. about half of all women are widowed in their forties
    d. women are more likely than men to marry again

18. The death of a spouse in late adulthood is particularly difficult for many people because
    a. friends and family give little support
    b. friends and family continue discussing the impact of the death
    c. they have structured their lives around a spouse
    d. all of the above

19. The people who seem to make the best adjustment to widowhood are those who
    a. have been widowed only a short time
    b. are self-reliant
    c. like to sit back and reflect on the past
    d. keep busy and develop new roles

20. A widow is most likely to seek assistance from
    a. friends (especially other widows)
    b. social agencies
    c. children and siblings
    d. none of the above

21. What is the most common reason why older people decide to remarry?
    a. They are forced to by circumstances beyond their control.
    b. They want better housing.
    c. They want more money.
    d. They want companionship and relief from loneliness.

22. One study of older people who remarried found that most of them
    a. had been divorced rather than widowed
    b. had known their new partners during their first marriages
    c. described their new marriages as less calm than marriages early in life
    d. all of the above

23. Among older people, which of the following are especially important in maintaining family relationships?
    a. siblings of either sex
    b. brothers
    c. sisters
    d. children and grandchildren more than siblings

24. Which of the following statements best describes the basis for friendship among the elderly?
    a. Friends are likely to live close by.
    b. Friends are likely to be of the same race, sex, age, and marital status.
    c. Friends are likely to be of the same socioeconomic status.
    d. all of the above

25. The longing to transcend mortality by investing oneself in the lives of future generations is most often reflected in
    a. grandparenthood
    b. charitable and philanthropic donations
    c. remarriage
    d. relationships with siblings

## Matching

Match each of the lettered items in the box with the appropriate description in the numbered list that follows the box.

---

a. integrity versus despair
b. activity theory
c. disengagement theory
d. elder abuse
e. broader self-definition
f. transcendence of the body
g. transcendence of the ego
h. integrated
i. armor-defended
j. passive-dependent
k. unintegrated
l. wisdom
m. despair
n. emotional health in late adulthood
o. control by residents

---

1. defining one's self beyond work _____
2. Erikson's eighth and final stage _____
3. disorganized with poor control of emotions _____
4. characteristic of a good nursing home _____
5. achievement-oriented _____
6. neglect or abuse of dependent older people _____
7. seeks comfort from others or is apathetic _____
8. accepting the certainty of death _____
9. more activity produces better aging _____
10. the result of unsuccessful resolution of the final crisis _____
11. overcoming concerns with bodily condition _____
12. the clear ability to play, work, and love _____
13. aging as a process of mutual withdrawal _____
14. the virtue of Erikson's eighth stage _____
15. functioning well with a complex inner life _____

## Completion

Supply the term or terms needed to complete each of the following statements.

1. Erikson's eighth crisis in personality development is _____ versus _____ .
2. Peck's first crisis in late adulthood is ego differentiation versus _____ .
3. Overcoming concerns about one's physical condition and finding compensating satisfactions is what Peck calls _____ versus _____ .
4. Disengagement theory sees aging as a process of _____ withdrawal.
5. Research suggests that the happiest elderly people are involved in _____ activities; whereas _____ activities have a negative effect.
6. Of the four major personality types mentioned in Neugarten's classic study, _____ people had low activity levels and low life satisfaction.
7. _____ is the largest source of income for older people in the United States.
8. _____ percent of older people live in the community, and about _____ percent in institutions.
9. Many _____ elderly people gain strength and resilience from their extended families and friends.
10. Elderly people who reside in the _____ report higher levels of well-being than those who reside in _____ .
11. It is estimated that up to _____ percent of the people who go into nursing homes do not actually need nursing care but have no better alternative.
12. According to one study, _____ is still the most important factor for success in marriage in late adulthood.
13. _____ in late life is rare; if a couple are going to take this step, they usually do it at an earlier stage.
14. A widow is more likely to seek out her _____ when she is worried or depressed, but she will turn to her _____ for financial help.
15. Researchers have found from questionnaires and interviews that _____ can be a vital force throughout life.

## ANSWERS FOR SELF-TESTS

### Multiple-Choice

1. b (page 501)
2. b (501)
3. c (501)
4. d (502)
5. a (502)
6. d (502)
7. c (502)
8. b (503–504)
9. a (504)
10. a (505)
11. c (507)
12. b (507)
13. d (509)
14. b (512)
15. a (512)
16. d (513)
17. b (515)
18. c (515)
19. d (516)
20. c (516)
21. d (517)
22. b (517)
23. c (518)
24. d (519)
25. a (524)

### Matching

1. e (page 501)
2. a (501)
3. k (505)
4. o (511)
5. i (505)
6. d (512)
7. j (505)
8. g (502)
9. b (503)
10. m (501)
11. f (502)
12. n (502)
13. c (504)
14. l (501)
15. h (505)

### Completion

1. integrity; despair (page 501)
2. work role preoccupation (501)
3. body transcendence; body preoccupation (502)
4. mutual (504)
5. informal; formal (*or* structured) (504)
6. unintegrated (505)
7. social security (507)
8. 95; 5 (507)
9. minority-group (508)
10. community; institutions (509)
11. 40 percent (511)
12. being in love (513)
13. divorce (514)
14. children; siblings (516)
15. sexuality (517)

# CHAPTER 18

# DEATH AND BEREAVEMENT

## INTRODUCTION

**Chapter 18,** the final chapter of the text, examines the final chapter of life—death and bereavement.

■ The chapter begins with a discussion of three aspects of death: biological, social, and psychological.

■ Attitudes toward death and dying are discussed, as well as the idea of confronting one's own death and dealing with bereavement, mourning, and grief.

■ Two important and controversial issues related to death and dying are discussed: euthanasia and suicide.

■ The chapter concludes with as examination of finding a purpose and meaning in life and death.

## CHAPTER OUTLINE

### I. THREE ASPECTS OF DEATH

### II. FACING DEATH

A. ATTITUDES TOWARD DEATH AND DYING ACROSS THE LIFE SPAN

1. Childhood

2. Adolescence

3. Young Adulthood

4. Middle Adulthood

5. Late Adulthood

B. CONFRONTING ONE'S OWN DEATH

1. Changes Preceding Death

   a. Personality changes

   b. Near-death experiences

2. Stages of Dying: Elisabeth Kübler-Ross

C. BEREAVEMENT, MOURNING, AND GRIEF

1. Forms of Grief

   a. Anticipatory grief

   b. "Grief work": A three-phase pattern

   c. Other patterns of grieving

2. Helping People Deal with Dying and Bereavement

   a. Implications of research

   b. Grief therapy

   c. Death education

      (1) Goals of death education

      (2) Teaching children about death

   d. Hospices

   e. Support groups and services

### III. CONTROVERSIAL ISSUES OF DEATH AND DYING

A. EUTHANASIA AND THE RIGHT TO DIE

B. SUICIDE

1. Patterns of Suicide

   a. Suicide among children

   b. Suicide among adolescents

   c. Suicide among adults

2. Preventing Suicide

### IV. FINDING A PURPOSE IN LIFE AND DEATH

A. THE MEANING OF DEATH

B. REVIEWING A LIFE

## KEY TERMS

active euthanasia (page 544)

anticipatory grief (538)

bereavement (538)

death education (541)

durable power of attorney (545)

grief (538)

grief therapy (541)

hospice care (543)

life review (550)

living will (545)

mourning (538)

near-death experiences (534)

passive euthanasia (544)

thanatology (530)

## LEARNING OBJECTIVES

After finishing Chapter 18, you should be able to:

1. Describe *thanatology* and recent developments in the field.

2. List and define three aspects of death.
   a.

   b.

   c.

3. Describe young children's attitudes toward death, and explain why they are often more realistic than adolescents' attitudes.

4. Discuss attitudes of people of different ages as they face their own death.

5. Identify some intellectual and personality changes which people often undergo shortly before death.

6. Describe the results of studies of *near-death experiences*.

7. Explain Kübler-Ross's five stages of coming to terms with death.
   a. denial

   b. anger

   c. bargaining

   d. depression

   e. acceptance

8. Describe, compare, and contrast the following concepts.
   a. *bereavement*

   b. *mourning*

   c. *grief*

9. Describe three forms of grief.
   a.

   b.

   c.

10. Describe the mourning customs of traditional Jews.

11. Describe the three-phase pattern of "grief work."
    a.

    b.

    c.

12. Explain how the following are ways of helping people deal with dying and bereavement.
    a. *grief therapy*

    b. *death education*

    c. *hospice care*

    d. support groups and services

13. Discuss the following controversial issues regarding death and dying.
    a. *euthanasia* and the right to die

    b. suicide

**14.** Define the following and differentiate between them.
  **a.** *active euthanasia*

  **b.** *passive euthanasia*

**15.** Outline the provisions of a *living will*.

**16.** Describe patterns of suicide among different age groups.

**17.** Discuss the challenge of finding a purpose in life and death, and factors which most influence attitudes toward life and death.

**18.** Discuss the *life review* and its benefits.

---

## SUPPLEMENTAL READING

---

The following excerpt is from a book in progress, *Companion through the Darkness: Inner Dialogues on Grief*, by Stephanie Ericsson. The book is structured with two different voices: "Meditation" speaks to the collective, universal experience; "Journal" is the private reporting of the bereaved. Each chapter addresses a facet of grief seldom discussed.

## The Agony of Grief

### Stephanie Ericsson

MEDITATION

What is there to say about grief? Grief is a tidal wave that overtakes you, smashes down upon you with unimaginable force, sweeps you up into its darkness, where you tumble and crash against unidentifiable surfaces, only to be thrown out on an unknown beach, bruised, reshaped, and unwittingly better for the wear.

Grief means not being able to read more than two sentences at a time. It is walking into rooms with intentions that suddenly vanish.

Grief is three-o'clock-in-the-morning sweats that won't stop. It is dreadful Sundays, and Mondays that are no better. It makes you look for a face in a crowd, knowing full well there is no such face to be found in that crowd.

Grief is utter aloneness that razes the rational mind and makes room for the phantasmagoric. It makes you suddenly get up and leave a meeting in the middle, without saying a word.

Grief makes what others think of you moot. It shears away the masks of normal life and forces brutal honesty out of your mouth before propriety can stop you. It shoves away friends, scares away so-called friends, and rewrites your address book for you.

Grief makes you laugh at people who cry over spilled milk, right to their faces. It tells the world that you are untouchable at the very moment when touch is the only contact that might reach you. It makes lepers out of upstanding citizens.

Grief discriminates against no one. It kills. Maims. And cripples. It is the ashes from which the phoenix rises, and the mettle of rebirth. It returns life to the living dead. It teaches that there is nothing absolutely true, or untrue. It assures the living that we know nothing for certain. It humbles. It shrouds. It blackens. It enlightens.

Grief will make a new person out of you, if it doesn't kill you in the making.

JOURNAL

The denial moves in. It must be a sick joke. He's really there, and as soon as I round this next corner, he'll be there, standing with that stupid grin on his face. As soon as I open the door, he'll be there. Answer the phone, it will be him. Look in that direction, and I know, I just know I'll catch a glimpse of him. I'm sure I do see him out of the corners of my vision, but he is never there when I focus, never there when I turn my head to catch him. The man sitting at the sushi bar with the aviator glasses, like the ones he used to wear, makes me jump up and then sit down quickly again, before someone sees me, looking for my husband. Not him. I speak to my friends and they all have this look on their faces like they are watching me lying on the pavement with my belly sliced open. The expression is one of mixed pity and disgust. They want to avert their eyes, but they can't. Propriety? Fascination? Did I say disgust?

And then there's the inertia. You know the walk has to be shoveled and instead of saying, "In a minute . . ." you say, "Maybe next week . . . ." You know there's a million things to do, but you just have to sit for a while. Just for a while. And a while turns into months.

People say "How are you?" and they have that look in their faces again. And I look at them like they're crazy. I think, how do you think I am? I'm not strong enough for talk. The phone rings incessantly with the damned question, how are you, how are you, how are you, how are you. Finally, I say "Fine." Just so they'll stop. And maybe they'll stop calling because they feel better now. Then one day, my strength is down, and I actually tell someone how I am and they can't handle it, they can't understand, and I never hear from them again.

A woman said to me, in a comforting tone of conspiracy, "My mother had breast cancer and lost her right breast . . . ." "Oh," I say, "that's awful . . . ," and wonder if that is supposed to be some sort of comparison. A tit, a husband—same thing? Strange how people want to join you in your intensity, your epiphany, by trying to relate—grabbing at straws of a so-called "like" experience while simultaneously they are repulsed by the agony. They see you on the street, driving by and pretending they don't see you. Shit, we all have our stuff to deal with. I suppose it's hard enough dealing with your own.

I can't tell them to shut up, not because I'm not rude by nature (it takes too much energy to be polite) but because I am afraid they'll go away. One more abandonment. "I lost my father two years ago . . . ," and I think, schmuck, that's supposed to happen, it's a natural part of becoming adult—children are supposed to outlive their parents. Did you lose the only other person in the world who would love your child the way you do? Did you lose the person you held all night, who slept next to you, warmed your bed so much you didn't need an extra blanket in the winter? Do you know how many blankets it takes to replace a husband? Did you lose the person who would worry about bills with you? Screw in a light bulb when you were busy with the baby? Don't reduce this experience to something logical, universal. Even if it is, I walk alone amongst the dead, it's my death, my pain. Don't pretend you know it, like you know batting averages. Don't sacrilege all over my crucifixion.

The most idiotic thing I heard was "It was meant to be." I wonder who meant it to be? Who is this grand designer who didn't consult me? And I look at them wondering if I'm supposed to feel better now. Thanks, I think, for reminding me how powerless I am. How utterly powerless I am over my own life. I invested in a person, my soul, my heart, my very body, and now I should feel better because it was meant to be. Ha! If I ever thank God for this experience, it will be my own decision.

Somebody says they want to hold me and I stand stiff and foreboding, hoping it will end soon, this too-closeness. If it doesn't end soon, if they touch me too long, I know I'll fall apart, and that could be messy. Pieces of a soul all over the pavement. Bloody shame.

And the conversations with God go something like this: "Imbecile, is this some kind of sick joke? Where were you when I needed you? You're supposed to be some kind of loving God? Ha! You're fired!" People worry about me because I'm talking to myself. Exactly, I think, I'm talking to myself because there's *nobody out there.*

The only thing I know for sure is that I don't know a bloody thing anymore. I was bopping along, confident in tomorrows, in the next moments, in I'll-have-time-to-tell-him thoughts, and some sick cosmic architect erased our future. Ambushed by the grim reaper. Broad-sided by the crowbar of fate. I wonder if I could have seen it coming. If I really look, from now on, really watch everything carefully, maybe I'll see it coming next time and get my head out of the way of the next grand slam. Maybe I could have gotten him out of the way. I could have tied and gagged him and dragged him to the doctor, after all! And when I drive over bridges, now, I'm sure they'll fall down.

The guilt emerges like a thick fog that permeates every airspace available, surrounds everything, tucks itself away in corners and hovers close to the ground, waiting to trip me. What did I withhold telling him out of principle? Out of laziness? Out of a stupid confidence that I had time to tell him? Did I tell him *that day* that I loved him? That week? Somehow, the only thing I can think was important was telling him I love him. I talk to the ground, to the air, to the pillow, I get on my knees on his snowy grave and weep the words into the snow, melting it, but finding only frozen ground beneath. I confess all to a dead body, waxen-faced in a coffin, that doesn't look a thing like him. I only want to crawl in next to him while I am simultaneously repulsed at the makeup morticians have smeared all over any part of him that might show.

That's grief.

## Questions about the Reading

1. How do peoples' responses to the death of a parent or older person differ from their responses to the death of a spouse or child?

2. Do you think that the phases of normal grief described in the textbook would be the same for an anticipated death as for a sudden, unexpected death? Why?

## SELF-TESTS

### Multiple-Choice

Circle the letter of the response which best completes or answers each of the following statements and questions.

1. The study of death and dying is known as
   a. thanatology
   b. mortology
   c. mortuary science
   d. deathology

2. Generally, death is most accurately defined, in biological terms, as cessation of
   a. heart activity
   b. brain activity
   c. bodily processes
   d. blood flow

3. Social aspects of death most properly include
   a. saying goodbye to friends before dying
   b. paying all debts before dying
   c. funeral and mourning rituals
   d. severance of all social contacts in preparation for death

4. Children below about age 5 often believe that death is
   a. universal
   b. functional
   c. permanent
   d. reversible

5. Which of the following is *not* one of the three aspects of dying?
   a. social
   b. psychological
   c. environmental
   d. biological

6. Which of the following characteristics of death are children able to grasp?
   a. that it is irreversible
   b. that it is universal
   c. that it is nonfunctional
   d. all of the above

7. Adolescents are generally more concerned, not with how *long* they will live but rather with
   a. how long their *parents* will live
   b. *how* they will live
   c. how much fun they can have *before* they die
   d. how long their *friends* will live

8. The period of life when feelings about imminent death are most likely to be strongest is
   a. childhood
   b. adolescence
   c. young adulthood
   d. middle adulthood

9. The age at which most people really *know,* deep inside, that they are going to die is
   a. childhood
   b. adolescence
   c. young adulthood
   d. middle adulthood

10. Many people who have come close to death from drowning, cardiac arrest, and other causes have reported a kind of experience called
    a. predeath
    b. after-death
    c. near-death
    d. quasi-death

11. Research has shown that, compared with people who were not near death, people within a year of death tended to
    a. score higher on cognitive tests
    b. be less introspective
    c. be more aggressive
    d. be less docile

12. Which of the following statements about attitudes toward death in late adulthood is the most accurate?
    a. Older people, realizing and accepting their own mortality, tend to be less anxious about death than other age groups.
    b. Older people, realizing that death is drawing closer, become more fearful and anxious about death.
    c. Older people who feel that their lives have been full and meaningful are less able to accept the prospect of death.
    d. Older people—who have lost many friends to death and are losing their own physical vigor—resent younger, healthier people.

13. The person credited with having sparked the current interest in the psychology of death and dying is
    a. Jean Piaget
    b. Elisabeth Kübler-Ross
    c. Erik Erikson
    d. Lawrence Kohlberg

14. A dying person who says, "Why me?" is probably in which stage of dying?
    a. anger
    b. bargaining
    c. acceptance
    d. denial

15. A dying person whose first thought is, "This can't be happening to me," is probably in which stage of dying?
    a. anger
    b. bargaining
    c. acceptance
    d. denial

16. A dying person who prays, "If I can just see my son get married . . ." is probably in which stage of dying?
    a. anger
    b. bargaining
    c. acceptance
    d. denial

17. A dying person who says, "My time is very close now, and it's all right," is probably in which stage of dying?
    a. anger
    b. bargaining
    c. acceptance
    d. denial

18. Behavior associated with death, such as an Irish wake or a Jewish *shiva,* is known as
    a. mourning
    b. acceptance
    c. bereavement
    d. grief

19. The objective fact of loss is called
    a. mourning
    b. acceptance
    c. bereavement
    d. grief

20. The emotional response of a person experiencing loss is called
    a. mourning
    b. acceptance
    c. bereavement
    d. grief

21. In grief work, the final stage is called
    a. preoccupation
    b. summative
    c. denial
    d. resolution

22. Which of the following is *not* part of the three-phase pattern of grief work
    a. shock and disbelief
    b. resolution
    c. anger
    d. preoccupation with the memory of the deceased

23. Killing a terminally ill person at his or her own request, or to end suffering, is called
    a. anticipatory grief
    b. active euthanasia
    c. passive euthanasia
    d. morbid grief

24. In one study, children diagnosed as suicidal had which of the following traits?
    a. They were more aggressive.
    b. They seemed more depressed.
    c. They were less likely to cry after being hurt.
    d. all of the above

25. Reminiscence that enables a person to see the significance of his or her life is known as
    a. life review
    b. anticipatory grief
    c. preparatory morbidity
    d. living will

## Matching

Match each of the lettered items in the box with the appropriate description in the numbered list that follows the box.

```
a. mourning
b. anticipatory grief
c. living will
d. thanatology
e. acceptance
f. active euthanasia
g. grief therapy
h. hospice care
i. life review
j. shock and disbelief
k. passive euthanasia
l. bereavement
m. denial
n. grief
o. depression
```

1. final stage of dying _____

2. emotional response to loss from death _____

3. programs to help the bereaved cope with loss _____

4. initial phase of grief work _____

5. family-centered care for terminally ill patients _____

6. behavior of friends after a death _____

7. withholding life-prolonging treatment _____

8. initial response to impending death _____

9. a person's written wishes about treatment for terminal illness _____

10. grief for loss of one's own life _____

11. study of death and dying _____

12. grief expressed before a death _____

13. objective fact of a loss due to death _____

14. deliberately taking a life out of mercy _____

15. reminiscence to realize life's meaning _____

## Completion

Supply the term or terms needed to complete each of the following statements.

1. Before the twentieth century, more than _____ of all babies died in infancy; now, infant mortality has fallen to about _____ percent in the United States.

2. A healthier attitude toward death is shown in a growing interest in _____ , the study of death and dying.

3. Though legal definitions vary, in general _____ death is considered the cessation of bodily processes.

4. It is usually around the ages of 5 to 7 that children come to understand that death is _____—that a dead person, animal, or flower cannot come to life again.

5. At about ages 5 to 7, children realize that death is _____ (all living things inevitably die) and that a dead person or thing is _____ (all life functions end at death).

6. Of the different age groups, _____ tend to have highly "romantic" ideas about death.

7. _____ changes often begin to take place even before physiological signs indicate that a person is dying.

8. The five steps in coming to terms with dying, as proposed by Elisabeth Kübler-Ross, are _____ (refusal to accept the reality of what is happening), anger, bargaining for extra time, depression, and ultimate acceptance.

9. _____ refers to the behavior of the bereaved and the community after a death.

10. _____ with the memory of the person who has died is the second phase of grief work.

11. The initial phase of normal grief—when survivors often feel lost, dazed, and confused—is known as the stage of _____ .

12. A program to help the bereaved cope with their losses is called _____ .

13. The _____ movement began in response to a need for warm, personal patient- and family-centered care for the terminally ill.

14. Many controversial issues of death and dying have arisen because of _____ advances such as antibiotics and wonder drugs, respirators, and organ transplants.

15. Older people's natural tendency to talk about the people, events, and feelings of previous years is an important part of the _____ process.

---

## ANSWERS FOR SELF-TESTS

---

## Multiple-Choice

1. a (page 530)
2. c (531)
3. c (531)
4. d (531)
5. c (531)
6. d (531)
7. b (532)
8. c (533)
9. d (533)
10. c (534)
11. b (534)
12. a (534)
13. b (535)
14. a (537)
15. d (537)
16. b (536)
17. c (537)
18. a (538)
19. c (538)
20. d (538)
21. d (540)
22. c (540)
23. b (544)
24. d (546-547)
25. a (550)

## Matching

1. e (page 537)
2. n (538)
3. g (541)
4. j (540)
5. h (542)
6. a (538)
7. k (544)
8. m (536)
9. c (545)
10. o (537)
11. d (530)
12. b (538)
13. l (538)
14. f (544)
15. i (550)

## Completion

1. one-third; 1 (530)
2. thanatology (530)
3. biological (531)
4. irreversible (531)
5. universal; nonfunctional (531)
6. adolescents (532)
7. psychological (534)